Fitz-Jol
Scap
of Second Manassas

Fitz-John Porter, Scapegoat of Second Manassas

*The Rise, Fall and Rise of the
General Accused of Disobedience*

DONALD R. JERMANN

McFarland & Company, Inc., Publishers
Jefferson, North Carolina, and London

LIBRARY OF CONGRESS CATALOGUING-IN-PUBLICATION DATA

Jermann, Donald R.
  Fitz-John Porter, scapegoat of Second Manassas : the rise,
fall and rise of the general accused of disobedience / Donald
R. Jermann
      p.   cm.
  Includes bibliographical references and index.

  ISBN 978-0-7864-3930-0
  softcover : 50# alkaline paper ∞

  1. Porter, Fitz-John, 1822–1901—Trials, litigation, etc.
2. Trials (Military offenses)—United States.   3. Judicial
error—United States.   4. Bull Run, 2nd Battle of, Va., 1862.
5. Generals—United States—Biography.   6. United States.
Army—Biography.   I. Title.
E473.772.J475   2009
973.7'8—dc22   2008049423

British Library cataloguing data are available

On the cover: Fitz-John Porter; Second battle of Bull Run, August
29, 1862 (Library of Congress).

Manufactured in the United States of America

McFarland & Company, Inc., Publishers
  Box 611, Jefferson, North Carolina 28640
  www.mcfarlandpub.com

To my wife, Florence

Acknowledgments

I would like to thank my daughter, Mary Jermann Amozig, who provided invaluable assistance in the preparation of this book.

Table of Contents

List of Maps

Preface

August 30, 1862, was possibly the darkest day in the history of our country since Valley Forge. The Union had just suffered a disastrous defeat in the second battle of Manassas and it appeared that Washington was lost.

Major General John Pope accused Major General Fitz-John Porter of being responsible for the loss. The charges were misbehavior before the enemy and failure to obey orders. The case wound its way through the military justice system for more than twenty years. All of the principal players, including Generals Pope, Porter, McDowell, Hunter, and Schofield, were career officers of long standing.

The profession of military officer is unique. It is the only profession where one has surrendered the option to walk away from unpleasantness, tedium, boredom, hardship, danger, and even death. The profession has its own mores and customs, and its own legal system. One can be punished and even imprisoned for conduct "unbecoming a gentleman" and sentenced to death for failing to carry out an order.

I have served all my adult life as a career military officer, covering a period of three wars. I have served as a member of courts-martial and have presided over courts-martial. Hence, I felt that I could bring a unique, insider perspective to the case.

This work is not a mere recounting of events, and not just a biography of General Porter. Rather, it is an analysis of the case. Was Porter guilty or not? If not, who was responsible for the loss of second Manassas? This work addresses both questions.

Introduction

We often hear that such and such trial was the "trial of the century." A leading contender for this distinction for the nineteenth century certainly must be the trial of Major General Fitz-John Porter. In 1862, the Union was fighting for its life in the great Civil War and was desperately in need of heroes. One stepped forward. He was the handsome, personable, young Maj. Gen. Fitz-John Porter—a darling of the press. He seemed able to prevail where others could not. Then, something went terribly wrong. The Union suffered a crushing defeat in the second battle of Manassas. It seemed that even Washington might be lost. It was one of the darkest days of the war.

Union army commander General John Pope came forward and said that it was all Gen. Porter's fault. Charges were filed against Porter—five for disobeying orders and four for shameful conduct before the enemy.

The trial involved more than a mere matter of guilt or non-guilt. Porter's supporters contended not only that Porter was blameless, but that his actions were meritorious; it was he who actually saved the army from complete destruction. The legal and political moves relating to Porter's guilt or heroism raged on for more than twenty years. Was Porter his country's savior—or a Benedict Arnold? This book will present the evidence. You be the judge.

This is a tale about Civil War generals, who differed in two ways from those that preceded or followed. First, the Civil War entailed the most rapid expansion of the U.S. military that ever occurred. A single U.S. military of fewer than 16,500 men in 1860 was to grow into two huge militaries involving over one and a half million in less than two years. Second, the same pool of pre-war officers was to fill the ranks of both of the combating armies.

The usual path to becoming a general is to complete four years of officer training and then to advance from second lieutenant to first lieutenant, to captain, to major to lieutenant colonel, to colonel, and, finally, to brigadier general. This normally required twenty-five to thirty years of service after commissioning. Consequently, one became a general in his fifties or late forties at best.

At the outbreak of World War II, the average age of Americans who were ultimately to receive the rank of five star general was 57.6 years and the youngest was 48. The experience of America's enemies was almost identical. The average age of Germans who were to achieve top rank during the war was 54.7 and the youngest was 48. In the Mexican War and World War I, generals tended to be even older.

In the spring of 1862, the general-in-chief of the U.S. Army, General George B. McClellan, was thirty-four years old. Of the twenty-one Union generals mentioned by name in this narrative (aside from members of the court), ten were in their thirties and most of the rest in their early forties. The Confederate situation was similar. In fact, numerous Civil War generals were in their twenties, and one, General Galusha Pennypacker, was not even old enough to vote.

Then too, there is the matter of experience. In the normal course of events, most officers rising to the rank of general have commanded a platoon, a company, a battalion, and a regiment. In addition, most have served on the staff of a general. In the case of Civil War generals, many had never previously commanded a body of men larger than a company (one hundred men), most had never served on a general's staff, and many had never risen high enough even to interact with a general or to observe how a general functions.

Being promoted from captain to general, as young men were in 1861–62, did not involve merely more of the same. The world of a general was vastly different from the world of a captain. A general commanded too many men to attend to all the details of command himself; he, unlike a captain, had a staff. The staff included experts in various disciplines and was headed by a chief of staff. A good chief of staff relieved the general of many problems, allowing him to concentrate on the larger issues. One will note when examining the official records that most

Major General Fitz-John Porter, United States Volunteers: was he the loser or the hero of Second Manassas? (courtesy the Massachusetts Commandery Military Order of the Loyal Legion and the U.S. Army Military History Institute).

orders emanating from the general were signed by his chief of staff, and most reports intended for the general were addressed to his chief of staff. Many of the young men now being promoted to general had never served on a staff and did not know how a staff functioned or was organized. Consequently, some tended to get enmeshed in details at the expense of the larger picture, and others treated their chiefs of staff as a general purpose flunky who served as a combination messenger and secretary.

Then too, captains were specialists. A captain of infantry commanded a company of infantry. A captain of artillery commanded a battery of artillery, and a captain of cavalry commanded a troop of cavalry. There were also special duty types that the captain did not command, such as engineers, paymasters, and surgeons. A general's command, particularly at corps or army level, contained elements of infantry, cavalry, and artillery, plus the various specialists.

Generals also possessed certain judicial powers that captains did not possess. Under the articles of war, generals commanding corps or armies could appoint courts-martial. They could also approve or mitigate the sentences meted out.

Most of the generals named in this narrative came from a common source—West Point. Of the twenty-two Union generals named, seventeen were graduates of West Point. Of the eight Confederate generals named, seven were graduates of West Point. Inasmuch as the generals from opposite sides were from a common source, they tended to know each other. Around the time of the Civil War, a typical graduating class at West Point had about fifty members. An individual who attended classes daily with forty-nine other members, lived with them, and socialized with them for four years tended to know them very well indeed. For example, Confederate corps commander "Stonewall" Jackson and Union army commander George McClellan were four-year classmates, as were Confederate division commander A. P. Hill and Union corps commander Ambrose Burnside, and as were Union army commander John Pope and Confederate corps commander James Longstreet. Similar examples are too numerous to mention. Thus, in the Civil War, far more than in any other war, a general was far more likely to evaluate what a particular enemy general was likely to do, rather than to consider what an unknown and presumably competent enemy general could do. Confederate General Robert E. Lee was particularly adept at estimating what known opponent generals were likely to do in a given situation. (See Appendix 1 for data on the generals involved in the Porter case.)

In the Civil War there was no radio, and telegraph did not service the battlefield. There was also no aerial reconnaissance (except for Professor Thaddeus S. C. Lowe's balloons, which played no part in this episode). Thus, battlefield decisions had to be based in large part on what one could see with one's own eyes. By the time one became a corps commander, as Gen. Porter was, he was giving orders to subordinate division commanders. In time of battle, these division commanders were usually too far apart for verbal consultation—and what one could see, the other usually could not. Thus, the normal means of communication between a corps commander and his division commanders was the written word delivered by courier. The corps commander controlled his battle by the written word.

Written orders containing good ideas were not enough. The manner of phrasing was all-important. Often in battle, it took far longer to deliver a message by courier than one might think. This was particularly true after dark. In this narrative, we have a case of over six hours elapsing between the time a courier was given a message and the time it was delivered to the intended recipient three miles away. Certain rules for order writing were elementary. Every order should contain a time of origination. Every order should indicate where the originator could be found. Every order should indicate who else has a copy. And finally, every order should be receipted with the time of delivery indicated. In the case of Gen. Porter, these most elementary rules were consistently violated—sometimes with tragic results.

Above and beyond these basic rules, an order must clearly express what the commander wants the recipient to accomplish and, preferably, why (but not how). An order must also give the recipient some leeway, because the situation confronting the recipient may be radically different from that visualized by the originator. Peremptory orders such as "capture that hill" or "take that hill at any cost" could have tragic results. They could result in a recipient wasting his men against a position he knew to be impregnable. This portion of the war is replete with confusing, ambiguous, and unnecessarily imperative orders that no experienced general would write.

There is another area where generals of this time were often remiss when more experienced generals might not be. At the time of the Civil War, there were few maps of country roads, and those that did exist were notoriously inaccurate. Furthermore, there was a dearth of signs on country roads. Many, if not most, were unmarked. An experienced general ordering a subordinate unit to proceed from point A to point B would, if possible, place a guide at each crossroads to ensure the correct route was followed. In the second battle at Manassas, a general lost one third of his force while within sound of the battlefield for failing to follow this simple procedure.

In summation, the typical Civil War general in 1862 was not stupid and was not lacking in courage or leadership skills. However, he was apt to be inexperienced, unseasoned, and sometimes even immature.

The background of this narrative is the conflict between Robert E. Lee's Confederate Army of Northern Virginia and Union General John Pope's Army of Virginia. Here, all advantages of leadership lay with the Confederate side. The South had already assembled a magnificent leadership team for the Army of Northern Virginia consisting of Generals Robert E. Lee, James Longstreet, Stonewall Jackson, and J.E.B. Stuart. All were career officers, although Jackson technically was not in the army at the outbreak of the war. However, as professor at the Virginia Military Institute, he was very much enmeshed in military affairs. All four were graduates of West Point. Lee had risen to the rank of colonel in the pre-war army, and the general-in-chief, General Winfield Scott, considered him the best officer in the army. Stuart, although a very young general, had unusual capabilities. This talented team worked harmoniously together and was never to be equaled by either side during the war.

The situation in the Union Army of Virginia was vastly different. It had been cobbled together from disparate units just before the crisis erupted. The commanding officer was called in from another theater and was actually junior on the seniority list to all three of his corps' commanders. The army was then hurriedly reinforced from the Ninth Corps, the Army of the Potomac, and the Washington Defense Force—right up to the day of the commencement of the second battle of Manassas. Some of these reinforcements were commanded by generals who disliked Gen. Pope, resented serving under him, or had never met him in person. Thus were assembled all the ingredients for a massive Union defeat.

1

The Situation in Late August 1862

Washington and Richmond, the two capitals, were only one hundred miles apart. Each was of great psychological significance. The loss of either would be a damaging blow. Richmond, unlike Washington, was more than a governmental center. It was also a prime manufacturing center for armaments. Thus, its loss would be disastrous for the South.

The Army of the Potomac was the main Union army in the East. It was larger than all the other Union field forces in the area put together. Its commanding general was the young George B. McClellan, sometimes referred to as "the Young Napoleon." McClellan had a plan for capturing Richmond. He would not proceed overland from Washington to Richmond through one hundred miles of hostile territory with an ever lengthening, vulnerable supply line. Rather, he would capitalize on Union sea superiority. He would transport his army by sea to Fortress Monroe, which the Union held, at the tip of the peninsula between the York and James rivers (see Map 1). He would then march up the peninsula and seize Richmond from the east. In this way, his flanks would be protected by gunboats on the two rivers, and he would always be ensured of supplies by water. Thus, in May 1862, began what has become known as McClellan's Peninsular Campaign.

There was one thing President Abraham Lincoln did not like about McClellan's plan. It left no Union forces between Washington and the Confederate army defending Richmond. Lincoln feared that the Confederate army might abandon the defense of Richmond and seize Washington. Lincoln worried that, if this were to happen, it would create the appearance that the South was winning—and foreign powers would then recognize the Confederacy, and the Union would be dissolved.

McClellan assured Lincoln he need not worry. He argued that the Confederate army could not withdraw if it were locked in combat with his army. Furthermore, even if it did withdraw, Washington had forts and a strong garrison that could hold out long enough for him to reinforce it from the sea. After all, reinforcements could come all the way from the peninsula to the M Street

Map 1—McClellan's Plan

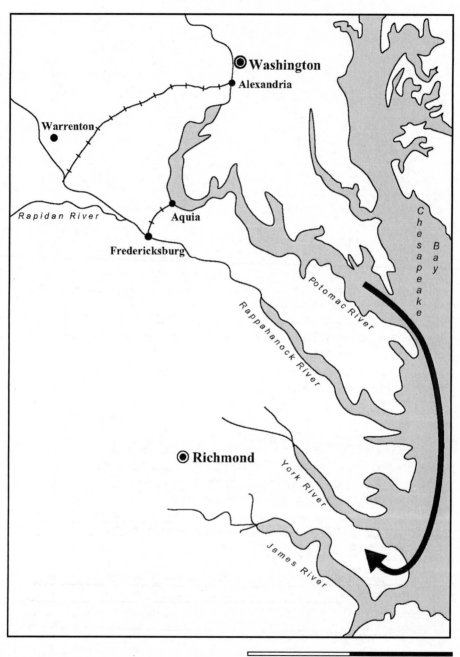

MILES　0　　　　　　　　　　25　　　　　　5(

docks in downtown Washington in little more than twenty-four hours. Events later in the war proved McClellan right. Lincoln, however, was not mollified.

On June 26, 1862, Lincoln ordered the creation of a new Union army, the Army of Virginia. This army was to operate between Washington and the Confederate army. The Army of Virginia was to be created by consolidating three small Union field commands that were operating in various parts of the state. These three were the commands of John Fremont (later Sigel), McDowell, and Banks. The three independent commands were to become three corps in the new army. For the new army commander, Lincoln sent for Gen. Pope, who was then in the West. This new army initially contained about thirty-five thousand men. Its function was twofold: it was to maintain a blocking position between Washington and Richmond, and it was to threaten the Confederate army defending Richmond so as to draw off forces and permit McClellan to seize Richmond. But literally hours after the Army of Virginia was created, events transpired that were to change its mission.

Up to late June, things seemed to be going well for McClellan on the peninsula. Then, between June 21 and July 1, the Confederate army, under Robert E. Lee, seized the initiative. In the so called "Seven Days Battle," Lee seemingly inflicted a defeat on McClellan, saved Richmond, and put McClellan on the defensive. The Peninsula Campaign now looked like a failure. The general-in-chief of the Union Army, Henry Halleck, decided that a new strategy was needed. He decided to withdraw the Army of the Potomac from the peninsula by sea to the Washington area. It would then unite with the Army of Virginia. This united, giant army would then steam-roller its way overland to Richmond.

This new plan was not without risk. It was feared that once Lee realized that the Army of the Potomac was being withdrawn from the peninsula, he would immediately march north and attack Pope before the two Union armies could unite. This is, in fact, precisely what Lee did.

Withdrawing the entire Army of the Potomac from the peninsula was no small matter. It contained over one hundred thousand men, over thirty thousand horses, and over three thousand supply wagons. This was without even mentioning the removal of the sick and hospitalized, the artillery, the ammunition, the supplies, the commissary, and the fodder. Nineteen days were to elapse between August 3, when McClellan received the order to withdraw, and the first man's arrival at the Army of Virginia.

The new mission of the Army of Virginia was to hold a defensive position until it could be joined by the Army of the Potomac. One thing was unclear at this point. Who was going to command the new super army once united? Pope? McClellan? Henry Halleck?

Halleck decided that the defensive line would be the line of the Rappahannock River. As Pope was withdrawing to the Rappahannock, he had his first clash with the advancing forces of Lee on August 9 at a place called Cedar Mountain. This was a minor success for the Confederates and an omen of what was to come.

The Line of the Rappahannock

The Rappahannock is a major river in northern Virginia. It is about one-third of the way from Washington to Richmond. It runs across the entire state on a diagonal from northwest to southeast. It starts in the Blue Ridge Mountains and ultimately empties into Chesapeake Bay (see map 2). From its mouth at Chesapeake Bay up to Port Royal, a distance of about seventy miles, it is tidewater and sufficiently wide and deep to be controlled by the navy alone. From Port Royal to its main tributary, the Rapidan, a distance of about thirty miles, it can be crossed only by bridging, as by pontoon bridges. Up river, beyond the confluence of the Rapidan and Rappahannock, it can be crossed at numerous fords, and when low, by cavalry and infantry almost anywhere. However, even in its upper stretches, the river can rise rapidly after rain and become uncrossable for two or three days. Thus, even in its upper stretches, it can pose a severe military danger. An army crossing could be divided into parts for days and be subject to destruction.

As Gen. Pope gradually drew his army behind the Rappahannock with his headquarters at Warrenton, Gen. Halleck considered the possibility that the Confederates might strike farther down the river. Consequently, he ordered General Burnside and his Ninth Corps to move by sea from Newport News to Aquia, and thence down to Fredericksburg (see map 3). By August 3, Burnside was setting up his headquarters at Falmouth, on the north bank of the Rappahannock opposite Fredericksburg. Thus Pope was with the Army of Virginia defending the upper reaches of the Rappahannock, and Burnside was with his Ninth Corps, the lower reach. Burnside's Ninth Corps was not subordinate to Pope. In fact, Burnside was senior to Pope.

Soon after Burnside and Pope took up positions, it became evident that the Confederates were going to strike in Pope's sector. Consequently, the War Department began transferring troops from Burnside to Pope. These troops constituted Pope's first reinforcements. By August 18, Pope was ensconced behind the Rappahannock and the Confederate army was taking up position on the opposite bank with Longstreet to the east and Jackson to the west.

Landings and Routes for Reinforcements

The two landings nearest to the front on the Rappahannock where ships could debark troops and cargo were Aquia and Alexandria (see map 3). Both were on the Potomac—Alexandria just outside Washington, and Aquia on an inlet fifteen miles farther downstream. Both Alexandria and Aquia were at the

Map 2—The Line of the Rappahannock

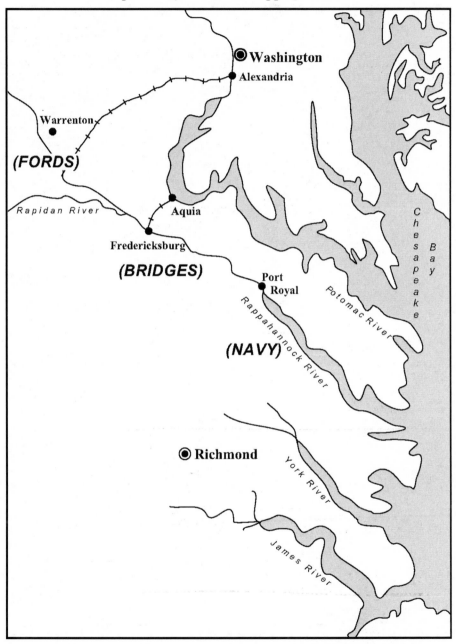

MILES 0   25   50

Map 3—Landings and Routes

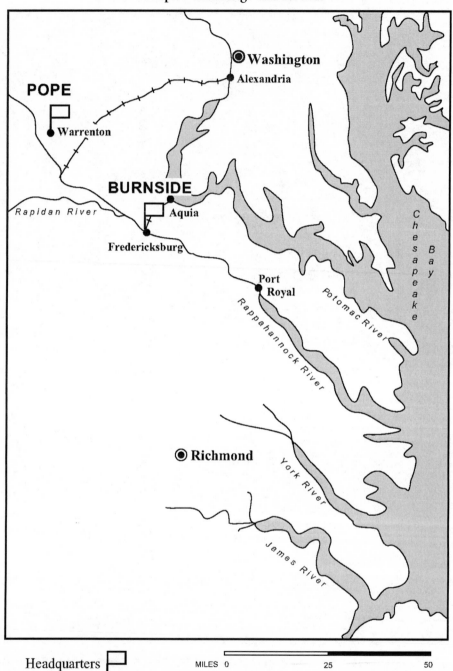

Headquarters ⌐

MILES 0   25   50

head of railroads that led south to the Rappahannock. The railroad at Alexandria was the Orange and Alexandria and it was about fifty rail miles from Alexandria to Rappahannock Station. The railroad at Aquia was the Richmond and Potomac and it was about thirty miles to Fredericksburg. The Orange and Alexandria was the primary supply line for Pope, and the Richmond and Potomac the primary supply line for Burnside. If one wanted to get troops to Pope in a hurry, Alexandria was obviously preferable. If troops were landed at Aquia, they still had a full day's march up the Rappahannock from Fredericksburg to reach Pope's sector. After August 22, all troops destined for Pope were debarked at Alexandria. Before that date, both sites were used because of the crowding of the facilities at each.

Reinforcements for Pope

The first reinforcements for Pope came up the Rappahannock from Burnside's Ninth Corps. They consisted of two divisions under Reno, numbering about eight thousand, that arrived on August 15. Beginning on August 22, the floodgates were opened when units from the Army of the Potomac began flowing in. General S.P. Heintzelman's Third Corps, consisting of the divisions of Joseph Hooker and Philip Kearny, came down the railroad from Alexandria. They numbered about ten thousand. John Reynolds came up the Rappahannock with his division numbering another forty-seven hundred, and then A.S. Piatt came down the railroad from Alexandria with another thousand.

Then, on the night of August 26, something went terribly wrong. The authorities at Alexandria noted that the telegraphic communications to Pope's headquarters at Warrenton Junction suddenly ceased. Then it was noted that trains that had carried troops and supplies south to Pope were no longer returning for reloads. What had happened?

To the surprise of all, Jackson, with three Confederate divisions, was on the railroad between Pope and Alexandria. He had marched completely around Pope's army, covering fifty-four miles in forty-eight hours. He was now busy destroying trains, blowing up bridges, pulling up rails, and burning warehouses full of supplies. (See Map 4 for an overview of the area where the second battle of Manassas took place.)

Pope was to get one more reinforcement before the crunch. Porter, from McClellan's Army of the Potomac, was marching up the Rappahannock with his corps from Fredericksburg and would join him on the twenty-seventh. Porter had about ten thousand men. With Porter's arrival, Pope would have received approximately 25,700 reinforcements since the twenty-second. This gave him a force of about seventy thousand—a comfortable margin over Lee's approximately fifty thousand. Furthermore, Pope had tens of thousands of additional potential reinforcements accumulating at nearby Alexandria waiting for transportation. Lee had none nearby.

Map 4—Area of the Second Battle of Manassas

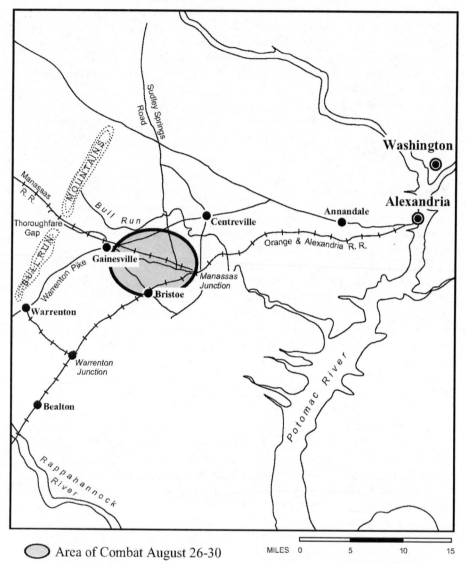

⬭ Area of Combat August 26-30

MILES 0   5   10   15

Pope's numerical advantage, however, was not all that it seemed to be. McClellan's Army of the Potomac was arriving at Alexandria and Aquia in chaotic fashion. Some ships carried just troops, others just horses, and yet others just wagons or just artillery. There was a tendency to ship the troops off to Pope immediately with the rest to follow. Thus, most units were arriving without any transport, some without horses, and others with only the ammunition the men had on their persons. Worse yet, the entire cavalry division of the Army of the Potomac was still on the peninsula awaiting shipping. The units of the Army of the Potomac would have to operate without their usual cavalry support, other than that which could be provided by Pope.

Trouble in the Making

Secretary of War Edwin M. Stanton, General-in-Chief Halleck, and probably President Lincoln and Gen. Pope, all suspected that Gen. McClellan resented having his peninsular campaign terminated and his troops taken from him; that he was dragging his feet in turning his troops over to Pope; and that he might even be pleased to see Pope defeated and humiliated. Their suspicions were deepened by the Franklin incident.

Major General George B. McClellan of the United States Volunteers was known as "the Young Napoleon" (courtesy the Massachusetts Commandery Military Order of the Loyal Legion and the U.S. Army Military History Institute).

General W.B. Franklin was a corps commander in the Army of the Potomac and a friend and favorite of McClellan. Franklin and his corps arrived at Alexandria by sea on the twenty-sixth. Although the railroad was cut by Jackson that night, Halleck urged that very night that Franklin and his corps proceed immediately to Centreville (near Manassas) by foot. After all, Centreville was less than twenty-five miles from Alexandria by road—a distance Jackson could easily have covered in one day. Despite Halleck's repeated urgings, McClellan kept responding with reasons (or excuses) as to why Franklin could not move. Franklin finally started at 6 A.M. on the twenty-ninth, and at the end of the day was only at Annandale, six miles from Alexandria. Franklin was not to reach the battlefield until late on the thirtieth after Pope had been decisively defeated (see map 5).

By the twenty-eighth, Secretary of War Stanton was already sufficiently exasperated to send Halleck the following message:

War Dept
Washington City, D.C.
Aug 28, 1862

Map 5—Franklin's March

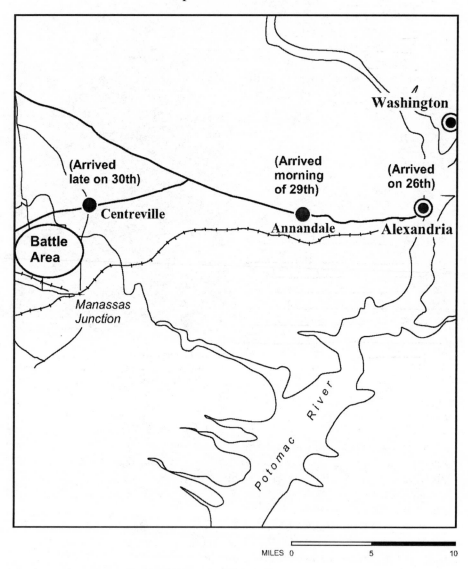

Maj. Gen H. W. Halleck
Commander-in-Chief

General: I desire you to furnish me information on the following points:
    1st. At what date you first ordered the general commanding the Army of the Potomac to move from James River.
    2nd. Whether that order was or was not obeyed according to its pur-

port with the promptness which, in your judgment, the national safety required, and at what date the movement commenced.

3rd. What order has been given recently for the movement of Franklin's corps, and whether it was obeyed as promptly as national safety required.

4th. You will furnish me copies of the orders referred to in the foregoing inquiries.

Edwin M. Stanton
Secretary of War[1]

Halleck responded to Stanton's message on August 30, giving a lengthy catalogue of times and dates. (The full text of Halleck's response is contained in Appendix 2.)

While the Franklin episode was unfolding, Gen. Porter, with the Fifth Corps of the Army of the Potomac, was marching up the Rappahannock from Fredericksburg to join Pope, which he did on August 27. If Franklin was a close friend of McClellan's, Porter was a closer friend. McClellan closeted himself with Porter for advice and discussion more than he did with any other general. As Porter advanced up the Rappahannock, he sent a stream of telegraphs to his friend, Gen. Burnside, that contained some highly disparaging references to Gen. Pope and Pope's capabilities. Unknown to Porter, these messages were automatically forwarded to the War Department, where they were read by Halleck, Lincoln, and possibly Stanton. To make matters worse, their contents were forwarded to Pope by someone unknown.

When Porter reported in to Pope on the morning of August 27, the two already had reason not to like each other. Within hours, their relationship was going to take a turn for the worse. Within days, Pope was to blame Porter for the loss of the second battle of Manassas, and would arrange to have charges filed against him.

2

The Second Battle of Manassas

Porter's were the last troops to join Pope before the bottom dropped out for Pope. In its most simplified form, the second battle of Manassas can be summarized as follows (see map 6):

AUGUST 25: The two armies face each other on the Rappahannock.

AUGUST 26: Jackson takes three of Lee's eight divisions and marches completely around Pope's army and seizes the railroad in Pope's rear.

AUGUST 27–28: Pope re-opens the railroad and becomes obsessed with destroying Jackson's force before it can reunite with the other five Confederate divisions commanded by Longstreet.

AUGUST 28–29: Jackson does not retreat toward Longstreet as expected, but takes up a strong defensive position along an unfinished railroad north of the Warrenton pike to wait for Longstreet.

AUGUST 29: Pope believes that he still has time to destroy Jackson before Longstreet can arrive. He believes that Longstreet cannot arrive before late on the thirtieth. He is wrong. Longstreet is already taking up position on Pope's flank on the twenty-ninth.

AUGUST 29–30: Pope makes a maximum effort against Jackson late on the twenty-ninth and early on the thirtieth. Longstreet, who is on Pope's flank, attacks and rolls up Pope's army.

LATE AUGUST 30: Franklin belatedly arrives at the battle scene but can do little more than slow the Union retreat.

SEPTEMBER 1: Jackson intercepts retreating Federals at Chantilly (currently the site of Washington's Dulles Airport) and defeats the Federals again. Union division commanders Isaac Stevens and Philip Kearny are both killed.

The Union authorities in Washington were slow to recognize the magnitude of Pope's defeat. McClellan told Halleck that it was serious and recommended that Halleck go to the front and see for himself. Instead, Halleck sent Colonel J.C. Kelton of his staff. Kelton returned and told them that it was a disaster of unprecedented magnitude; that it was worse than any of them thought. Lincoln, Stanton, and Halleck now feared that Washington was lost.

Chaos reigned in Washington. The streets were jammed with stragglers, broken units, and wagons. The banks began shipping their money to New York. A gunboat steamed up the Potomac to pick up Lincoln. At this point

Map 6—The Second Battle of Manassas

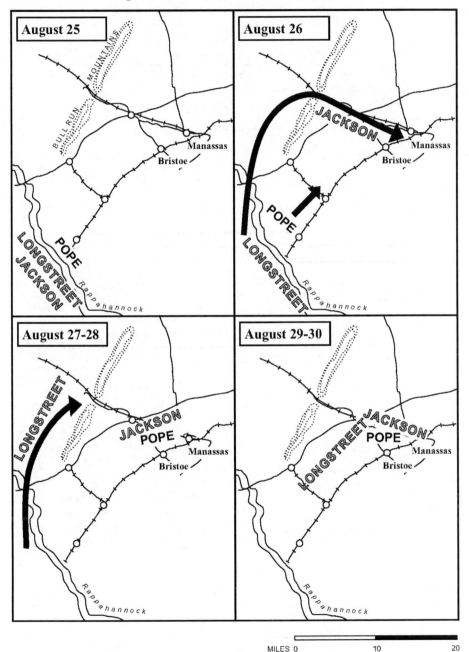

Lincoln turned to McClellan. Although he was ambivalent in his feelings toward McClellan, he recognized that McClellan had great organizational and leadership capabilities. If anyone could bring order out of chaos, it was McClellan. McClellan "guaranteed" Lincoln that he could save Washington. Lincoln then put him in command of all the Union forces in and around Washington. Pope's Army of Virginia was dissolved and Pope was ordered off to an unimportant command in Minnesota to fight Indians.

McClellan had landed on his feet and was now more important than ever, while Pope was in disgrace. Pope was furious. In his heart of hearts, he believed that McClellan had done all in his power to ensure his failure. He considered that it was all McClellan's fault and not his. McClellan was beyond Pope's reach. Two of McClellan's top assistants, however, were not. These were Porter, who had been directly subordinate to Pope, and Franklin, who had been ordered to join Pope but did not arrive in time. Pope filed charges against both. Technically, the charges were filed by Pope's inspector general, General Benjamin S. Roberts. Porter was charged with disobedience of orders and misbehavior before the enemy. Franklin was charged with disobedience of orders. These were serious charges and could result in the death penalty. Both generals were relieved from command and placed under arrest awaiting trial. The crisis, however, was still in full swing. McClellan said that he needed his two assistants and requested that both be restored to their commands until the crisis was resolved. Halleck relented and both Porter and Franklin were restored to command, at least temporarily.

In the meantime, Lee, following his smashing victory at Manassas, crossed the Potomac to the west of Washington and invaded Maryland. No one in the North knew his true objective. Was it Washington? Baltimore? Philadelphia? Actually, it was none of the above. It was Harrisburg, Pennsylvania. By marching up to and capturing Harrisburg, Lee hoped to accomplish two things. First, he would cut three of the four arteries between East and West (the Baltimore and

T.J. "Stonewall" Jackson, Confederate major general and Pope's nemesis (courtesy the Massachusetts Commandery Military Order of the Loyal Legion and the U.S. Army Military History Institute).

Ohio Railroad, the Pennsylvania Railroad, and the Chesapeake and Ohio Canal). Second, by capturing a northern state capital, he hoped to create the appearance of victory and thus gain foreign recognition of the Confederacy.

Back in Washington, McClellan, employing his usual energy and organizational skills, brought order out of chaos. He then marched out with a reorganized and rejuvenated Army of the Potomac to maintain a blocking position between Lee and Baltimore and Washington.

As Lee advanced, there was one plum he could not resist. There was now a large Union garrison at Harpers Ferry in his rear that was cut off and isolated. Before he continued on to Harrisburg, Lee decided to divide his army into components so as to close in on the garrison on all sides and capture it. This was risky. If McClellan realized that Lee's army was divided, he could destroy it piecemeal. However, Lee calculated that he could capture the garrison and reunite before McClellan realized what was happening.

As luck would have it, the Confederates lost a copy of Lee's secret plan and it ended up in McClellan's hands. McClellan now had an unparalleled opportunity to destroy Lee, but he had to act with dispatch. Acting with dispatch was not his forte, but he did act. It was now a race against the clock with each hour golden—the Confederates rushing to reunite, and McClellan rushing to destroy them before they did. In the race, McClellan scored two minor victories, one at South Mountain and one at Crampton's Gap. The nearest place that the Confederates could reunite was a site known as Sharpsburg in the South and Antietam Creek in the North, and here they did. It was a photo finish.

In the gigantic battle of Antietam, the bloodiest day ever in the northern hemisphere, the Confederates managed to reunite just in time to avoid destruction, but were forced to terminate their invasion. McClellan was now at the height of his popularity, but his days were numbered. Powerful figures in the Lincoln administration, such as Secretary of War Stanton, detested him. Lincoln insisted that McClellan rigorously press the Confederates. McClellan procrastinated. Lincoln visited McClellan in person and insisted. McClellan still procrastinated. Finally, Lincoln relieved McClellan as commander of the Army of the Potomac and ordered him to report to his home to await further orders. Such orders never came. The next we hear of McClellan is when he reappeared as the candidate of the Democratic Party to run against Lincoln in the 1864 presidential elections.

With McClellan gone, Porter and Franklin lost their patron and protector. Within days of McClellan's departure, Porter was ordered to stand trial. Franklin managed to dodge the bullet. He had an unassailable defense. He had no freedom of action on those fateful days in August. He was under McClellan's command until he appeared on Pope's battlefield on August 30. Porter alone was left to face the wrath of Pope. (See Appendix 3 for the organization of the two contending armies at the second battle of Manassas, and the positions occupied by the generals.)

3

Courts and Courts-Martial

In 1862, military justice was governed by the so called "Articles of War." Porter was charged with violating Article Nine and Article Fifty-two. Franklin was charged with violating Article Nine. The two articles read as follows:

Article Nine

Any officer or soldier who shall strike his superior officer, or draw or light upon any weapon, or offer any violence against him, being in the execution of his office, on any pretense whatsoever, or shall disobey any lawful command of his superior officer, shall suffer death, or such other punishment as shall, according to the nature of this offense, be inflicted upon him by the sentence of a court-martial.[1]

Article Fifty-two

Any officer or soldier who shall misbehave himself before the enemy, run away or shamefully abandon any fort, post or guard which he or they may be commanded to defend, or speak words inducing others to do the like, or shall cast away his arms and ammunition, or who shall quit his post or colors to plunder and pillage, every such offender, being duly convicted thereof, shall suffer death, or such other punishment as shall be ordered by the sentence of a general court-martial.[2]

Under the articles, a commissioned officer could be tried only by a general court-martial. The articles specified that a general court-martial could consist of any number of commissioned officers from five to thirteen, but was not to have less than thirteen when that number could be convened "without manifest injury to the service."[3] Furthermore, none of the officers of the court were to be of lower rank than the accused if it could be avoided.

The senior officer of the court presided and was known as the "president." Each member of the court had one vote as to the accused's guilt or innocence on each charge. The junior member of the court voted first, and so on, up to the senior member. A simple majority was sufficient for conviction, except in the case of a death penalty, where a two-thirds majority was required. If the accused was a general officer, and the sentence involved either loss of life or dismissal from the service, the sentence had to be approved by the president of the United States.

The judge advocate, or some person deputed by him, prosecuted the case in the name of the United States. However, he had the dual responsibility of ensuring that the accused's rights were not violated. Before the trial commenced, the judge advocate was required to administer the following oath to each court member:

> You, A. B., do swear that you will well and truly try and determine according to evidence, the matter before you, between the United States of America and the prisoner to be tried, and that you will duly administer justice, according to the provisions of an act establishing rules and articles for the government of the armies of the United States, without partiality, favor or affection; and if any doubt should arise, not explained by said articles, according to your conscience, the best of your understanding, and the custom of war in like cases; and you do further swear that you will not divulge the sentence until it shall be published by the proper authority; neither will you disclose or discover the vote or opinion of any particular member of the court-martial, unless required to give evidence thereof, as a witness, by a court of justice, in a due course of law.
>
> So help you God.[4]

The articles provided that any general commanding an army, or colonel commanding a separate department, could appoint a general court-martial. However, whenever a general commanding an army was the accuser of an officer under his command, the court-martial must be appointed by the president. Thus, Pope himself could not accuse Porter and then appoint a court-martial to try him. If Pope was, in fact, the accuser, President Lincoln would have to appoint the court-martial. Had the issue been put to Lincoln, he may well have demurred and directed the War Department to resolve the matter without a trial that could be embarrassing to the administration. This, however, was avoided in the Porter case by Gen. Roberts, Pope's inspector general, filing the charges against Porter instead of Pope filing them. Whether or not this was the result of collusion between Roberts and Pope is unknown. The court-martial for Porter was appointed by the adjutant general's office of the headquarters of the army. Thus, the individual selecting the court members was General-in-Chief Halleck or Secretary of War Stanton, or both.

The activating order for the court-martial was dated November 25, 1862. It appointed nine generals as members, seven of whom were junior to Porter. As previously noted, Article Sixty-four of the Articles of War required thirteen members where that number could be convened "without manifest injury to the service," and Article Seventy-five provided that no officer shall be tried by court-martial by officers inferior in rank to himself "if it can be avoided." These criteria were not met because of the time of the court-martial. The country was enmeshed in a desperate war with the outcome still very much in doubt.

Most generals at the time had more pressing things to do than sit on a court-martial and, inasmuch as Porter was the twentieth senior general in the army, there was no way, under the circumstances, that thirteen generals senior to him could be assembled. The War Department did the best it could under the circumstances. It appointed those who happened to be available at the time.

The nine designated members were: Major Generals D. Hunter and E. A. Hitchcock of the U.S. Volunteers; Brigadier Generals Rufus King, B. M. Prentiss, James Ricketts, Silas Casey, James Garfield, and N. B. Buford of the U.S. Volunteers; and BVT Brigadier General W. W. Morriss of the U.S. Army. The designated judge advocate was Colonel J. Holt of the U.S. Army. Before the trial began, Brig. Gen. Morriss was replaced by Brigadier General J. P. Slough of the U.S. Volunteers.

Of the nine members, General Hunter was senior and was thus court president. Hunter was sixty years old, a graduate of West Point class of 1822, and one of only two court members senior to Porter. Except for a six year hiatus before the Mexican War, Hunter had remained on active duty in the army from the time of his commissioning in 1822 until appointed to the court-martial. Throughout his long and relatively undistinguished career, Hunter had demonstrated a knack for controversy. In fact, it was his latest controversy that caused him to be in Washington at the time and available for the court-martial. In March 1862 he had been placed in command of the federally occupied areas of South Carolina, Georgia, and Florida. In this capacity, he managed to enrage the governments of both the Union and the Confederacy. Prior to Lincoln's Proclamation of Emancipation, Hunter issued his own. He then began recruiting ex-slaves into regiments. President Lincoln repealed Hunter's decrees and ordered him relieved for exceeding his authority. President Davis put a bounty on his head and ordered him executed if captured. After the Porter trial, Hunter chaired the commit-

Major General David Hunter of the U.S. Volunteers was president of Porter's court-martial (courtesy the Massachusetts Commandery Military Order of the Loyal Legion and the U.S. Army Military History Institute).

tee investigating the loss of Harpers Ferry. He was then returned to field duty, where he continued his erratic performance until his retirement in 1866.

The next general on the court was Maj. Gen. E. A. Hitchcock. Hitchcock was sixty-four at the time of the trial and had graduated from West Point way back in 1817. He had much experience fighting Indians on the frontier and, by the time of the Mexican War, had risen to become inspector general of the army. In 1855, he resigned from the army because of an altercation with then secretary of war Jefferson Davis. At the outbreak of war, he returned to active duty but, because of his age, spent most of his time on administrative duties.

The third general on the court was Brig. Gen. Rufus King. He was forty-eight years old and, like Hunter and Hitchcock, a scholar of West Point, having graduated in 1833. King, however, did not follow a military career, but resigned from the army three years after graduation. He was a member of a well-to-do, politically connected family that had deep roots in American history. King was active in the newspaper business, politics, and education. He had served as superintendent of schools for the city of Milwaukee and as a regent for the University of Wisconsin. At the outset of war, he was U.S. Minister to the Papal States. He took a leave of absence from this position to accept a brigadier general's position in the U.S. Volunteers. King suffered from epilepsy and, in 1863, resigned from the army because of ill health.

Next was forty-three-year-old Brig. Gen. Prentiss. Prentiss, unlike most of the other members of the court, was not a West Point officer and not a career army officer. He was a Yale graduate and his occupation was the law. However, he did participate in the Mexican War as a junior volunteer officer and did continue active in the Illinois militia. At the outbreak of the war, he was a militia colonel and, when incorporated into the federal service, became a brigadier general. Prentiss was prominent in the battle of Shiloh and was captured by the Confederates. He was exchanged just before the Porter court-martial and thus found himself in Washington and available when the court members were selected.

Brig. Gen. Ricketts was a forty-five-year-old career officer who had graduated from West Point in 1839. At the outset of the war he was a captain in the regular army. He participated in the first battle of Manassas, where he was severely wounded and captured. He was exchanged just in time to participate in Pope's second battle of Manassas campaign. Afterwards, he participated in the battle of Antietam in September 1862, where he was again wounded. While recovering, he was assigned to a desk job in Washington. He was thus available when the assignments for the Porter trial were made.

Brig. Gen. Silas Casey was another old-timer from the regular army. Casey graduated from West Point in 1826 and, at the time of his appointment to the court-martial, was fifty-five years old. He had served continuously since his commissioning, and was renowned primarily for his authorship of the army's standard manual on infantry tactics that was commonly known as "Casey's

Tactics." Casey had seen combat in the Indian Wars, the Mexican War, and during McClellan's Peninsula Campaign. However, at the time of his appointment to the court, he was on desk duty in Washington.

The youngest of the court members was thirty-one-year-old Brig. Gen. James Garfield. Garfield had no pre–Civil War military experience. He had served as professor of ancient languages at Hiram College in Ohio, and then as president of the college. Garfield entered politics shortly before the war when he was elected to the Ohio State Legislature. He then became prominent for his anti-slavery rhetoric. At the outset of the war, he raised a company of volunteers and offered his services. In August 1861, he was sworn in as lieutenant colonel. Garfield demonstrated considerable military talent and, by the time of the trial, was a brigadier general and in Washington between assignments. He was thus available for assignment to the court-martial. Among Garfield's post-war accomplishments was being elected the twentieth president of the United States.

The eighth member of the court was Brig. Gen. N. B. Buford. The N. B. stood for Napoleon Bonaparte. Buford was fifty-five years old at the time of the trial. He had graduated from West Point in 1827 but resigned his commission in 1835 and did not pursue a military career. At the outset of hostilities, he raised a regiment and was made its colonel. Buford saw much action in the West in the early phases of the war but, by the fall of 1862, became seriously ill. During his convalescence, he was sent to Washington for desk duty, and hence ended up as a member of the court. Buford was the older brother of Brigadier General John Buford, whom we shall encounter later.

The last member of the court was Brig. Gen. John P. Slough. Slough was a thirty-three-year-old lawyer-politician with no pre-war military experience. He ended up as a member of the court because he was there. At the time of selection of members, he was military governor of nearby Alexandria, Virginia, a suburb of Washington.

Col. Joseph Holt, the designated judge advocate, was probably the most prominent of all those associated with the trial. He was fifty-five years old and, for many years, a prominent jurist. He served as postmaster general and then as secretary of war in the Buchanan cabinet. He did, however, support the war; Lincoln, in gratitude, appointed Holt the first adjutant general of the army with the rank of colonel.

To summarize, of the nine members of the court, six had graduated from West Point, and five had put in long years of service before the war. Most, or possibly all, happened to be in Washington at the time for one reason or another, and their availability may have constituted the main reason for their appointments.

Of great surprise to many was the appointment of General King and General Ricketts to the court. These two were the division commanders of McDowell—and McDowell, next to Pope, was the most damaging witness against

Porter. The conduct of all three (McDowell, King, and Ricketts) in the second battle of Manassas was subject to criticism by many. Some even considered it more worthy of censure than the conduct of Porter. For a time during the battle, King was actually directly subordinate to Porter—and most unsettling of all, King, as a member of the court, was called as a court witness.

The Articles of War did permit the accused to challenge a member of the court. It also provided that the court members themselves would decide upon the challenge. However, Porter made no challenge.

The first meeting of the court where all the members were present and substantive business was conducted occurred on Wednesday, December 3, 1862. Several events took place. Porter requested that the trial be open to the public and press. This was granted. Porter was asked if he objected to any member of the court. He did not. The nine charges against him were read. Five were against Article Nine (disobeying orders) and four were against Article Fifty-two (shameful conduct before the enemy). The judge advocate announced that the fourth charge against Article Fifty-two was being dropped. Eight charges remained. Porter pled "not guilty" to all eight charges.

The court began taking testimony on Thursday, December 4. Court President Hunter pushed matters at an accelerated pace. Hearings were usually conducted six days a week and the court took only a single day off for Christmas and a single day off for New Year's Day. Despite this, Secretary of War Stanton was not satisfied with the length of the trial and, on January 5, sent the court the following message:

War Department
Washington City, D. C. January 5, 1863

Major General Hunter, President etc.

General: The state of the service imperatively demands that the proceedings, having been pending more than four weeks, should be brought to a close without unnecessary delay. You are, therefore, directed to sit without regard to hours, and close your proceedings as rapidly as may be consistent with justice and the public service.

Yours truly,
Edwin M. Stanton
Secretary of War [5]

The court completed its hearing and rendered its verdict on January 10, less than a week after Stanton's letter.

By the time of the trial, shorthand had progressed to the point where the court recorder was able to keep a verbatim record of the proceedings as the trial progressed. This record has been preserved in the *Official Records of the War of the Rebellion*, which provides a complete description of the trial.

4

Charge 1, Specification 1

Charge 1st.—Violation of the Ninth Article of War
Specification 1st.—In this, that said Maj. Gen. Fitz-John Porter, of the Volunteers of the United States, having received a lawful order, on or about the 27th August, 1862, while at or near Warrenton Junction in Virginia, from Maj. Gen. John Pope, his superior and commanding officer, in the following figures and letters, to wit:

Headquarters Army of Virginia,
Bristoe Station, August 27, 1862 6:30 P.M.

Maj. Gen. F. J. Porter, Warrenton Junction:

General: The major-general commanding directs that you start at 1 o'clock tonight, and come forward with your whole corps, or such part of it as is with you, so as to be here by daylight to-morrow morning. Hooker has had a very severe action with the enemy, with a loss of about 300 killed and wounded. The enemy has been driven back, but is retiring along the railroad. We must drive him from Manassas, and clear the country between that place and Gainesville, where McDowell is. If Morell has not joined you, send word to him to push forward immediately; also, send word to Banks to hurry forward with all speed, to take your place at Warrenton Junction. It is necessary, on all accounts that you should be here by daylight. I send an officer with this dispatch, who will conduct you to this place. Be sure to send word to Banks who is on the road from Fayetteville, probably in the direction of Bealton. Say to Banks also, that he had best run back the railroad trains to this side of Cedar Run. If he is not with you, write him to that effect.

By command of Major-General Pope:
Geo. D. Ruggles
Colonel and Chief of Staff

P. S. If Banks is not at Warrenton Junction, leave a regiment of infantry and two pieces of artillery as a guard until he comes up, with instructions to follow you immediately. If Banks is not at the junction, instruct Colonel Clary to run the trains back to this side of Cedar Run, and post a regiment and section of artillery with it.

By command of Major-General Pope:
Geo. D. Ruggles
Colonel and Chief of Staff

Did then and there disobey the said order, being at the time in the face of the enemy. This at or near Warrenton, in the state of Virginia, on or about the 28th of August, 1862.[1]

(See map 7 for the situation at the time of the specification.)

The defense's plea to charge 1, specification 1 was "not guilty."

The distance from the station at Warrenton Junction to the station at Bristoe was nine and a half miles. However, the area over which Porter's nine thousand some men were bivouacked was considerable, so that distances to be covered by individual units may have varied by as much as a half mile or more. The term "daylight," by which time Porter's men were required to be at Bristoe, is non-scientific and non-precise. However, the terms "sunrise" and "begin civil twilight" are. On August 28, 1862, sunrise at Bristoe was 5:35 A.M. and "begin civil twilight" was 5:07 A.M. "Begin civil twilight" defines the time at which the horizon becomes visible and objects are distinguishable without artificial lighting. Obviously then, it was by about 5 A.M. that Pope wanted Porter's troops to begin arriving at Bristoe. Pope's order for Porter to begin his march at 1 A.M. was not arbitrary. This provided a maximum time for rest and a reasonable amount of time for the troops to arrive at Bristoe under most conditions at the specified time.

The reason for moving the railroad cars up the tracks as the troops advanced was so that they were not left behind Union protection and thus subject to destruction by Confederate cavalry. There were over one hundred such train cars on sidings loaded with ammunition, commissary supplies, forage, and sick or wounded. The trains could not be moved up the tracks farther than Kettle Run because the Confederates had destroyed the trestle at that location (see map 7).

The Situation the Night of August 27–28

Pope's Army of Virginia's primary supply line was the Orange and Alexandria Railroad, and his main supply base was Alexandria. It was from Alexandria that he received commissary, forage, and ammunition; it was from Alexandria that he received massive reinforcements as troops from McClellan's Army of the Potomac debarked from ships and transferred to cars on the Orange and Alexandria.

On the night of the twenty-sixth, Jackson reached the railroad at Bristoe in Pope's rear and began destroying bridges and trestles, cutting telegraph lines, destroying trains, and burning warehouses containing accumulated supplies. During the day of the twenty-seventh, Jackson moved two of his three divi-

Map 7—Evening of August 27

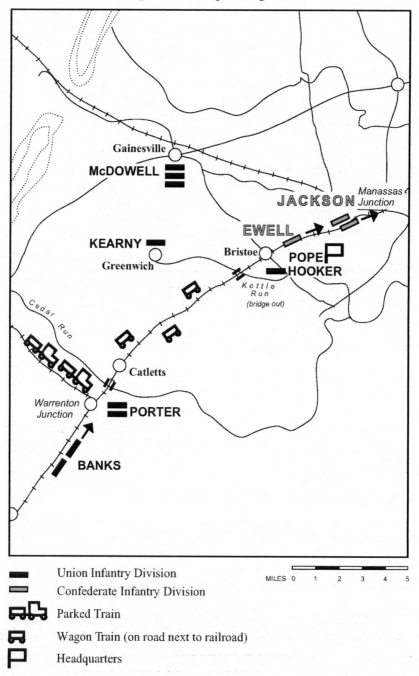

Gainesville

McDOWELL

JACKSON   *Manassas Junction*

EWELL

KEARNY   Bristoe

Greenwich   POPE
HOOKER

Kettle Run
(bridge out)

Cedar Run

Catletts

Warrenton
Junction   PORTER

BANKS

	Union Infantry Division
	Confederate Infantry Division
	Parked Train
	Wagon Train (on road next to railroad)
	Headquarters

MILES 0   1   2   3   4   5

sions up the railroad to Manassas, leaving his third division under his most
trusted subordinate, Richard Ewell, at Bristoe.

As Pope woke up at his headquarters-in-the-field at Warrenton Junction
on the twenty-seventh, he found both his supply line and telegraphic communications with Alexandria (and army headquarters at nearby Washington) cut
and the Confederates on the rail line just nine and a half miles above him at
Bristoe. Pope considered he had two tasks. First, he must drive Jackson from
the railroad and re-open his supply and communications with Alexandria; second, he must surround and destroy Jackson's isolated corps before it could be
joined by Longstreet.

Pope had the two divisions of Heintzelman's corps (Hooker and Kearny)
with him at Warrenton Junction. They had arrived by rail from Alexandria
between two and three days prior to Jackson's cutting the line. The infantry of
both divisions had been quickly transferred from ship to rail car at Alexandria
before their artillery, horses, and supply wagons arrived. Thus, they were at
Warrenton Junction without any of the three. Upon learning of Ewell at Bristoe, Pope ordered Hooker to proceed up the road paralleling the railroad direct
to Bristoe, and Kearny to take a road that angled off the railroad to the west,
so as to come in to the west of Ewell. As Hooker and Kearny marched off, the
only ammunition they had was the forty rounds that each man carried on his
person. Coincidentally, the Army of Virginia wagon train that had been heading up the same road that Hooker was now taking began arriving by the time
Hooker's last troops left, and continued on up following Hooker. The wagon
train was headed for the supply depot at Manassas.

As Hooker's and Kearny's troops were departing, Porter's corps began
arriving at Warrenton Junction, thus completing its long march up the Rappahannock to join Pope's Army of Virginia. Sykes's division arrived during the
morning, followed by Morell's. Porter personally reported to Pope, who then
set out with his staff by horseback for Bristoe, where the battle was undoubtedly going to commence when Hooker met Ewell.

By the time Pope arrived on the scene of combat, the battle was dying
down because of darkness. Hooker's men were now down to five rounds of
ammunition with no replenishment immediately available. Hooker could not
withdraw because his division was all that stood between the Confederates and
the vulnerable wagon train on the road in his rear. If the Confederates re-
opened the battle at dawn, it could be curtains for Hooker. It was in this environment that Pope sat down at 6:30 P.M. to write his order for Porter. He then
handed the order to his aide, Captain Drake DeKay, for delivery.

Porter received the order before 10 P.M. He immediately directed Colonel
Clary to move the railroad cars up to the break in the line at Kettle Run, but
did not order his troops to begin their march to Bristoe until 3 A.M. The head
of his column finally arrived at Bristoe Station at 10:20 A.M. on the twenty-
eighth. The crisis at Bristoe had passed before Porter's arrival; General Ewell

had withdrawn up the railroad to Manassas during the night rather than attacking Hooker at dawn as Pope feared.

The Prosecution's and Defense's Cases

The prosecution set out to demonstrate that, though the order required Porter to begin his march to Bristoe at 1 A.M. and to arrive at daylight (i.e., by 5 A.M.), he did not begin his march until after 3 A.M., and the head of his column did not arrive at Bristoe until 10:20 A.M. on the twenty-eighth. The prosecution also introduced evidence to indicate that Porter received the order by 10:00 P.M. on the twenty-seventh and thus had ample time to read it and implement it. Lastly, the prosecution introduced evidence to show that Porter was contemptuous of Pope and his abilities, which could have served as a reason for Porter's reactions to Pope's orders.

The defense attempted to demonstrate that Porter did everything possible that a reasonable and competent man could do to comply with Pope's order, but because of circumstances beyond his control, he could not comply to the letter. The defense put forward as factors precluding exact compliance the fatigue of Porter's troops from earlier marching, the darkness of the night, the blockage of the road by the wagon train, and the impossibility of moving the artillery along the road under such circumstances. The defense also attempted to rebut the allegation that Porter bore a contempt toward Pope.

The Trial—The Prosecution's Case

The first witness called by the prosecution was Gen. Pope. Pope affirmed that the text of the order contained in the specification was identical to the one he issued.

Pope testified that he was at Warrenton Junction with his staff when Porter arrived with Sykes's division between 7 and 10 A.M. He said that Porter reported in to him personally. Shortly thereafter, about noon, Pope, his staff, cavalry escort, and twelve to fifteen headquarters wagons set out for Bristoe, where it was assumed that Hooker's division would enter into action against Ewell's Confederates. The group hit the road to Bristoe shortly beyond Cedar Run. Pope stated that the road was in good condition, sometimes running on one side of the railroad, sometimes crossing over to the other side, and sometimes running on both sides. Although they encountered wagons on the road heading toward Bristoe, Pope alleged that they posed no particular problem to the passage of his group. Upon reaching Kettle Run, the group reached the scene of earlier combat, which had now moved farther up the tracks toward Bristoe. Pope made several stops to observe the dead and wounded. Despite some relatively long stops, the group reached Bristoe about 5 P.M.

As Pope's group moved up the road from Cedar Run to Bristoe, he noted an almost continuous stream of stragglers from Hooker's division walking along the railroad to join Hooker at Bristoe. Pope estimated their number as fifteen hundred. Their preferred route was obviously the railroad tracks rather than the road. Pope stated that there was no impediment to their progress on the tracks whatsoever all the way to Kettle Run.

Shortly after 5 P.M., Pope testified that he was approached by Hooker and Heintzelman at Bristoe. It was now getting dark and the battle had wound down. Hooker advised Pope that his men were now down to five rounds of ammunition each and that there was no replenishment readily available. Furthermore, Jackson and his other two Confederate divisions were just a few miles farther down the track at Manassas; if Jackson learned of Hooker's weakness, he might decide to reinforce Ewell that night and attack Hooker at daylight. If that happened, it would be disaster for Hooker, Heintzelman, and Pope. It was in this environment that Pope dictated to his chief of staff, Colonel Ruggles, his order for Porter. Upon the completion of the drafting of Pope's order, Pope gave it to his aide, Capt. Drake DeKay, for delivery to Porter.

Pope testified that he chose 1 A.M. as the starting time for Porter's troops to allow them a maximum of rest and to still get them off in sufficient time to easily arrive at Bristoe by daylight. In fact, he estimated that they would arrive not later than 4 A.M.

Pope stated that the night, although moonless, was not particularly dark and that he had marched larger numbers of troops than Porter had under worse conditions. He stated that after a long day, he lay down to sleep on the ground, without shelter, and slept soundly, and had there been inclement weather during the night, this would not have been possible. He stated that upon awakening, he sent more than one officer to find the status of Porter and to hurry him along; and that all reported that Porter was making slow progress.

Pope testified that he was at Bristoe Station when the head of Porter's column finally arrived, and that he looked at his watch and it was 10:20 A.M.

Pope acknowledged that the wagons in the road might have posed a problem for Porter's artillery but insisted that the infantry could easily have been at Bristoe at the specified time. Pope stated that he was surprised to learn that Porter had ordered the railroad cars to be moved up to the break in the line at Kettle Run before Porter marched his infantry. Porter thus denied his infantry the use of the rail tracks. Pope said that it was neither his expectation nor his intention that Porter should move the rail cars first.

In general, Pope proved to be a very effective witness for the prosecution. He appeared to answer each question precisely and with great thought, and always differentiated what he had seen with his own eyes, what he had learned from others, and what he merely thought.

The questioning of Pope by the defense was ineffective and, in fact, was counterproductive and detrimental to Porter. It concentrated on two instances. The first was a conversation Porter had with Pope after Porter's arrival at Bristoe on August 28, and the second was a conversation that Porter had with Pope at Fairfax Court House on September 2, after the battle.

The defense attempted to demonstrate that Pope had no criticism of Porter either during the action (August 28) or after its completions (September 2) and, in fact, in the September 2 conversation stated that he was satisfied with Porter's performance and planned no further action.

Pope initially appeared defensive and feigned a lack of memory as to just what was said in each instance. He eventually expanded upon the conversation of September 2 and said, among other things, that he had learned from friends in Washington that Porter "had written letters or sent dispatches to General Burnside, dated before he (Porter) had joined me, that criticized my conduct, my military capacity, and the campaign which I was conducting, very severely and which exhibited an exceedingly unkind spirit."[2] Pope's treatment of Porter in the subsequent conversation (according to Pope) was a model of moderation, reasonableness, and charity.

Pope's divulging of the "Burnside dispatches" constituted the prosecution's opening salvo in its attempt to demonstrate that it was Porter's contemptuous attitude toward Pope that constituted a motivation for Porter to disobey Pope's orders. (This point did not relate to a single charge or specification, but appeared at various points in the trial and related to all charges and specifications, and will be addressed as a separate subject in a separate chapter.)

The next witness for the prosecution was Capt. Drake DeKay, Gen. Pope's aide-de-camp who was entrusted with delivering the order to Gen. Porter. Pieced together from various answers to various questions, Capt. DeKay's story is as follows:

He took the dispatch from Col. Ruggles at Bristoe and set out for Warrenton Junction. Warrenton Junction was nine to ten miles from Bristoe. DeKay did not read the dispatch but knew its contents. The night was moonless and cloudy but not particularly dark. There was no rain. There was a large number of wagons on the road heading in the direction of Bristoe. DeKay passed the last wagon on the road before he got to Catletts Station. He then passed a large park of wagons camping for the night between Catletts and Warrenton Junction. He arrived at Gen. Porter's tent at about 9:30 P.M. He gave the dispatch to Porter and advised him that he was directed to guide Porter's troops to Bristoe when they departed at 1 A.M.

He further advised Porter that the road was good, that he had difficulty because of the large number of wagons in the road, but that he passed the last wagon in the road before he got to Catletts. He also told Porter that the infantry could walk along the railroad track, and that when he had accompanied Pope on the road to Bristoe during the day of the twenty-seventh, he noted that most all of Hooker's stragglers used that as the preferred route.

When DeKay entered Porter's tent, Porter was not alone. He was conversing with his two division commanders, Gen. Sykes and Gen. Morell. General Butterfield, a brigade commander, was also there or entered soon thereafter. Upon reading the dispatch, Porter commented to all in general that his troops had just got into camp; they had been marched hard that day and would be good for nothing if they started that time of night and that if their rest was broken, they would be good for nothing on coming up with the enemy.

As the discussion continued, it became evident to DeKay that they were not going to march before dawn, so his services were not going to be required that night. He decided to go to bed. He was invited to bed down in Gen. Porter's tent, which he did. It was now about 11 P.M. The next DeKay remembers was being awakened for breakfast. It was now just getting daylight. DeKay could not remember whether they used candles for breakfast. Porter's column started out for Bristoe at about 4 A.M. with DeKay at its head.

When they reached the point between Warrenton Junction and Catletts where DeKay had seen the large camp of wagons the previous night, the camp was now largely empty, most wagons having entered the road on their trip to Bristoe. Porter joined DeKay at the head of the column near Catletts. The column moved at a normal pace with no evidence of urgency. Occasionally they encountered jumbles of wagons in the road which blocked their progress. In these instances, Gen. Porter acted very vigorously to clear the way. DeKay estimated that the head of the column arrived at Bristoe about 10 A.M.

DeKay also testified that he had been with Gen. Pope at Warrenton Junction on the morning of the twenty-seventh, until Pope and staff departed for Bristoe. DeKay said that about 10 A.M. he visited with a number of officers from Sykes's division whom he had previously known. He could thus testify that Sykes's division was there at that time.

The accused's examination of DeKay was ineffective and largely counterproductive for the defense. It served mostly to validate DeKay's story.

The next prosecution witness was Brig. Gen. B. S. Roberts. Roberts was inspector general of Pope's Army of Virginia. Most of Roberts's testimony related to other charges and specifications than charge 1, specification 1, and to Porter's attitude toward Pope. This testimony is treated elsewhere. Following is a summary of Roberts's testimony relative to charge 1, specification 1:

As inspector general, Roberts was a member of Pope's staff, was close to the person of Pope, and was thoroughly knowledgeable of Pope's plans and orders. On the morning of August 27, Roberts was at Warrenton Junction, and by 9 or 10 A.M., a part of Porter's corps had already arrived. Roberts saw Gen. Pope with Gen. Porter at about 10 A.M. The troops that had arrived and were arriving belonged to Gen. Sykes's division, and Roberts met a large number of officers from that division by noon. At about noon, Gen. Morell's division began to arrive and Roberts met with Gen. Morell at that time. Gen. Morell was quite sick and Roberts had a lengthy conversation with him. Among other things, Gen. Morell divulged that the condition of his troops was quite good.

When Gen. Pope left Warrenton Junction for Bristoe about 1 P.M., Roberts accompanied him. The condition of the road was generally good. The first three or four miles passed through open country with some woods intersecting it. Some bridges had been burned, and passing over the streams was the only difficulty Roberts recalled. Even this, though, was not a problem, as numerous wagons passed over them without difficulty.

At Bristoe Station, Gen. Pope dictated an order for Porter in Roberts's presence. Roberts identified the order as the one in charge 1, specification 1. The order was written about sundown, probably between 5:30 and 6 P.M. The order was then given to Capt. DeKay for delivery. DeKay departed between 6:30 and 7 P.M. Roberts could not say what time Porter's column arrived at Bristoe Station, as he was not there at the time.

The defense questioned Roberts about the conditions of the night of August 27–28. Roberts responded that, according to his recollection, it was moonless and at times cloudy and quite dark. He had been sleeping on the ground without cover and, at about midnight, it appeared to be threatening rain so he got up and got into a wagon. When questioned as to how far he could see that night, he responded that he could not answer that question; their entire camp was under the glow of fires that the Confederates had left and were still burning.

The next two prosecution witnesses had much to offer about other matters, but little to offer relative to charge 1, specification 1. The first of the two was U.S. Army Surgeon Robert O. Abbott. Abbott was medical director of the Fifth Corps (Porter's). In fact, Abbott said nothing about the events of August 27 and 28 during examination by the prosecution. It was only upon questioning by the defense that Abbott revealed his involvement in the march of the Fifth Corps during the night of August 27–28.

Abbott testified he was with Porter's corps at Warrenton Junction at the time Porter was ordered to proceed to Bristoe. Reveille sounded very early on the twenty-eighth. Abbott could not give the hour but recalled that they started soon after daylight. However, there were troops that started in advance of his unit and he did not know what time they started. It was a dark night, the road was a great deal blocked with wagons, and Gen. Porter exerted great effort to clear the way. This terminated Abbott's testimony. Abbott did not amplify why being a "dark night" had anything to do with the march if they started, as he had said, at daylight.

The next witness was Colonel Thomas C. H. Smith. Smith identified himself as an aide-de-camp on the staff of Gen. Pope. Smith had much to say about Porter's attitude toward Pope, but the only testimony he gave relating to Porter's march from Warrenton Junction to Bristoe consisted of a description of the route as he observed it while traversing it earlier in the day. Smith said that he departed Warrenton Junction for Bristoe late in the afternoon on the twenty-seventh, he estimated between 4:30 and 5 P.M. He gave a confusing description of the route:

> For the first mile and a half, until you get to Cedar Run, the road was bordered on either side by open fields, or open woods, over which troops could march easily, in great part without going on the road. Indeed, I doubt whether there is any road a good part of the way up. The troops (Hooker's) marched through the fields to Bristoe Station. A road has been worn by the troops I suppose. At Cedar Run, just above the railroad, on the west side there was a bridge, and a ford with it, and men coming this side of Cedar Run soon struck a small piece of woods, which is perhaps [less] than a quarter of a mile. I give these things as I remember them. I may be mistaken in this point. There it is rather a bad road for marching. Then for a considerable distance, and for most of the way until you get to Kettle Run, the road was practicable, and also the fields on either side of it. I remember that distinctly, for at Catlett's Station I saw something of the character of the country, as I stopped there a few moments. At Kettle Run there was another bad place. There was, however, a very practicable ford there; a narrow ravine, the road running down, with high banks to it, on either side. I should say that there was a half a mile or three quarters of a mile of the road in which, if there was a wagon train, the march of troops would be badly impeded. The railroad track was good, all that I saw of it; men could march upon it.[3]

Next up for the prosecution was Maj. Gen. Heintzelman. Heintzelman was commanding general of the Third Corps, which consisted of the divisions of Kearny and Hooker. It was thus Heintzelman's troops that were in action at Bristoe on the twenty-seventh. It was Heintzelman's troops that Porter had been called upon to support in the events described in charge 1, specification 1. In the questioning by the prosecution, Heintzelman affirmed that Hooker was short of ammunition after the battle at Kettle Run on the twenty-seventh and that he made known this fact to Gen. Pope.

The accused then questioned Heintzelman on the condition of the road from Warrenton Junction to Bristoe. Heintzelman stated that it was in tolerable good condition; it was narrow and in places ran through some woods. There were a few little ditches that were bad crossings, and he thought that the road crossed the railroad once or twice and he considered the railroad crossings bad. There was a large wagon train on the road that did not belong to his troops, but was proceeding between the rear of his troops and Porter's at Warrenton Junction, and this constituted a considerable obstruction for troops coming up from Warrenton Junction. As for marching on the railroad, it would be very difficult at night, as some of the rails were torn up, ties were piled on the tracks, culverts destroyed, and bridges burned.

When questioned as to the darkness of the night of August 27–28,

Heintzelman responded that it was very dark, and during the course of the night there was a drizzling rain. Heintzelman acknowledged, however, that it would not have been impossible for troops to march along the road that night but alleged that there would have been many stragglers.

Heintzelman's description of the condition of the railroad for marching is very different from the description of other witnesses. Others testified that there was no impediment to marching on the railroad all the way to the break at Kettle Run. Furthermore, no one disputed that trains ran back and forth along the tracks all the way to Kettle Run that night. The discrepancy between Heintzelman's testimony and others can be attributed entirely to the time of observations. No one saw fit to ask Heintzelman the time he passed along the road and made his observations. The fact that Heintzelman said that the wagon train was behind him clearly indicates that his observations were made during the morning of the twenty-seventh, when he undoubtedly accompanied Hooker's troops (his own corps) on their march from Warrenton Junction to Bristoe. Pope had ordered that the railroad be brought into full operating condition all the way to Kettle Run on the twenty-seventh, and this was done. Heintzelman observed the railroad while the work was in progress and others observed it after it was complete.

The next three prosecution witnesses—Maj. Gen. McDowell, telegraph operator Theodore Moreland, and Colonel Speed Butler—had no information relative to charge 1, specification 1. Next was Lieutenant Colonel Frederick Myers, chief quartermaster to Gen. McDowell. He was in charge of the wagon train that was strung out on the Bristoe–Warrenton Junction road behind Hooker's division. The train consisted of over two thousand wagons and was en route to the Union supply depot at Manassas.

Myers testified that he was at the head of the wagon train following behind Hooker's division. Just before dark, when the head of the train was about one and a half miles short of Kettle Run, Gen. Pope and staff rode up. Myers informed Pope that Hooker was in action in front of him and asked Pope if he should continue on or go into park. Pope told him to use his own judgment. Myers decided that, inasmuch as they had already traversed a normal day's distance of twenty miles, they would go into park. Myers passed the word back along the train. Thus, the head of the train went into park about one and a half miles short of Kettle Run with no wagons in advance of that position. Myers had no specific knowledge of what wagons behind him did, but testified that he heard movements during the night as wagons continued to move, seeking places to park. After spending the night in park, the head of Myers's column commenced moving at daylight. Myers stated that the condition of the road was excellent, that it was a dark night, but he could not offer any opinion of the night in the hours before daylight. When questioned as to whether he knew of anything that would have hindered the movement of troops that night, Myers replied: "I do not know of anything to hinder troops moving along the railroad there. There was a road running each side of the railroad. I should think it would have been easy for troops to move along there, although I may be mistaken in that."[4]

The final four witnesses for the prosecution were Major S. F. Barstow, Col. Benjamin Smith, Lieutenant Edward P. Brooks, and Captain W.B.C. Duryea. Col. Smith had no testimony relative to charge 1, specification 1. Maj. Barstow and Capt. Duryea both belonged to components of Maj. Gen. McDowell's corps. Each testified that he participated in a march along the Warrenton pike during the night of August 27–28. Barstow said that the night was "very much like other nights"[5] and Duryea said that they encountered no unusual problems. McDowell's corps was of course not Porter's corps, and the Warrenton pike was not the Warrenton Junction–Bristoe road. They were, however, nearby—and this did constitute evidence that marching was possible that night.

Lt. Brooks did have considerable information that bore directly on the charge and specification. He was carrying a dispatch for Gen. Kearny late on the twenty-seventh. At the time, Kearny was located at Greenwich, which is five and a half miles to the west of Bristoe (see map 7). Brooks's itinerary was as follows: departed Warrenton Junction about 4:30 P.M.; arrived at Bristoe about 7 P.M.; departed Bristoe about 9 P.M.; arrived at Greenwich 12:10 A.M. (August 28); went to bed at Greenwich about 1 A.M. (August 28). Brooks described the road from Warrenton Junction to Bristoe as "very good." He stated that he passed wagons on the road, but as he passed they were in the process of going into park. He said that the night was "not very dark—not so dark but what I could find my way through the woods."[6]

This constituted the prosecution's case. The prosecution had thus produced evidence to indicate that:

(1) The order in the specification was the one dictated by Pope and delivered to Porter.

(2) The order was delivered to Porter by 10 P.M., giving him ample time to act upon it.

(3) Porter made no effort to start out at 1 A.M. as required by the order. In fact, he did not start out until 3 A.M. at the earliest, but probably later.

(4) Once he did start out, he did not hurry.

(5) He did not arrive at Bristoe at daylight as required by the order and, in fact, the head of his column did not arrive until after 10 A.M. on the twenty-eighth.

(6) The road to Bristoe was in good condition and the wagons in the road were already going into park before Porter was required to start.

(7) There was no obstacle to marching along the railroad all the way to Kettle Run.

(8) The night was not so dark as to prevent marching. In fact, others did so the same night and in the same general area.

The Defense Case

The defense called twenty witnesses. Nine were generals, two of whom were senior to Gen. Pope and to all the members of the court. Thirteen of the twenty had testimony that related to charge 1, specification 1. Four had testimony that only related to Porter's attitude toward Pope, which is applicable to all the charges and specifications (the testimony of these will be treated in Chapter 9). The remaining three only had testimony that related to charges and specifications other than charge 1, specification 1.

The first of the thirteen was Col. Robert E. Clary. Although Col. Clary did not indicate his position when called, he was the same Col. Clary who was referred to in specification 1. It was Clary that Porter was to order to move the railroad trains up the tracks beyond Cedar Run.

Clary testified that he was at Warrenton Junction on the night of the twenty-seventh. At 10 P.M., he received a note from Gen. Porter to move the trains beyond Cedar Run toward Bristoe Station. He gave the necessary orders and the moving of the trains began immediately. He was occupied with the trains until 2 A.M. on the twenty-eighth. At that time, he set out by horseback with a group of ten or twelve for Bristoe. They came to a fork in the road with both roads looking equally well-traveled, and then took the wrong road and became lost. They then waited about two hours for daylight, corrected their route, and proceeded on to Bristoe. The night was generally dark and cloudy. For the first three miles out of Warrenton Junction, the road was clear and the bridge over Cedar Run was intact. They then ran into an obstruction of wagons on the road that extended three miles. Because of this obstruction, it was very difficult for their group to pass by.

Upon examination by the prosecution, Clary admitted that it would have been possible for troops to pass over the road that night, but only if an advance party had been sent out to clear the obstruction.

The next defense witness was Captain B. F. Fifield. Fifield identified himself as commissary who was attached to Gen. Pope's headquarters and was in charge of the transportation and railroads for the Department of the Army of Virginia.

Capt. Fifield was in bed when Col. Clary approached at about 10:30 P.M. Clary read Fifield the order to move the trains. As Fifield recalled, the trains were to be moved from Warrenton Junction as close as possible to Bristoe Station. This would be at Kettle Run since the bridge was down at that point. The trains were to be moved by 1 A.M., as the army was to be under march at that time and there would be no rear guard to protect the trains. The cars to be moved were loaded with quartermaster and commissary stores, a large amount of ordnance stores, and camp equipage that belonged to the units of the Army of the Potomac that had joined Pope's army.

Fifield had more cars to move than engines to move them. Consequently, some engines had to make four trips up and back to Kettle Run. The last cars and engine were not parked at Kettle Run until about 4 A.M. on the twenty-eighth. There was much coming and going on the track up to that time, making the track too dangerous for infantry marching.

Fifield started out for Bristoe as a member of the Clary party at about 2 A.M. They were on horseback. As indicated by Clary, the party got lost and did not arrive at Bristoe until after daylight. Fifield stated that they encountered wagons on the road. They were stationary in a jam about three miles long. The jam commenced after they had passed Catletts Station. For some portion of the way where the jam occurred, there was timbered country. It was very dark. In some places it would have been very difficult to have moved the wagons without great trouble. In other places, they could have been moved out of the road with reasonably energetic action.

The court asked Fifield: "With 100 efficient men, commencing at 10 P.M. that night, do you think you could have cleared the wagon road so as to have rendered it passable for troops?"[7] Fifield responded: "If I could have had command of the wagon road, and a sufficient force when the wagon trains commenced their movement, I think I could have kept them from a jam."[8] Fifield thus dodged the question. When he was questioned as to the character of the night, he responded: "The early part of the night was an ordinary starlight night of summer, without any moon; about half past 11 o'clock it commenced overcastting and threatened rain; very black clouds came up, and it did sprinkle a little. It was very dark from this time till toward morning."[9]

Captain George Montieth was next up for the defense. He was aide-de-camp to Gen. Porter. His story was as follows: During the evening of the twenty-seventh, Gen. Porter sent Montieth and Captain McQuade out on a mission to find the road to Greenwich. (This is the road that Gen. Kearny and his division took that morning.) Montieth assumed that they were being so tasked because Gen. Porter expected to move his corps by that road in the morning. Upon reaching Catletts Station on the Warrenton Junction–Bristoe road, they noticed a road angling off to the left. It appeared to be un-traveled and, consequently, they were in doubt if it was the Greenwich road. They noticed a house with a light on and went to inquire. The house proved to be that of Mr. Catlett, namesake of the station. Catlett affirmed that that was the Greenwich road. There were no wagons on the Greenwich road. Upon reaching Catletts Station on their way back, they encountered a wagon train on the Warrenton Junction–Bristoe road. Some of the wagons were moving and some were stopped. It was a very dark night and they had trouble getting back to Porter's tent. Montieth reported to Porter that they had located the Greenwich road, but could not recall if he told him about the wagons.

Montieth estimated that Porter's march for Bristoe commenced at about 3 A.M. while it was still dark. Between 4 and 5 A.M., when it was already becoming light, Gen. Porter tasked Montieth and Lt. Weld, along with about six cavalry men, to go forward and clear the road for the infantry. They encountered wagons as far as Montieth could see. In some places the road was so narrow and the trees so dense on both sides that they could not get the wagons off the road, and had to move them forward to a wider section, or one without impediment to their moving off the road. Montieth understood later that, after his group left on their mission, Gen. Porter sent off a second group under his chief of staff, Colonel Locke, with the same mission.

Upon examination by the prosecution, Capt. Montieth made some additions and explanations to his testimony. Montieth said that it was about one half hour before sunset when he set out on his mission to find the Greenwich road, and it was after dark, between seven and eight o'clock, when he returned to make his report. As for his testimony that Porter's troops started out their march to Bristoe at about 3 A.M., he stated that they were not actually in motion at 3 A.M., but soon after they formed and started to move and quickly got into confusion with a battery or two of artillery. The actual onward march commenced about dawn.

The defense then called Lt. Weld, Capt. Montieth's companion in clearing the road on the morning of the twenty-eighth. Weld's testimony relative to charge 1, specification 1, was brief and was limited to the condition of the night of August 27–28. When asked what kind of night it was, he responded: "It was very dark indeed. I went to bed about 10 o'clock, and then the night was very dark indeed. I heard someone, I think it was General Morell, who came into camp before I went to bed, say that he was trying to find General Sykes' headquarters, but had lost his way. General Sykes' headquarters were very near ours [Porter's]. In the morning I got up by 3 o'clock, and it was then drizzling."[10]

Next up for the defense was Lt. Col. Frederick T. Locke, Porter's chief of staff. Locke testified that sometime during the day of the twenty-seventh, the time of which he could not remember, Porter received an order from Gen. Pope to march to Greenwich. However, about 10 P.M., a second order changing this was brought to him by Capt. Drake DeKay. This order was to march to Bristoe, and the order called for him to start at 1 A.M. Earlier that evening, about 8 P.M., Gen. Porter had received a report on the status of the road to Bristoe. The report was that the road was very much blocked with wagons, and that there were several bad places in the road. Porter ordered the corps to begin its march to Bristoe at 3 A.M.; reveille was between 1 and 2 A.M.

Locke stated that the men were very much fatigued, that a part had marched seventeen to eighteen miles before coming into camp, and that the other part had marched eleven or twelve miles. He further testified that the march actually started about 3 A.M., that it was dark, and that they immediately ran into difficulties. The difficulties, aside from the darkness, were caused by the wagon trains on the road. Locke said that he personally injured himself groping about in the dark, but did not elaborate. Once the march commenced,

Locke contended that they moved as fast as they could. He said that Gen. Porter made great personal exertions to clear the road, and said that he used his staff and all available cavalry for the same purpose.

The questioning of Locke by the prosecution did not elicit any new significant information. The court, however, did submit a question to Locke that drew an embarrassing admission. As we will recall, Locke had testified that Porter had learned that the road was bad, that he received an order to march at 1 A.M., and that he had ordered the march to begin at 3 A.M. The question put to him was, "In case of an order for the movement of troops at a specified time, to meet an emergency, would a report of bad roads be a reason for commencing the march before or after the time fixed in the order, if the time is to be varied from at all?"[11] Locke replied: "If the time were to be varied from, it would be better to have it prior to the fixed time than after."[12] The court then asked Locke if he thought Porter's troops could have made more rapid progress if they had started at 1 A.M. rather than 3 A.M. Locke replied that he thought not.

Next up for the defense was Captain A. P. Martin. Martin was in command of the artillery in Morell's division. Martin testified that reveille the night of August 27–28 was about 1 A.M. The troops were ordered to march at 3 A.M. and the actual movement forward was between 3 and 4 A.M. The night was very dark and Martin's artillery encountered problems almost immediately upon leaving camp. There was a creek bordering the camp and many of the carriages got stuck. Some could not be extricated until after daylight.

The defense then called Maj. Gen. George W. Morell, the senior of Porter's two division commanders and thus next in line to command the Fifth Corps after Porter. Morell said that he himself arrived at Warrenton Junction in the middle of the afternoon on the twenty-seventh. His division arrived throughout the afternoon with the last brigade arriving just before sunset and stragglers after that. Two of his brigades had marched from Kelly's Ford, and the third from Barnett's Ford. The distance from Warrenton Junction to Kelly's Ford was about seventeen miles, and to Barnett's Ford was about nineteen or twenty miles.

Morell said that when his troops arrived at Warrenton Junction, they were much exhausted. From the time they left the James River on August 14 until they arrived at Warrenton Junction, they had been marching daily, and sometimes at night, with the exception of their day and night sea trip from Fortress Monroe to Aquia, and a rest on August 25.

Morell testified that he was present in Gen. Porter's tent the night of the twenty-seventh when Capt. DeKay arrived with Gen. Pope's order. This was about 10 P.M. He said that Gen. Sykes and Gen. Butterfield were also either present or arrived soon thereafter. Gen. Porter informed them that they were ordered to march at 1 A.M. that night, but did not read the order to them. As Gen. Morell recollected, Capt. DeKay said nothing about a problem of Gen.

Hooker running out of ammunition as a reason for Porter's early presence. Furthermore, Morell believed that he was present for the full length of the conversation between Porter and DeKay. Upon hearing that they were required to march at 1 A.M., the three subordinate generals all spoke up. They pointed out the darkness of the night and the fatigue of the troops, and opined that they would make better progress if they started at daylight.

After hearing his subordinates out, Porter decreed that they would start at 3 A.M. At this, Morell left Porter's tent to prepare the march. Morell elaborated on the condition of the night. He said that it was very dark, cloudy, threatening to rain and, in fact, did rain before morning. Reveille was sounded about 1:30 or 2 A.M., providing the men enough time to get their breakfast before starting. They started about 3 A.M. When Morell's troops did get started, they immediately ran into problems caused by a small stream directly in front of their camp. Sykes's division was scheduled to go first, and when Morell's troops reached the road, they had to stop and wait until Sykes had passed. This wait extended into daylight hours.

In conclusion, the court asked Morell if he thought they could have made better progress by starting at 1 A.M. Morell replied that he did not believe they could.

The next witness for the defense was Brig. Gen. Charles Griffin. Griffin was a brigade commander in Morell's division of Porter's corps.

Griffin testified that his brigade left Barnett's Ford on the Rappahannock at about 7 A.M. on August 27. The day was warm and the march was fatiguing. There were many stragglers. The brigade arrived at Warrenton Junction about sundown. The distance covered was eighteen to nineteen miles. The night of August 27–28 was very dark. It sprinkled about 10 P.M.

About midnight, Griffin received an order to move his brigade at 3 A.M. Reveille was at 1:30 A.M. and the infantry started out at 3 A.M. They had marched about 1 mile, using candles to find their way through the woods to the road, when the division commander, Gen. Morell, called a halt. The reason was that the brigade had become separated and the halt was to allow it to close up. The reason for the separation was that some artillery had become stuck in the mud or water of a creek near the camp. About two hours of daylight elapsed before forward motion was resumed.

Griffin opined that they would actually have made better progress had they started at daylight, as the artillery then would have avoided becoming mired down. In any event, Griffin stated that there were some bad places on the Warrenton Junction–Bristoe road that would have been nearly impossible for artillery to traverse in the dark. One such place was near Catletts Station, where there was a steep hill, winding roads, and woods.

In response to questioning by the court, Griffin acknowledged that some infantry could probably have gotten through to Bristoe in the dark if they had had no artillery. The tenor of Griffin's answers to questions posed by the court was that moving the artillery in the dark was the main problem; that the corps always marched one brigade, one battery of artillery, one brigade, one battery, etc. That's the way they always marched. Finally, the court put the following question: "Did you mean to say, in answer to the question about moving an army, when positively ordered to do so, that it is not common in emergencies to move infantry in the night, and leave a force to bring up the artillery afterward?"[13] Griffin replied: "I have yet to know an instance of leaving our division artillery when we have been moving by land."[14]

The next witness for the defense was Brig. Gen. John F. Reynolds. Reynolds was in command of a division that was normally part of Porter's corps. However, Reynolds had reported to Pope before Porter arrived with his other two divisions, and Pope assigned Reynolds's division to McDowell's corps. On the night of August 27–28, Reynolds's division was not at Warrenton Junction with Porter, but was ten miles away on the Warrenton pike with McDowell. Consequently, Reynolds's testimony relative to charge 1, specification 1, was limited to his estimate of the feasibility of marching under the conditions of the night.

Reynolds stated that, although his division went into camp at dark the night of August 27–28, he was up much of the night. He considered that the night was very dark, and he did not think it feasible to march large masses of troops over unfamiliar country unless they were on a road and had a guide. Even then, if the road was blocked, it would be difficult.

The prosecution put the following question to Reynolds: "You say that the night of 27 August was too dark to have marched troops over a country not known to them, without a guide or a road to follow. Suppose they had a road, and a guide who had passed over the road a few hours before, who was acquainted with it; or professed to be acquainted with it, who proposed to conduct the army, and that army was to march during that night over one of the country roads of Virginia, would it have been practicable to do so?"[15] The prosecution thus presented Reynolds with precisely the situation confronting Porter, except for mentioning possible blockage on the road. Reynolds's answer to the question was: "I suppose it would."[16] Thus, Reynolds's testimony was not helpful to the defense and may even have been counterproductive.

Major George Hyland, Jr., was up next for the defense. Hyland was a major of the Thirteenth New York, the second regiment in the first brigade of Gen. Morell's division of Gen. Porter's corps. He testified that he was with his regiment on the march from Kelly's Ford to Warrenton Junction on the twenty-seventh. He said that the regiment arrived about dusk, the men were much worn out, and that they had no provisions that day to any amount. He then said that the march to Bristoe commenced about 3 A.M. the following morning. Neither the prosecution nor the court had any questions relative to this testimony.

The next witness for the defense was perhaps the most important of the trial in determining the guilt or innocence of Gen. Porter to charge 1, specification 1. The witness was Brig. Gen. George Sykes. Sykes was the junior of Porter's two division commanders. It was Sykes's division that was scheduled to take the lead in the march to Bristoe. Thus, no one would have departed from Warrenton Junction before the head of Sykes's column departed, and no one would have arrived at Bristoe Station before the head of Sykes's column arrived. The time Sykes's column departed Warrenton Junction would inevitably be considered the time Porter departed, and the time the head of Sykes's column arrived at Bristoe Station would be the time Porter arrived. All others of Porter's corps were, in a sense, following the leader.

Sykes testified:

> About 10 P.M. on the 27th of August General Porter sent for me. We were then encamped at Warrenton Junction, Virginia. In his tent I met General Morell, General Butterfield, and Captain Drake DeKay. General Porter informed me that he had received an order by the hands of Captain DeKay, directing his corps to march at 1 o'clock A.M. on the 28th. We talked it over among ourselves, and thought that nothing was to be gained by moving at midnight or 1 A.M. rather than at dawn. I was very positive in my opinion, and gave General Porter my reasons; They were, first, that a night march is always exceedingly fatiguing and injurious to troops; that my command had already marched from 12 to 14 miles that day; that I thought the darkness would cause confusion; that a constant stream of wagons had passed ahead of us from the time my command reached Warrenton Junction until dusk; and, above all, as I thought that but two hours or three hours at most would elapse between 1 o'clock and daylight, we could make the march in much better order, and march more rapidly, by starting at dawn than if we started at the hour prescribed. I might add that General Porter made his decision not to move until daylight, and I took it that the decision was based upon his own experience and upon the opinions of the three general officers in his corps next in rank to himself.[17]

Sykes was then asked if he understood that the hour for the movement of the troops had been fixed at 3 A.M. He replied: "I cannot say that I did. But as my division led, I know the hours at which I fixed the reveille and the advance. Reveille in my own division was beaten at 2 or 2:30 A.M., and the advance was sounded as soon as I could distinguish the road. I generally allow an hour and one half or two hours between reveille and the advance."[18] Sykes was next asked about the condition of the night. He replied: "The night was unusually dark. Before I directed the advance to be sounded, I sent an aide-de-camp to find the road, so as to lead the column upon it. He returned in a short time and told me that the darkness was so great that he could not distinguish the road. He also told me that he was assisted in that search by several soldiers."[19]

Sykes was then asked to describe any difficulties he met on the road to Bristoe. He replied:

> As I anticipated, we ran upon this train of wagons within 2 miles of my camp; they encumbered the road for miles. Myself and staff officers were constantly engaged in opening the way for the head of my column. On several occasions I had to take my mounted escort, and place them on the road, with drawn sabers, to prevent the wagons from closing up any interval that occurred. I do not think that in my military life I had so much trouble with a train as I had that day. The wagon masters and teamsters alike were insubordinate. About 2 miles from Bristoe Station a stream crossed the road. On the Bristoe side of the stream, General Porter and his staff officers directed and compelled all those wagons to be parked, so that none of them should precede my troops. That order was carried out. I was compelled to halt the head of my command on the Bristoe side of that stream for fully an hour, in order that my rear brigades might be united with the brigade in advance; and the cause of the separation was the trains on the road.[20]

Sykes was then asked if anything would have been gained by leaving at 1 A.M. He responded that there would have been no advantage whatsoever. Had there been any military necessity for the movement to start at 1 A.M., it was not evident to him. When they arrived at Bristoe at 10:30 A.M., they did nothing and remained there all day. He added that upon arrival, his men were fresh and could have gone wherever desired. This constitutes the conclusion of the defense questioning of Sykes.

The prosecution asked if Porter, upon receiving the order, read it aloud to Sykes, Morell and Butterfield in the tent on the night of the twenty-seventh. Sykes responded: "I do not know that it was read; I think General Porter passed it to us all; we all read it."[21]

The prosecution then asked Sykes if he was acquainted with the urgent nature of the order, stating by all means that Gen. Porter must be at Bristoe by daylight the next morning. Sykes answered: "No sir, I think not; for I am satisfied that, if that urgency had been made known to us, we would have moved at the hour prescribed."[22] The prosecution then read the order to Sykes and asked him if it was the one he read on the night of the twenty-seventh. Sykes replied: "I suppose it is, but I cannot recollect it at this distance."[23]

The prosecution's final question was: "Do you, or not, believe that the terms of that order are sufficiently urgent, so that if they had been impressed upon you at that time you would have felt it to be the duty of the command to advance in accordance with it?"[24] Sykes replied: "Well sir, knowing the obstacles that we would have to encounter, taking into consideration the darkness of the night, and believing, as I did, that we could reach the point we were desired to reach by moving at daylight as well as that hour, those considerations would have influenced me, as they did, not to move until dawn."[25]

The court then asked Sykes what time his division actually started its march to Bristoe. Sykes replied that he could not say the precise hour, but they commenced as soon as he could distinguish the road. He thought it was about 3:30 A.M. The court then asked if, once the march began, it continued without stopping until it reached Bristoe. Sykes responded that they only made the usual halts that all commands have, except for the lengthy stops at Kettle Run that he previously described. The court then asked if it would have been practicable to have moved the infantry (less artillery) to Bristoe Station at 1 A.M. as ordered. Sykes replied: "It would not have been impracticable, but I think it would have resulted in so much breaking up of the command and so much confusion that it would have been a false military movement."[26]

Next up for the defense was Brig. Gen. Daniel Butterfield. Butterfield was a brigade commander in Morell's division and third in seniority to Porter, after Morell and Sykes. Gen. Butterfield entered Porter's tent just after Capt. DeKay delivered Pope's order to Porter. Butterfield testified:

> The order, I believe, was for general Porter to move his forces at 1 o'clock in the morning to Bristoe Station. He handed the order to General Morell or General Sykes, who were present, and said that there was a chance for a short nap, or something of that sort (I do not remember the exact words), indicating that there was but little time for preparation. General Sykes or General Morell, I do not remember which (one or both of them), spoke with regard to the fatigue our troops had endured, the darkness of the night, and the fact that, in their judgment, the troops would be of more service to start at a later hour than they would be to start at the hour named. In reply to these remarks, General Porter spoke rather decidedly, that there was the order; it must be obeyed; that those who gave the order knew whether the necessities of the case would warrant the exertions that had to be made to comply with it. I do not state that as his exact words, but as the substance of what he said. Captain DeKay, who brought the order, was then present, and was asked some questions about the road. He stated that it was very dark, and that the road was full of teams. General Sykes, I think, suggested that it would be impossible for us to move at the hour named, if the road was full of teams; that they could not find the way. General Porter called two aides, and sent them off to investigate the condition of the road, and to ask General Pope to have the road cleared, so that we could move up. When we got outside, the darkness was so apparent (to use such an expression), and it seemed to be such a matter of impossibility to move, that General Porter said, "In consideration of all of the circumstances, I will fix the hour at 3 o'clock instead of 1. You will be ready to move promptly." And I subsequently wrote an order, in General Porter's tent, for my command to be in line of march at 3 o'clock.[27]

Butterfield then said that Capt. DeKay then made some comment about the condition of the road, something to the effect that he would have a hard time finding his way back to Bristoe. Butterfield said that he did not read the order himself. He testified that his troops were much fatigued; that they had marched all the way from Kelly's Ford that date in the dust, without water. However, in accordance with Porter's order, he did indeed prepare his troops to march at 3 A.M. He had his column formed and sent staff officers to notify him when he could take his place in the line of the march. His brigade was to be at the rear of Morell's division, which was to follow Sykes's division.

When the march did begin, Butterfield noted that there were large numbers of wagons on the road and alongside the road, and he had to be very attentive to avoid being separated from the units ahead. From time to time the column halted, but he could not ascertain the reason for the halt, as his unit was at the rear of the column. His unit arrived at Bristoe station about noon.

Earlier witnesses had testified to the existence of a stream adjacent to the camp that had impeded the start of the march. One testified that the artillery had become bogged down in this stream, delaying the march. The prosecution put the following question to Gen. Butterfield: "What do you know, if anything, about the forces having been impeded or brought to a halt in their march on the morning of the 28th August last, a little stream or creek not far from Warrenton Junction, in the direction of Bristoe Station?"[28] Butterfield replied: "I know that after it had got to be about daylight, I went out to the head of my column, and I found a difficult place to cross; that there was difficulty in getting the troops across. I could see that it had been dark, and the troops had been impeded, but they began to go on more rapidly as light broke. I did not know that that had been the original cause of delay in moving the column. I knew nothing further than I saw there."[29]

It is very easy to miss the significance of Butterfield's answer here. He said, "After it had got to be about daylight, I went out to the head of my column and I found a difficult place to cross...." This statement clearly indicates that "after it had got to be about daylight," Butterfield's men had not yet crossed the stream at the edge of their camp. Obviously then, if they had not yet reached the road to Bristoe at "about daylight" they were not going to be at Bristoe ten miles down the road at daylight, as ordered.

The defense had just one more witness with testimony related to charge 1, specification 1. It was Lieutenant Colonel Joseph P. Brinton, lieutenant colonel of the Second Pennsylvania Cavalry, which was then located at Catletts Station. Brinton's regiment was not a part of Porter's command. During the evening of the twenty-seventh, one of Brinton's scouts brought him information (subsequently proven false) that Brinton felt must be made known to the senior officer in the area, who happened to be Porter. Brinton set out with two other officers on horseback from Catletts for Warrenton Junction at about 10 P.M. He said that the night was very dark and overcast, that it was difficult to distinguish the road, and that the road was blocked with wagons (stationary) for about the first half mile out of Catletts. The road near Catletts was narrow and passed through some woods. They would run into a tree on one hand and a wagon on the other.

Brinton did not know exactly where to find Porter and spent considerable time inquiring at various wagon encampments as to Porter's location. Brinton finally succeeded in locating Porter at about midnight and delivered his message. Porter made inquiries regarding the condition of the road and requested that, when Brinton got back to his unit at Catletts, he have his unit clear the road for Porter's troops.

Brinton also testified as to the condition of the railroad bridge over Cedar Run (between Warrenton Junction and Catletts). However, it is not clear whether he provided this information to Porter. He said that the bridge could be safely passed over by troops during the day, but that it was not safe at night because there were loose planks. He also said that there was a ford close to the bridge.

Brinton spent about an hour returning to his unit at Catletts. He could have made it considerably sooner, but spent time trying to locate his regiment's wagons in the dark. He reached his unit at Catletts at about 1 A.M. and told an adjutant to send out some men to clear the road. He did not, however, know what was done.

The court asked Brinton how far away in the dark he could see a wagon in the wooded part of the road. Brinton stated that he did not believe that he could distinguish a wagon five meters off. The court then asked Brinton that, if in his opinion, it would have been possible to move large masses of troops along the road between 12 and 1 A.M. Brinton replied as follows: "I do not know as I should answer that question. The court are more able to draw an inference than I am. I give simply the facts. I can give my judgment if it is desired. I should think it would have been very difficult to move a body either of infantry or cavalry over that road at night—almost impossible. They might have been marched in file, following each other in that way."[30] Brinton then added that artillery could not have been moved without moving the wagons. This concluded Brinton's testimony and the case of the defense against charge 1, specification 1.

The defense's case was thus:

1. Porter did the best he could to comply with the order.
2. He could not comply to the letter because:
    (a) the night was too dark
    (b) the road was blocked with wagons
    (c) the troops were fatigued from earlier marching that day
    (d) even when they started in the dark, the artillery became stuck and they could not extricate it until daylight.

The Enemy

When we consider what one side is capable of doing in war, we must consider what the other side is capable of doing. One does not set the standards for oneself. The enemy sets the standards one must exceed. In war, to finish in second place is to lose.

Testimony has shown that among the reasons for Porter not marching at 1 A.M. were that it was too dark, that the troops were too fatigued, that the road was blocked with wagons. It was suggested that, if the artillery was the main problem, the infantry might have left at 1 A.M. and the artillery have followed at daylight. To this, the response was that the Fifth Corps always marched with its artillery; one brigade, one battery. If they changed this pattern, confusion would result.

In the real world, if it is too dark for you but not too dark for your enemy, you lose. If you are too fatigued to continue but your enemy is not, you lose. If you do things in a prescribed way but your enemy finds a better way, you lose. In this instance, the enemy was the corps of Jackson supported by the cavalry of Stuart.

On August 26, Jackson departed Salem before dawn and arrived at Bristoe after dark. The distance covered was over thirty miles. He then directed Gen. Trimble, with his infantry brigade, to proceed a further five miles up the railroad that very night, without a significant rest, and to defeat the garrison at Manassas Junction and capture the supply depot. This Trimble did in a night battle in which he captured two batteries of artillery and over three hundred prisoners. Thus, within a period of about twenty-four hours, Trimble covered thirty-five miles and fought and won a significant battle, much of it at night.

During the day of the twenty-seventh, Jackson took two of his three divisions the five miles up from Bristoe to Manassas Junction, leaving his most trusted subordinate, Ewell, with his division at Bristoe. During the afternoon of the twenty-seventh, Jackson fought and won a battle with Brigadier General Taylor's brigade coming down from Alexandria, while Ewell fought a significant engagement with Hooker's division coming up from Warrenton Junction. During the night of August 27–28, Jackson moved ten miles up from Manassas Junction to Groveton, where he set up a defensive position; Ewell moved the five miles up the railroad from Bristoe Station to Manassas Junction.

Stuart conducted a raid on Pope's headquarters at Catletts Station on the night of the 22nd while Porter was still marching towards Warrenton Junction. Stuart said in his report: "A terrific storm set in.... We found ourselves in the midst of the enemy's encampment on the darkest night I ever knew ... amid the darkness and a perfect torrent of rain ... the only light left to guide us was the flash of the enemy's guns...."[31] In the darkness and the rain, Stuart managed to capture three hundred prisoners; Pope's uniforms, money chest, and dispatch book (containing secret orders); and part of Pope's staff.

Two days after Stuart returned to the Rappahannock from his raid, on the night of the twenty-fifth, he was called into Lee's tent. He was ordered to depart at 2 A.M. with his cavalry division and overtake Jackson, who had departed for Bristoe that morning, and support Jackson on the mission. Stuart reported:

> I was to start at 2 AM, and arriving at the brigades that night at 1 AM, I had reveille sounded and preparations made for the march at 2 o'clock. In this way I got no sleep, but continued in the saddle all night. I followed by direction the route of General Jackson through Amissville, across the Rappahannock at Henson's Mill, 4 miles above Waterloo; proceeded through Orleans, and thence on the road to Salem, until getting near that place, I found my way blocked by the baggage trains and artillery of General Jackson's command. Directing the artillery and ambulances to follow the road, I left it with the cavalry and proceeded by farm roads and by-paths parallel to General Jackson's route to reach the head of his column.[32]

The Confederates not only marched the night that Porter could not, but they were more active—marching more, resting less, and throughout operating under decisive, determined, and resourceful leadership. It is interesting to compare the Confederate activity with the discussion of Porter's generals that fateful night as to the possibility of their marching ten miles, uncontested by the enemy, during the seven hours elapsing between 10 P.M. and 5 A.M. They decided they could not.

Railroads, Roads, and Wagons

Confederate Major General J.E.B. Stuart, a cavalry commander (courtesy the Massachusetts Commandery Military Order of the Loyal Legion and the U.S. Army Military History Institute).

To get to Bristoe from Warrenton Junction on the night of August 27–28, Porter's troops had to march on the railroad, the road, or both. The distance along the railroad from Warrenton Junction to Bristoe was nine and a half miles (see map 8). There was one station between the two, Catletts Station. Catletts Station was approximately two miles from Warrenton Junction and hence seven and a half miles from Bristoe. There were two major bridges on the railroad; the first was over Cedar Run, about two thirds of the way from Warrenton Junction to Catletts Station; the second was over Kettle Run, eight miles

Map 8—Night of August 27–28

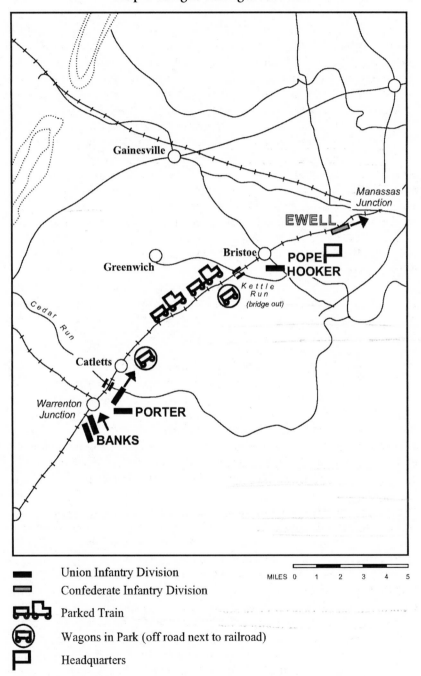

▬	Union Infantry Division
▭	Confederate Infantry Division
🚂	Parked Train
⊖	Wagons in Park (off road next to railroad)
Π	Headquarters

MILES 0 1 2 3 4 5

from Warrenton Junction and one and a half miles short of Bristoe. The bridge over Cedar Run was intact and useable by trains. However, it had loose planks that made it treacherous for foot traffic after dark. The bridge over Kettle Run was destroyed by the Confederates. By the afternoon of the twenty-seventh, the railroad was fully useable up to the destroyed bridge at Kettle Run. By that time, there were no obstacles on the track that would impede either foot traffic or trains. There were no trains operating on the section between Warrenton Junction and Kettle Run for the simple reason that they had no place to go. They could not get beyond the destroyed bridge at Kettle Run.

When Gen. Pope traveled from Warrenton Junction to Bristoe the afternoon of the twenty-seventh, he noted that all of the stragglers to Hooker's division proceeding to Bristoe (estimated at over a thousand) chose to walk along the railroad tracks rather than on the road. The reason for this was obvious. The railroad was straight, while the road ran back and forth; and the railroad was level, while the road went up and down hills, and one had to ford a number of steams in the valleys. Thus, the railroad route was both shorter and easier and less fatiguing, and allowed one to keep one's feet dry. Furthermore, as there were no trains, it was safe.

During the day of the twenty-seventh, when Porter arrived at Warrenton Junction, there were over a hundred rail cars there loaded with supplies (mostly ammunition, commissary and forage) and a number of cars containing sick and wounded. In addition, there were four locomotives.

Pope's order to Porter showed a concern for these supplies and for the sick and wounded. He wanted the cars to be moved up the line to the break at Kettle Run before Warrenton Junction was vacated by Union troops. Gen. Banks's corps was moving up the rail line following Porter's corps, but Pope did not know how far behind Banks was. Consequently, in his order, he directed Porter to leave a detachment behind until Banks arrived if the rail cars had not yet been moved. As it turned out, Banks was very close behind, and the first of Banks's troops could easily have entered Warrenton Junction before the last of Porter's left. There was thus no need for a quick removal of the cars up the line to Kettle Run.

As we have seen, the first thing Porter did upon receiving Pope's order was to order the cars moved. There were only four locomotives and well over one hundred cars, so each locomotive had to make several runs pushing cars up to the break and then return for more. Thus, there was heavy two way traffic on the tracks between Warrenton Junction and Kettle Run until the last cars and locomotive were parked at Kettle Run. This did not occur until 4 A.M. For the critical hours of 10 P.M. on the twenty-seventh until 4 A.M. on the twenty-eighth, Porter unnecessarily deprived himself of the use of the tracks for marching.

The road was a typical Virginia unpaved country road of the time. Most witnesses who commented on the condition of the road considered it good. While the railroad ran straight and level, the road, while roughly paralleling the railroad, followed the lay of the land. It went up hills and down valleys and crossed the railroad four times. At times it was on one side of the railroad, at times on the other side, and sometimes on both. In addition to the fords at Cedar Run and Kettle Run, it forded four small creeks. Most of the way to Cedar Run and all of the way from Kettle Run there was open country on both sides of the road, permitting easy egress of wagons for night camping. Nearing Cedar Run, there were some hills and narrow stretches and, at places, woods crowded the road on both sides. A second sticky wicket was the area of the ford at Kettle Run. All in all, though, the road was as good as most that troops marched on, and better than many.

The wagon train consisted of over two thousand wagons. The most important single witness regarding the wagons was undoubtedly prosecution witness Lt. Col. Frederick Myers. Myers was in command of the wagon train and at the head of the column. He categorically stated that there were no wagons ahead of him. At about dark, when about one and a half miles short of Kettle Run, Myers ordered the wagons into park for the night. The wagons near him went into park at that location. Myers said that he passed the word down the line but could not vouch for what the wagons out of sight behind him did. Myers then testified that the train re-entered the road at daylight and continued its journey toward Manassas Junction.

Myers's testimony was not only uncontested, but validated by other witnesses. Capt. DeKay, who passed down the road from Bristoe to Warrenton Junction between 7 and 10 P.M., stated that he encountered the last wagons on the road before he reached Catletts and then saw a large park of wagons between Catletts and Warrenton Junction. Lt. Brooks, who passed up the road in the other direction between 4:30 and 7 P.M., stated that, as he passed, the wagons on the road were going into park.

From other witnesses, it is clear that some wagons remained on the road throughout the night. Presumably, these included those looking for a place to park and those unable to get off the road for one reason or another. It appears that those on the road included a jam some three miles long.

Porter's attempts to clear the road before 1 A.M. were anemic at best. When Lt. Col. Brinton from Catletts visited Porter at midnight, Porter asked Brinton to clear the road after he got back to Catletts. When Brinton got back, he told someone else to see to it and gave no further thought to the matter.

Myers's wagons did re-enter the road from park at daylight as Myers testified. When Capt. DeKay, at the head of Porter's column, after daylight on the twenty-eighth, reached the point between Warrenton Junction and Catletts, where DeKay had noticed the large wagon park the night before, the park was now largely empty, the wagons already having entered the road. There were far fewer wagons on the road during the hours from 1 A.M. to 5 A.M., when Porter was ordered to make the march, than there were after daylight when he did make the march.

The testimony of witnesses such as Generals Morell, Sykes, and Griffin about the wagons that they encountered on the road is moot as far as a defense is concerned, because their testimony relates to the situation on the road later than the time the order required them to be at Bristoe.

It was generally agreed that the night was moonless and that it sprinkled a little or threatened to do so at a couple of points. Beyond that, the testimony varied widely from a normal starry night to an unusually dark night. These discrepancies may be attributed at least in part to the fact that the witnesses made their observations at various times and at various places. However, darkness didn't stop Ewell's troops from marching that night and Jackson's troops throughout that night in the same general area that Porter was located.

Guilty or Innocent

The court did not pronounce its verdict on any charge and specification until it had considered all of the testimony on all of the charges and specifications, and the verdicts won't be presented here until the end either. However, some opinions as to Porter's guilt or innocence will be given at the end of the chapter on each charge and specification.

First to be considered is the order Porter received. It was faulty in the extreme. Pope testified that he sent the order to Porter because Hooker was nearly out of ammunition, and that he feared that reinforced Confederates would renew the battle at daylight. He was later to add, outside the trial, that Hooker could not retreat because he was all that stood between the Confederates and the vital wagon train in his rear. None of this was divulged in the order, and the bearer of the order, Capt. DeKay, did not divulge this either. The order, as presented to Porter, stated: "The enemy has been driven back, but is retiring along the railroad. We must drive him from Manassas, and clear the country between that place and Gainesville...."[33]

From this, Porter might reasonably conclude that his corps was not going directly into action upon reaching Bristoe, but was going to be subjected to further marching. Under these circumstances, Porter might have concluded that it would be best to have his whole corps arrive rested, in an orderly fashion, and with all its artillery.

Suppose the order reflected the very situation that Pope feared. Suppose the order read: "Hooker had big battle with the Confederates this afternoon and is almost out of ammunition. He cannot retreat as his is the only unit standing between the Confederates and the vulnerable wagon train. I fear that the reinforced Confederates will renew the battle at daylight. Get here with all you can by daylight."

Had Porter received the above order, would he have been at Bristoe at daylight? I suspect he would have. Furthermore, an order like the above would have given Porter a better idea how to handle the rail cars than the confused instructions he received. Among the rail cars at Warrenton Junction were some that contained more ammunition than Hooker could use.

The order as received by Porter did contain some specific commands as follows: "...directs that you start at 1 o'clock tonight ... so as to be here by daylight ... it is necessary on all accounts that you should be here by daylight...."[34]

The bottom line was that Pope wanted Porter, with his corps, to be at Bristoe at daylight. The order to start at 1 o'clock was superfluous and even insulting. Porter was in a better position than Pope to know when he must start to be at Bristoe by daylight.

Porter had two divisions, those of Sykes and Morell. Sykes's division had arrived at Warrenton Junction during the morning after a 12 mile march, and Morell's division had arrived in the afternoon after a 17 or 19 mile march, depending on the starting points of the three brigades. Thus, Sykes's division was the more rested and should start first. This Porter so ordered. Porter ordered that the march begin at 3 A.M.

If Sykes was to lead the column, it all depended on him. No matter what Morell did, he was not going to get to Bristoe before Sykes. From their own testimony, we see that Morell, who was to leave after Sykes, called reveille earlier than Sykes, who was to leave first. Sykes, by his own testimony, called reveille at between 2 and 2:30 A.M. Morell called reveille between 1:30 and 2 A.M. Sykes further testified that he normally called reveille from one and a half to two hours before start time. Thus, it appears clear that Sykes had no intention of starting at 3 A.M. Furthermore, Capt. DeKay, who was to lead Sykes's column, testified that he was awakened for breakfast at dawn. DeKay further testified that when the head of the column reached the location of the wagon park he had noticed the previous night (about one mile from the start point), it was largely empty, the wagons having re-entered the road at daylight.

It is thus abundantly clear that the head of Porter's column did not depart Warrenton Junction at 3 A.M. but much later—at daybreak. If it departed at daybreak, obviously it could not be arriving at Bristoe, nine and a half miles down the road, at daybreak as ordered. We might thus add to disobedience a large dose of incompetence. The tired division got up before the rested division and then stood in line waiting for the rested division to take the road.

The author's verdict—guilty as charged.

Epilogue

The consequences of an action often determine the degree of legal action that follows. For example, if I drive through a stop sign and nothing happens, I may get off with a $25 fine and a warning. However, if I drive through a stop sign and cause a school bus to swerve and go over the embankment and 25 children are killed, it will be quite another matter. In the case at hand, Porter's late arrival at Bristoe had absolutely no adverse consequences. His troops remained idle at Bristoe throughout the remainder of the day. It would appear that bringing Porter to trial for this matter, where up to his life was at stake, was unusual and excessive. Actually, it was a matter of "piling on." This was just one more in a series of things. It was for other matters that the prosecution was out to get Porter.

Gen. Pope's impression of the matter is thus:

> It was possible, however to mass his whole force at Manassas Junction and assail our right (Hooker's division), which had fought a severe battle that afternoon, and was almost out of ammunition. Jackson with A. P. Hill's division, retired through Centreville. Thinking it altogether within probabilities that he might adopt the other alternative, I sent the orders above mentioned to General Porter. He neither obeyed them nor attempted to obey them, but afterward gave as a reason for not doing so that his men were tired, the night was too dark to march, and that there was a wagon train on the road to Bristoe. The distance was 9 miles along the railroad track, with a wagon road on each side of it most of the way; but his corps did not reach Bristoe Station until 10:30 o'clock next morning, six hours after daylight; and that the moment he found the enemy had left our front he asked to halt and rest his corps. Of his first reason for not complying with my orders, it is only necessary to say that Sykes' division had reached Warrenton Junction at 11 o'clock on the morning of the 27th, and had been in camp all day. Morell's division arrived later in the day at Warrenton Junction, and would have been in camp at least eight hours before it was ordered to march. The marches of these two divisions from Fredericksburg had been extremely deliberate, and involved little more exercise than is needed for good health. The diaries of these marches make Porter's claim of fatigue ridiculous. To compare the condition of this corps and its marches with those of any of the troops of the Army of Virginia is a sufficient answer to such a pretext. The impossibility of marching on account of the darkness of that night finds its best answer in the fact that nearly every other division of the army, and the whole of Jackson's corps, marched during the greater part of the night in the immediate vicinity of Porter's corps, and from nearly every point of the compass. The plea of darkness and of the obstruction of a wagon train along the road will strike our armies with some surprise in the light of their subsequent experience with night marches. The railroad track itself was clear and entirely practicable for the march of infantry....[35]

5

Charge 1, Specifications 2 and 3; Charge 2, Specifications 1, 2, and 3

Charge 1, specifications 2 and 3, and charge 2, specifications 1, 2, and 3 are all closely related and all arose out of the same situation. That situation was Porter's failure to bring his corps into action on the twenty-ninth to assist Pope in his battle against Jackson, even though Porter was within sound of the battle throughout the day. The five are as follows.

Charge 1, Violation of the Ninth Article of War

Specification 2d.—In this the said Maj. Gen. Fitz-John Porter, being in front of the enemy, at Manassas, Va., on or about the morning of August 29, 1862 did receive from Maj. Gen. John Pope, his superior and commanding officer, a lawful order, in the following letters and figures, to wit:

Headquarters Army of Virginia,
Centreville, August 29, 1862

Generals McDowell and Porter:

You will please move forward with your joint commands toward Gainesville. I sent General Porter written orders to that effect an hour and a half ago. Heintzelman, Sigel, and Reno are moving on the Warrenton turnpike, and must now be not far from Gainesville. I desire that as soon as communication is established between this force and your own, the whole command shall halt. It may be necessary to fall back behind Bull Run, at Centreville tonight. I presume it will be so on account of our supplies. I have sent no order of any description to Ricketts, and none to interfere in any way with McDowell's troops, except what I sent by his aide-de-camp last night, which were to hold his position on the Warrenton Turnpike until the troops from here should fall on the enemy's flank and rear. I do not even know Ricketts' position, as I have not been able to find out where General McDowell was until a late hour this morning. General McDowell will take immediate steps to communicate with General Ricketts, and instruct him to join the other divisions of his corps as soon as practicable. If any considerable advantages are to be gained by departing from this order, it will not be strictly carried out. One thing must be held in view: that the troops must occupy a position from which they can reach Bull run to-night or by morning. The indications are that the whole force of the enemy is moving in this direction at a pace that will bring them here by to-morrow night or the next day. My own headquarters will be for the present with Heintzelman's corps at this place.

John Pope
Major General Commanding
[Referred to as the "Joint Order"]

Which order the said Major-General Porter did then and there disobey. This at or near Manassas, in the State of Virginia, on or about the 29th of August, 1862.

Specification 3.—In this, that the said Maj. Gen. Fitz-John Porter, having been in front of the enemy during the battle of Manassas, on Friday, the 29th of August, 1862 did on that day receive from Maj. Gen. John Pope, his superior and commanding officer, a lawful order, in the following letters and figure to wit:

Headquarters in the Field
August 29, 1862—4:30 P.M.

Major General Porter:

Your line of march brings you in on the enemy's right flank. I desire you to push forward into action at once on the enemy's flank, and if possible on his rear, keeping your right in communication with General Reynolds. The enemy is massed in the woods in front of us, but can be shelled out as soon as you engage their flank. Keep heavy reserves and use your batteries, keeping well closed to your right all the time. In case you are obliged to fall back, do so to your right and rear, so as to keep you in close communication with the right wing.

John Pope
Major-General, Commanding
[Referred to as the "4:30 Attack Order"]

Which said order the said Major General Porter did then and there disobey, and did fail to push forward his forces into action either on the enemy's flank or rear, and in all other respects did fail to obey said order. This at or near Manassas, in the State of Virginia, on or about the 29th of August, 1862.

Charge 2, Violation of the Fifty Second Article of War

Specification 1st.—In this, that the said Maj. Gen. Fitz-John Porter, during the battle of Manassas, on Friday, the 29th of August 1862, and while within sight of the field and in full hearing of its artillery, did receive from Maj. Gen. John Pope, his superior and commanding officer, a lawful order to attack the enemy, in the following figures and letters to wit:

Headquarters in the Field
August 29, 1862—4:30 P.M.

Major General Porter:

Your line of march brings you in on the enemy's right flank. I desire you to push forward into action at once on the enemy's flank, and if possible, on his rear, keeping your right in communication with General Reynolds. The enemy is massed in the woods in front of us, but can be shelled out as soon as you engage their flank. Keep heavy reserves, and use your batteries, keeping well closed to your right all the time. In case you are obliged to fall back, do so to your right and rear, so as to keep you in close communication with the right wing.

John Pope
Major General, Commanding.
[4:30 Attack Order]

Which said order the said major-General Porter did then and there shamefully disobey, and did retreat from advancing forces of the enemy without any attempt to engage them, or to aid the troops who were already fighting greatly superior numbers, and were relying on the flank attack he was thus ordered to make to secure a decisive victory, and to capture the enemy's army, a result which must have followed from said flank attack, had it been made by the said General Porter in compliance with the said order, which he so shamefully disobeyed. This act at or near Manassas, in the State of Virginia, on or about the 29th of August, 1862.

Specification 2d—In this that the said Maj. Gen. Fitz-John Porter, being with his army corps, on Friday, the 29th of August, 1862, between Manassas Station and the field of a battle then pending between the forces of the United States and those of the rebels, and within sound of the guns and in the presence of the enemy, knowing that a severe action of great consequence was being fought, and that the aid of his corps was greatly needed, did fail all day to bring it on the field, and did shamefully fall back and retreat from the advance of the enemy, without any attempt to give them battle, and without knowing the forces from which he shamefully retreated. This near Manassas Station, in the State of Virginia 29 of August, 1862.

Specification 3d—In this, that the said Maj. Gen. Fitz-John Porter, being with his army corps, near the field of battle of Manassas, on the 20th of August, 1862, while a severe action was being fought by the troops of Major-General Pope's command, and being in the belief that the troops of said General Pope were sustaining defeat and retiring from the field, did shamefully fail to go to the aid of the said troops and general, and did shamefully retreat away and fall back with his army to the Manassas Junction, and leave to the disasters of a presumed defeat the said army, and did fail, by any attempt, to attack the enemy to aid in averting the misfortunes of a disaster that would have endangered the safety of the capital of the country. This at or near Manassas Station, in the State of Virginia, on the 29th day of August, 1862.[1]

Porter pleaded "not guilty" to all the charges and specifications.

The charges are closely related, and the disobedience of one and the same order can serve as the basis for two separate charges under two separate Articles of War. Charge 1 constituted a violation of the Ninth Article of War, and charge 2 constituted a violation of the Fifty-second Article of War. The ninth Article relates to disobedience of orders. The fifty-second relates to "misbehaving" before the enemy, or "shamefully abandoning" any post or guard, etc. Thus, proof of violations against Article 52 involve much more subjectivity. What one may consider a "shameful" retreat, another may consider a "prudent withdrawal."

The Situation on August 29

As of the twenty-eighth, Pope still believed that he could destroy Jackson's three divisions before the remaining five Confederate divisions under Lee and Longstreet could join them. Both Jackson and Pope knew that Longstreet would arrive through Thoroughfare Gap. However, Jackson knew that he would arrive on the twenty-ninth and Pope thought he could not arrive before the thirtieth. During the day of the twenty-eighth, Jackson took up a strong defensive position along an unfinished railway cut just north of the Warrenton pike. His right rested close to the turnpike near a town called Groveton, and his line then angled away from the turnpike to the north east (see map 9).

While Jackson was so engaged, Pope was gathering his forces at Centreville to attack. Pope also had two divisions of McDowell's corps to the west of Jackson; that is, between Jackson and Thoroughfare Gap. These prevented both Jackson's retreat and Longstreet joining Jackson. These two divisions were those of Ricketts, at the gap itself, and King, on the Warrenton pike. During the evening and night, Longstreet forced the gap with Ricketts's division retiring all the way to Bristoe. At the same time, King encountered Jackson's right flank and ultimately retired all the way to Manassas. When morning broke on the twenty-ninth, Pope had no one between Jackson and the gap.

Pope still believed that he had one more chance to bag Jackson before Longstreet could join him. Pope ordered Porter, who was at Manassas, to proceed down the Gainesville–Manassas Junction road to Gainesville and to join with Pope's left (see map 9). Pope would hold Jackson in place until Porter arrived, which was expected to be in the late afternoon. When Porter arrived, Jackson would be in the bag, as shown in map 10.

Porter led a formidable force as he headed down the Gainesville–Manas-

Map 9—Night of August 28–29

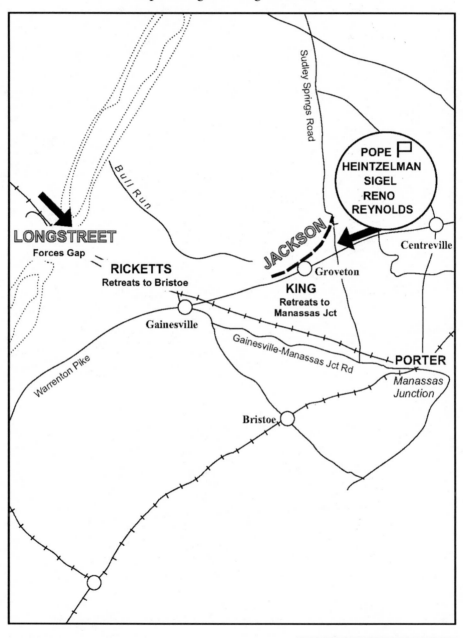

Map 10—August 29 (Pope's Hope)

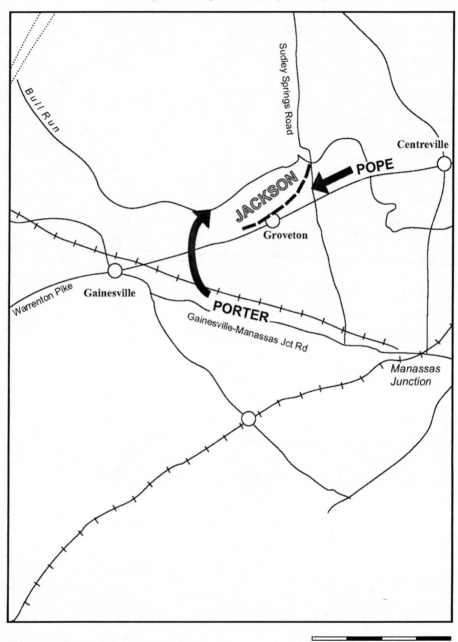

sas Junction road. He had his own two divisions of Morell and Sykes, and in addition, Pope had attached Piatt's large brigade to Porter's corps. Piatt's brigade belonged to the reserve corps of General Sturgis at Washington, and had been the last brigade to reinforce Pope before Jackson had cut the rail. In addition to this force, Pope ordered Porter to take King's division of McDowell's corps with him, as it happened to be at Manassas at the time. The reason Pope took the unusual step of assigning King to Porter was because King's normal corps commander, McDowell, had become lost during the night, and Pope did not know where he was or how to contact him. Thus, as Porter marched off down the Gainesville–Manassas Junction road, he commanded a force nearly as large as Jackson's (Morell and Sykes—nine thousand; Piatt—one thousand; and King—five thousand).

Porter had no sooner departed than McDowell showed up, reported to Pope, and requested that King again be placed under his command. Pope acquiesced and re-issued the order he had previously sent to Porter, now addressing it jointly to Porter and McDowell. Now the column proceeding down the Gainesville–Manassas Junction road had two commanders—Porter's corps in front and McDowell's following.

While Porter's troops were marching down the road to Gainesville, Longstreet's Confederates were pouring through the gap on the same road on a collision course. However, when Longstreet's troops reached the intersection of the Manassas road and the Warrenton pike, they turned up the turnpike (toward Groveton) to join Jackson (see map 11).

Early that morning, Jackson had sent Stuart with his cavalry, which had been supporting him, to join the oncoming Longstreet. Stuart met Longstreet during the morning on the Warrenton pike and was directed to take up a position on Longstreet's right flank (i.e., in the direction of the Gainesville–Manassas Junction road). Thus, Longstreet's troops halted for an hour as Stuart's troops crossed the turnpike in front of them to take up a position on Longstreet's right.

When Porter reached Dawkins Branch, which crossed the Gainesville–Manassas Junction road about three and a half miles short of Gainesville, he saw a Confederate force of unknown size lined up across the road on the other side of the creek. The Confederates were, of course, Stuart's troopers. Porter stopped to assess the situation and McDowell came forward to see what was going on. McDowell was senior to Porter, and it was McDowell's habit to take charge of any junior corps commander when they were operating together, even though it was Pope's intention that each corps commander operate directly under him.

McDowell gave Porter some instructions, the nature of which were disputed at the trial, and then advised Porter that he, McDowell, was going to take his own troops up the Sudley Springs road and join Pope, and that he would be operating on Pope's left, so it would be his troops closest to Porter's

Map 11—Night of August 27–28

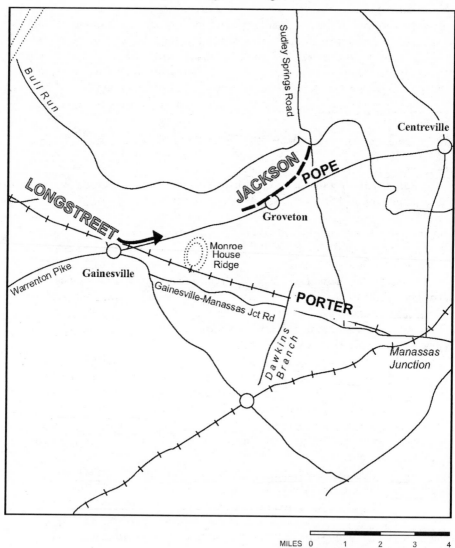

MILES   0   1   2   3   4

when they merged. In effect, McDowell visualized his corps filling part of the gap between Pope and Porter.

Porter was thus left alone to face the unknown ahead of him, but burdened by McDowell's instructions. Porter was further burdened by not having his usual cavalry detachment. The cavalry of the Army of the Potomac had not yet arrived from the peninsula when Porter's and Heintzelman's corps were rushed to Pope. In view of the absence of Porter's cavalry, Stuart was able to ascertain what was in front of him much more quickly than Porter could. Stuart correctly informed Longstreet that he (Stuart) was facing one corps at Dawkins Branch on the Gainesville–Manassas Junction road. Longstreet was thus in a position to afford Stuart reinforcements to the degree necessary.

Porter had great difficulty determining what was ahead of him. He could only get intermittent snapshot views of partial lines of troops through the woods. Furthermore, Stuart had horsemen drag branches behind them in the road from Thoroughfare Gap to his rear, creating great clouds of dust, thus giving the impression that masses of infantry were arriving and confronting Porter.

Porter could hear the battle raging to his right (Pope and Jackson) but could not see what was going on because of thick woods. Furthermore, he had no idea how far away to his right Pope's line lay. He sent scouts into the woods to find out, but none returned. Unknown to him, by late morning the woods were infested with Longstreet's troops. If Porter could have advanced just one mile farther up the road toward Gainesville, he would have come to a ridge that extended from the Gainesville–Manassas Junction road to the Warrenton pike. From the top of the ridge, one had a commanding view of the battlefield and could see both the point where Porter was to junction with Pope and the lay of Jackson's line. But alas, he never got that far.

While Porter was hung up at Dawkins Branch, Pope was anxiously peering down the line. He felt sure that Porter would be closing in on Jackson's flank for the coup de grace by late afternoon, but nothing happened.

Finally, at 4:30 P.M., Pope, in exasperation, sent a direct written order to Porter to attack Jackson's flank immediately. Pope then waited an hour or so for Porter to receive his message and prepare his attack. Finally, at a time when Pope anticipated Porter should be beginning his attack, he threw all of his forces against Jackson. Pope's attack was a minor success, but when dark terminated the fighting, Porter had still not appeared. Pope considered, and considered until his death, that had Porter entered the fray on Jackson's flank as ordered, the Union would have won a decisive victory.

Why did not Porter attack? Did he have justifiable reasons? This is the heart and substance of the legal confrontation in this chapter.

An Outline of the Prosecution's and Defense's Cases

The prosecution set out to prove that Porter disobeyed Pope's joint order to McDowell and Porter; that Porter also disobeyed Pope's 4:30 order to attack immediately; that Porter retreated from the enemy without any attempt to engage him; that, although within sight and sound of the battlefield at Groveton, Porter did not come to the aid of his comrades who were engaged in a desperate struggle with a greatly superior force; that when convinced that

Pope's troops were being driven and retreating, Porter retreated to Manassas Junction rather than coming to their aid.

The defense set out to demonstrate that while McDowell was with Porter, McDowell took charge and Porter was under his orders; that Porter's freedom of action was constrained by McDowell's last order even after McDowell left; that Porter had an enemy force in front of him that he believed was at least as large as his own command, and was separate and distinct from the enemy facing Pope; that he could not move cross-country to Pope's aid because of the enemy in front of him and the nature of the terrain between him and Pope; that when he received Pope's 4:30 order to attack, he attempted to implement it immediately, but that the order was delivered so late that darkness intervened; that he did, in fact, not retreat before the enemy, but held his position until ordered by Pope to leave.

The Prosecution's Case

The prosecution's first witness, Gen. Pope, testified that he issued four orders to Porter on the twenty-ninth, or, if one considers a superseded order, five orders. The orders were the result of his perceptions of a changing situation. The first order to Porter was sent while it was still dark, the exact time of which Pope could not remember. It called for Porter to march his corps to Centreville. By dawn, however, Pope realized that Jackson was not heading in that direction, but rather, was taking up a position along an unfinished railroad cut, north of the Warrenton pike, between Centreville and Gainesville. Consequently, at about 6:30 or 7:30 A.M., Pope issued new and changed orders to Porter. Porter, who was now at Manassas Junction, was to take the Gainesville–Manassas Junction road and march toward Gainesville. Pope also ordered Porter to take King's division of McDowell's corps with him. Pope said the reason for placing King under Porter was because he had lost contact with McDowell and did not know where he was. Shortly after issuing this order, McDowell reappeared and requested that Pope return King's division to his command. Pope did so by reissuing his earlier command to Porter as a joint command to Porter and McDowell. Pope identified this order as the one contained in charge 1, specification 2. Pope stated that he issued the joint order sometime between 8 and 9 A.M.

Pope elaborated on the joint order. At the time of issuance, it appeared that Jackson was retreating along the Warrenton pike toward Gainesville and thence to Thoroughfare Gap for a junction with Longstreet. Pope had a considerable force at Centreville consisting of the corps of Heintzelman, Sigel, and Reno. The Warrenton pike formed an angle with the Gainesville–Manassas Junction road with Gainesville at the junction. Thus, as the Heintzelman group pushed Jackson down the Warrenton pike, it would ultimately join with the Porter-McDowell force proceeding up the Gainesville-Manassas Junction road.

Pope did not want the thus united force to pursue Jackson beyond Gainesville for logistics reasons. The supply situation being what it was, Pope felt that he could not feed his troops or animals beyond that point.

Toward mid-afternoon, it became evident that Jackson was not retreating, but was locked in combat with the Heintzelman group. Consequently, inasmuch as the Jackson and the Heintzelman forces were stopped on the Warrenton pike, and the movements of the Porter-McDowell group on the converging Gainesville–Manassas Junction road were apparently unimpeded, Pope expected the Porter force to appear on Jackson's flank or rear at any time and thus decide the issue. When Porter still had not appeared at 4:30 P.M., Pope issued order number four. This order was to attack Jackson in flank or rear immediately upon receipt. Pope identified this order as the one contained in charge 1, specification 3. The Heintzelman group made its major effort against Jackson beginning about 5:30 to 6 P.M., anticipating Porter's attack on the flank and rear at about that time. Porter, however, did not appear. Pope alleged that had Porter attacked at any time up to about 8 P.M., the Jackson force would have been destroyed.

Pope testified that at around 5 P.M., Gen. McDowell's corps began arriving at the battlefield on the Warrenton pike. McDowell had taken his corps from Porter's rear on the Gainesville–Manassas Junction road and marched up the Sudley Springs road to report to Pope, and to join the Heintzelman group in its attack on Jackson (see map 12). Pope offered no criticism of McDowell in his testimony for this move.

Pope said that between 7 and 8 P.M. he was handed a message from Porter. It was actually addressed to Generals McDowell and King, but for unknown reasons was delivered to Pope. It was as follows:

> Generals McDowell and King
>
> I found it impossible to communicate by crossing the woods to Groveton. The enemy are in strong force on this road, and as they appear to have driven our forces back, the firing of the enemy having advanced and ours retired, I have determined to withdraw to Manassas. I have attempted to communicate with McDowell and Sigel, but my messengers have run into the enemy. They have gathered artillery and cavalry and infantry, and the advancing masses of dust show the enemy coming in force. I am now going to the head of the column to see what is passing and how affairs are going. Had you not better send your train back.
>
> F. J. Porter
> Major-General[2]

At 8:50 P.M., an exasperated Pope sent a scathing message to Porter ordering him to report his corps to the field of battle and ordering Porter to report to Pope in person. This order is the subject of another specification that will be treated in the next chapter.

Map 12—Day of August 29 (McDowell Joins Pope)

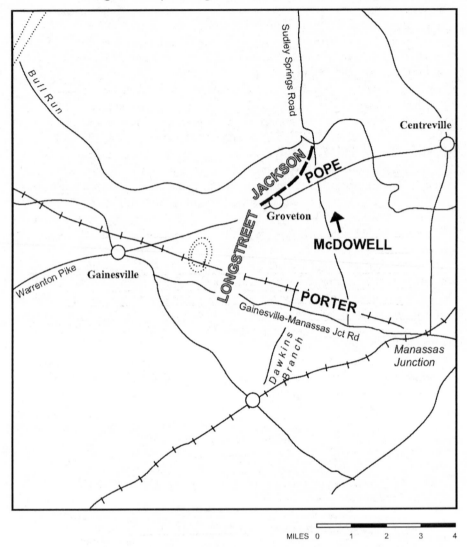

MILES 0   1   2   3   4

The Defense Questions Pope

Gen. Pope proved to be an extremely cagy witness. Much of the questioning by the defense served merely to fortify what Pope had testified for the prosecution. The defense's most effective questioning related to the question of whether or not Longstreet's troops were on the field on the twenty-ninth. This, of course, was the heart of Porter's defense. If Longstreet were in fact in front of him in force on the twenty-ninth, he obviously could not attack Jackson in the flank and rear as ordered.

As we will recall, Pope, in his joint order to Porter and McDowell on the morning of the twenty-ninth, clearly stated that he did not expect Longstreet on the twenty-ninth. To quote from the order: "The indications are that the whole force of the enemy is moving in this direction at a pace that will bring them here by tomorrow night or the next day."[3] Tomorrow, of course, in this instance meant August 30. Now, in questioning by the defense, Pope was brought to admit that Longstreet was expected on the afternoon of the twenty-ninth, and that he would join Jackson by the Warrenton pike. He still contended, however, that there were none of Longstreet's troops in front of Porter that afternoon at 4:30 P.M. Pope categorically stated: "I did not then believe, that at that time, nor do I now believe, that at that time any considerable portion of Longstreet's corps had reached the vicinity of the field."[4]

Pope was then asked: "Do you know whether at 5:30 P.M., or between that hour and 7 o'clock, the accused had the enemy immediately in his front?"[5] Pope replied:

> I do not know it, except from the report of others, though I would think it altogether likely that Jackson would have pushed out some force to observe the road between Gainesville and Manassas Junction. It is altogether likely, therefore, that some of Jackson's troops were in the presence of Porter's advance, though of my knowledge I do not know that.[6]

The defense was now prepared to put the clincher to Pope. Between 9 and 10 A.M. on August 29, Gen. Buford, McDowell's cavalry commander, had reported to McDowell that he had sighted a portion of Longstreet's command proceeding along the Warrenton pike, from the direction of Thoroughfare Gap toward Jackson. Buford reported the force as "seventeen regiments of infantry, one battery of artillery and about 500 cavalry."[7] Buford later testified that this force must have passed Gainesville by 9 A.M., and that the average strength of the regiments was eight hundred men. Thus, by 9 A.M. on the twenty-ninth, a significant portion of Longstreet's command was sighted and reported by a cavalry commander subordinate to Pope, and was within two hours' easy march from Jackson's position (or Porter's). The question now put to Pope was: "Are you now unable to say that you were informed or knew at 7 o'clock P.M. on the 29th of August that Longstreet's corps was up with Jackson in force?"[8] Pope answered:

> By 7 o'clock in the evening I knew from the report of General Buford that a portion of Longstreet's force—numbering, perhaps, one-half the force under General Porter, certainly not more than two-thirds, as General Buford estimated it—had passed through Gainesville and at that time, in all probability, had joined Jackson. The report of General Buford was in writing. He states the number of battalions, pieces of artillery I think, and

the cavalry which passed through Gainesville according to his observation. That information came to me quite late in the evening; certainly by 7 P.M., I think. The question put by the accused seems to imply that I have previously somewhere in my testimony said that I did not know at 7 o'clock in the evening that portions of Longstreet's force had joined Jackson. I have nowhere so stated.[9]

Just what did Buford sight and report that morning? In all probability, he sighted one of the five divisions of Longstreet that poured through Thoroughfare Gap on the night of the twenty-eighth and morning of the twenty-ninth. If this is correct, Buford's estimate of eight hundred men in each of the seventeen sighted regiments is too high. Longstreet's total force numbered about twenty-five thousand.

Pope's testimony as regards Longstreet can be summarized as follows: He said that he expected Longstreet to arrive to join Jackson on the afternoon of the twenty-ninth even though he had written on that very day that he did not expect him until the thirtieth. Furthermore, he said he did not believe any of Longstreet's men were in front of Porter at 4:30 P.M., even though a force of Longstreet's men had been sighted within two hours' march of joining Jackson seven and a half hours earlier—and they could have been assigned to Jackson's right flank, which would have placed them confronting Porter. In any event, Pope said he considered that the sighted Longstreet force was only half of that commanded by Porter. The last statement is questionable, inasmuch as seventeen regiments of eight hundred men each plus five hundred cavalry equals fourteen thousand one hundred, and Porter's force consisted of about ten thousand.

Questions by the Court

The court asked Pope what was the strength of his force confronting Jackson, and what was his estimate of Jackson's force. Pope replied that he had about twenty-five thousand men present, without counting an estimated twelve thousand of McDowell that joined him around 5 P.M. before his late afternoon attack. He estimated that Jackson had a minimum of twenty-five thousand. Later information, not then available, indicates that Jackson's force was probably about eighteen thousand. In any event, with any interpretation, Pope's force confronting Jackson, without Porter, was greater than Jackson's. This is significant since charge 2, specification 1, said Porter "did retreat from advancing forces of the enemy without any attempt to engage them, or to aid the troops who were already fighting greatly superior numbers...."[10]

The next two prosecution witnesses were Pope's aide-de-camp, Capt. Drake DeKay, and his inspector general, Brig. Gen. B. S. Roberts. DeKay had no information on the five specifications in question, but Gen. Roberts did.

Brigadier Gen. Roberts

Gen. Roberts attested that the orders in the specifications were the ones issued by Gen. Pope. Roberts testified that, from time to time, he was near the area from which Porter's attack was expected, but none materialized. He stated that both he and Pope expected Porter to attack Jackson's flank even before Pope issued his 4:30 P.M. order specifically requiring him to do so. He said that he considered that the order Porter was operating under was sufficient reason for doing so, even though it merely directed him to take the road to Gainesville and said nothing about an attack. He explained: "I had supposed that any general within hearing of an important battle, in whose power it was to engage in it—would do so; and I had supposed that General Porter's line of march from Manassas Junction would have brought him onto the right of the enemy's lines before 4 o'clock, and I had supposed that he would attack on coming onto those lines."[11]

Roberts said that the battle died down at dark, between 7:30 and 8 P.M., and that the advantages were in favor of Gen. Pope's army. He further stated that had Porter attacked Jackson's flank as he had been directed to do by Pope's 4:30 P.M. order, he did not doubt that "it would have resulted in the defeat, if not in the capture, of the main Army of the Confederates that were on the field at that time."[12]

Much of the accused's questioning of Roberts related to the arrival of Longstreet's troops. Roberts was asked whether Longstreet's troops, in whole or part, made a junction with Jackson's right between 4 and 5 P.M. Roberts replied that he thought not. He had been tasked with watching for Longstreet's arrival with a spy glass, and by observing clouds of dust in the vicinity of the Bull Run Mountains, became convinced that Longstreet could not make a junction with Jackson before late evening, and he so advised Pope.

The defense then asked if, based on the information that later became available to Roberts, up to the present, did he now believe that Longstreet could have made a junction with Jackson earlier; for example, between 5 and 6 P.M. or even earlier? Roberts responded that, based on information he later acquired, a force of Longstreet consisting of about seventeen battalions might have joined Jackson by 6:30 or 7 P.M. He estimated the force at about four or five thousand men. This was obviously a reference to the force reported by Buford. In the re-telling, this force gets ever smaller and arrives ever later. In being pressed by the accused, Roberts admitted that this force might have ended up in front of Porter. Roberts also admitted that he did not actually know what time Porter received the order to attack that Pope issued at 4:30 P.M.

The questioning of Roberts also introduced into the record the full text of the two orders to Porter from Pope on the twenty-ninth, which Pope could not produce at the trial but could only refer to from memory. These were Pope's order to Porter during the night of August 28–29 to march to Centreville, and Pope's order to Porter to take the Gainesville–Manassas Junction road that was superseded by his joint order to Porter and McDowell. The full text of these orders is as follows:

Headquarters Army of Virginia
Near Bull Run, August 29, 1862—3 A.M.

Major-General Porter:

General: McDowell has intercepted the retreat of Jackson. Sigel is immediately on the right of McDowell. Kearny and Hooker march to attack the enemy's rear at early dawn.

Major-General Pope directs you to move upon Centreville at the first dawn of day with your whole command, leaving your trains to follow. It is very important that you should be here at a very early hour in the morning. A severe engagement is likely to take place, and your presence is necessary.

I am, general, very respectfully, your obedient servant,

Geo. D. Ruggles
Colonel and Chief of Staff[13]

Headquarters Army of Virginia,
Centreville, August 29, 1862.

Maj. Gen. Fitz-John Porter:

Push forward with your corps and King's division, which you will take with you, upon Gainesville. I am following the enemy down the Warrenton turnpike. Be expeditious or we will lose much.

Jno. [sic] Pope,
Major-General, Commanding.[14]

Captain Douglas Pope

The next witness up for the prosecution was Captain Douglas Pope, an aide to Gen. Pope and the general's nephew. Nepotism was rampant during the Civil War, and it was common to find nephews and sons on generals' staffs. Capt. Pope testified that he was given Gen. Pope's 4:30 P.M. order to deliver to Gen. Porter. At the time, Pope's headquarters were near the Warrenton pike at the north end of the battlefield. Capt. Pope estimated the time of his departure only by the time on the order. He estimated the distance to Porter to be about three miles. On the way, he met Gen. McDowell, who asked to read the order. Capt. Pope estimated that he reached Porter at about 5 o'clock. Again, this was only an estimate of the time based on the time he thought he had left and an estimate of the travel time. He found Porter at the intersection of the Sudley Springs and Gainesville–Manassas Junction roads near the Bethlehem Church. (See map 13.)

Map 13—Headquarters Eve of August 29

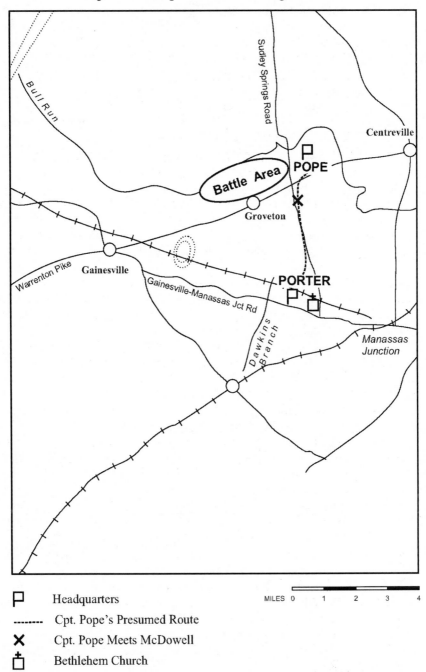

П   Headquarters

-------- Cpt. Pope's Presumed Route

✗   Cpt. Pope Meets McDowell

♁   Bethlehem Church

MILES 0   1   2   3   4

Capt. Pope spent about fifteen minutes with Porter. Porter, after reading the order, mentioned that the enemy had come down in front to attack him. Pope and Porter could hear cannon fire loud and clear coming from the battlefield along the Warrenton pike. Porter made no inquiry as to the progress of the battle, but an aide of Porter's did. While with Porter, Pope noticed troops on the road that he believed belonged to Sykes's division. Those in sight had their arms stacked.

Capt. Pope then left to return to Gen. Pope's headquarters. He had ridden no more than a mile or a mile and a half when he was overtaken by a messenger from Gen. Porter, who said that Gen. Porter wanted to see him. When Capt. Pope got back to Porter's headquarters, he did not see Gen. Porter, but saw an aide of his. The aide said that he had a message for Gen. Pope. It was that a scout had returned and reported that the rebels were retreating through Thoroughfare Gap. When Pope left Porter's headquarters a second time, an hour or so had elapsed since he first left Porter's headquarters, but he observed no evidence that any preparations for an advance of the troops in sight was in progress. This ended the prosecution's questioning of Pope, and it was now the turn of the defense.

Most of the defense questioning of Capt. Pope related to time. None of the times Pope had given were the result of having observed a clock. All were estimates and all were based on the premise that 4:30 P.M., the time he observed written on the order, was the time that he departed.

The next two prosecution witnesses had little or nothing to offer that related to the five specifications of this chapter. The first of the two was surgeon Robert O. Abbott, the medical director of Porter's corps. It was he who delivered Gen. Pope's joint order to Porter and McDowell on the twenty-ninth. He testified that the time of delivery was between 12 and 1 P.M., and at the time of delivery, Porter was about two miles down the road from Manassas Junction to Gainesville, and McDowell was about one mile in his rear. The second of the two prosecution witnesses was Lt. Col. Thomas C. H. Smith. Smith's testimony related almost entirely to Porter's attitude toward Gen. Pope and will be covered in Chapter 8.

What little testimony Smith had relative to Pope's battle with Jackson on the twenty-ninth was entirely opinion. Smith opined that Pope's forces alone could merely push Jackson back toward a uniting with Longstreet's force coming through Thoroughfare Gap, but that, had Porter attacked Jackson's flank and rear, he could have cut off Jackson's retreat.

The next two prosecution witnesses were two major generals, Heintzelman and McDowell. Gen. Heintzelman's testimony related solely to charge 1, specification 1, that was covered in the previous chapter. McDowell, however, was a major player in all of the five specifications treated in this chapter. Consequently, it was anticipated that his testimony would be key in the resolution of these five charges.

McDowell's Testimony

McDowell said in his testimony that he had difficulty in keeping track of the hours in the day, and the times he would give were estimates that could be off. Early on the morning of the twenty-ninth, he was with Reynolds's division of his corps, which was with the Sigel, Heintzelman, Reno group confronting Jackson along the Warrenton pike. McDowell gave instructions that Reynolds should support Sigel and then set out for Manassas Junction, where he heard that his divisions of King and Ricketts were near. On approaching Manassas Junction, McDowell met Gen. Porter and his corps moving up the road from Manassas Junction to Gainesville. McDowell entered into conversation with Porter, and Porter showed him the order he had that directed him to take King's division with him. Apparently, this caused some embarrassment, as King's division belonged to McDowell. Porter, however, offered that this would be no problem inasmuch as McDowell was senior to him and, if McDowell were along, McDowell would naturally be in command of the whole column (i.e., Porter's divisions and McDowell's).

McDowell, learning that his other division, that of Ricketts, was nearby, added Ricketts's division to the column behind King's. The column from front to back now consisted of Morell and Sykes's divisions of Porter's corps, and King's and Ricketts's divisions of McDowell's corps.

Somewhere along the road to Gainesville, McDowell could not say exactly when or where, McDowell was delivered a copy of Pope's joint order to McDowell and Porter (the one contained in charge 1, specification 2). It told them to do what they were already doing, that is, move up the Gainesville–Manassas Junction road toward Gainesville; but it also gave some discretionary authority. It contained the sentence: "If any considerable advantages are to be gained by departing from this order, it will not be carried out."[15] McDowell said that, at the time, he gave no particular thought to the question of whether or not, by Pope addressing the order to the two generals, Pope intended that each operate directly under him (Pope).

About this time, McDowell was handed a message from Gen. Buford. Buford was the commander of the cavalry of Banks's corps, but at the time, was operating under McDowell. Buford was watching the area of Thoroughfare Gap for the arrival of Longstreet's troops. Buford's message read:

> Headquarters Calvary Brigade—9:30 A.M.
> John Buford
> Brigadier General
>
> General Ricketts:
>
> Seventeen regiments, one battery, 500 cavalry passed through Gainesville three-quarters of an hour ago, on the Centreville road. I think this division should join our forces now engaged at once.

John Buford
Brigadier General[16]

McDowell said that he did not know whether the message was coming to him directly from Buford or from Ricketts. About this time, the column had stopped. McDowell rode forward to advise Porter of his receipt of the joint order and Buford's message, and to find the reason for the stop.

There was a church on the road from Manassas Junction to Gainesville at the intersection of the Gainesville–Manassas Junction road and the Sudley Springs road. By the time McDowell rode forward, the last of Porter's troops were a little past the church.

It was about noon when McDowell found Porter. Porter, with some staff members, was a little forward of his column. McDowell saw that Porter already had a copy of Pope's joint order, and he showed him Buford's dispatch. There was an open area several hundred yards in front of Gen. Porter, and McDowell could hear shots, as of skirmishing. There were woods to their right preventing them from seeing the Warrenton pike, which converged with their road at Gainesville. McDowell did not know how far away the Warrenton pike was at this point, but thought it not far. McDowell could hear large sounds of battle emanating from the direction of the Warrenton pike and noticed clouds of dust over the trees that were apparently being caused by troops marching up the pike from Gainesville toward the battle. McDowell presumed that this was caused by the troops Buford had sighted that morning. He said that his main consideration at this point was how soon could he bring the Porter-McDowell force into the battle raging beyond the trees to their right. Gen. Porter, however, was convinced that the enemy lay not only beyond the trees to his right, but in his front as well.

McDowell's parting words to Porter were: "You put your force in here, and I will take mine up the Sudley Springs road, on the left of the troops engaged at that point with the enemy,"[17] or words to that effect. McDowell felt that the joint order of Pope that they were operating under provided him sufficient discretion for this move.

McDowell apparently believed that he could extend Pope's line to the point where Porter could make a junction with him when Porter moved to his right through the woods. However, the distance between Porter's position on the Gainesville–Manassas Junction road and the converging Warrenton pike was almost two miles—probably a distance far greater than McDowell imagined. Furthermore, Jackson's position was more nearly parallel to the Warrenton pike than perpendicular to it, as McDowell probably imagined. Map 14 contains the situation as McDowell probably believed it to be, and as it actually was.

When McDowell departed from Porter, he firmly believed that they had an understanding that Porter was going to commit his force where he was.

Map 14—Jackson / Pope Positions, Afternoon of August 29

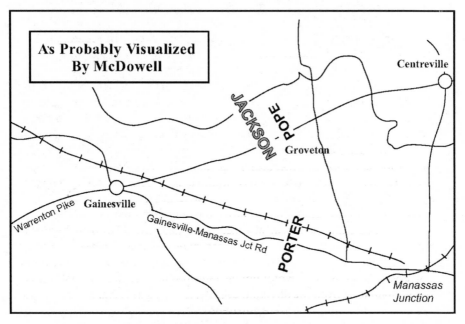

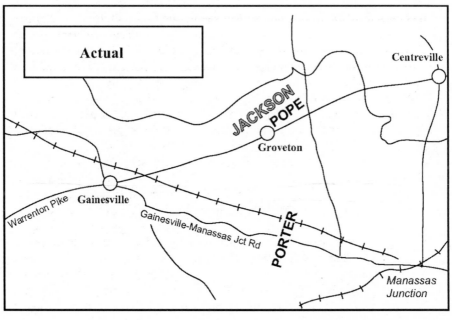

McDowell turned his two divisions up the Sudley Springs road and then rode on ahead of them. He said he met a courier coming the other way, carrying Gen. Pope's 4:30 P.M. order to Porter to attack Jackson's flank immediately. McDowell stopped the courier, read the order, and then sent him on his way. McDowell now felt that his perceived arrangement with Porter was entirely consonant with Gen. Pope's wishes.

Gen. McDowell considered that Porter was in the presence of the enemy when he left him. He said that he did not know what time Porter received Pope's 4:30 P.M. order to attack Jackson's flank, nor did he know how far from Porter Jackson's flank was. However, he did say that, had Porter turned off the road to his right when he left him or soon thereafter and acted with rapidity, he believed that Porter would have soon reached the enemy—and he had considered it Porter's duty to do just that. He further opined that, had Porter done so, Pope's army would have achieved decisive results.

There is a direct conflict between McDowell's testimony and that of a previous witness. (Other conflicts will surface later.) McDowell testified that, while proceeding up the Sudley Springs road, he met a courier carrying Gen. Pope's 4:30 order to Porter, stopped the courier, read the order, and sent the courier on his way. Previous testimony stated that the courier was Capt. Douglas Pope. McDowell, when questioned, said that he knew Douglas Pope and that he did not believe the courier was Douglas Pope.

The defense questioning of McDowell produced little if anything useful to the defense beyond one positive statement by McDowell regarding Porter's attitude and patriotism. In general, McDowell's answers were peppered with "I don't knows" and "I can't remembers." In general, McDowell proved himself a master of obfuscation. For example, when McDowell was asked how much time would have been required for the enemy troops that Gen. Buford had reported to reach Jackson, he replied: "It would depend on how fast they marched."[18] When asked how long he had conferred with Porter before their parting, he replied that he could not remember. When pressed and asked "was it five, ten, fifteen, or twenty minutes?"[19] he replied "Yes."[20]

The court posed a number of significant questions to McDowell. It asked if it were practicable for Porter to have crossed the wooded area to his right to attack Jackson's flank and rear. McDowell's answer was long and convoluted and was based on his experiences in the area earlier in the campaign and the movements of the enemy later in the campaign. His answer was affirmative and ended saying he had the "belief that troops could move through the country comprised between the Warrenton Turnpike and the Sudley Springs road and the road from Bethlehem Church to Gainesville. I will mention, further, that the country is a mixture of woods, cleared ground, and hills, and that it is easy for troops to march without being seen or seeing the enemy."[21] What McDowell failed to add was the reason why he did not take his own troops across this land to attack Jackson in the flank and rear, when he was lined up behind Porter on the Warrenton Junction-Gainesville road near the Bethlehem church.

The court then asked McDowell on what grounds he based his opinion that, if Porter had attacked the right wing of Jackson, the battle would have been decisive in the Union's favor. McDowell responded that as it was, the day's fighting ended up decidedly in the Union's favor, and the addition of Porter's twenty to thirty regiments being applied in such a favorable position, while Jackson was already fully engaged, would have proved decisive. The court then asked McDowell if he considered Porter to have been "in the presence of the enemy"[22] when they parted. McDowell replied that he did.

The defense then posed the question: Suppose Porter attacked and had been defeated? McDowell responded that Porter would have drawn off so many of the enemy's troops that, even if he had been defeated, the overall result would have been favorable to the Union.

McDowell's testimony was damning for the defense. He testified that: 1) Porter was in the presence of the enemy; 2) It was obvious from Porter's position that Pope was in a major conflict beyond the trees to Porter's right; 3) There was no significant impediment to Porter moving through the trees to enter the fray; 4) McDowell told Porter to do just that before they parted; 5) Had Porter done so, the Union would have won decisively that day; and 6) Porter did nothing.

The prosecution's last witness with information bearing on the events related to the five charges was Colonel Benjamin F. Smith, colonel of the One Hundred Twenty-sixth Regiment of Ohio Volunteers, which was part of Colonel Chapman's brigade of Sykes's division. Smith testified that on the morning of August 29, his column marched from Manassas Junction to Manassas Station, and then countermarched from Manassas Station to Manassas Junction. At Manassas Junction they turned off on the road to Gainesville. After marching a few miles toward Gainesville, the column was brought to a stop with his regiment on top of a rise. From here, they could see open country ahead over the tops of trees. Morell's division was deployed in front and below them, and the brigade of Smith was ordered deployed in line of battle. A Confederate battery opened on them and fired three or four shots. A Union battery replied and the Confederate battery withdrew.

Smith said that he could see dust over the tops of the trees (to his right?) as if a large number of men were marching, but he could not tell in which direction. After a short time, Smith's group was ordered to withdraw. Smith did not know the reason why. After heading back on the road toward Manassas Junction, they went into camp for the night. It was still afternoon when they did so. The next morning, they marched up the Sudley Springs road to the battle area.

The defense questioning of Smith elicited the information that the place they camped for the night of the twenty-ninth was within sight of the juncture of the Gainesville–Manassas Junction road and the Sudley Springs road, and within sight of the Manassas Gap railroad. Thus, Smith's unit had not retired all the way to Manassas Junction but, in fact, little farther back than its stopping point on the rise on the twenty-ninth. Inasmuch as Sykes's division, of which Smith was a part, was behind Morell's division in the advance toward Gainesville and ahead of Morell's in the retirement, Morell's division must have retired very little indeed back from the artillery exchange. The distance from Dawkins Branch to the road junction was about two and a half miles, and the distance from the road junction to Manassas junction was about one and a half miles.

Witness Charles Duffee was called by the court and not the prosecution. However, his testimony was part of the prosecution's case. On August 29 and 30, Duffee was a private orderly of the First Ohio Cavalry. At the time of his testimony, he was no longer in the service. Duffee was assigned to accompany Capt. Douglas Pope when Pope carried Gen. Pope's 4:30 P.M. order to Gen. Porter on August 29. The reason for Duffee's assignment was because Duffee claimed that he knew the road.

Duffee testified that they went at a pretty good clip, as fast as the terrain allowed. He estimated that they departed Pope's headquarters at about 4:30 P.M. They came across Gen. McDowell's headquarters about two miles from their starting point. Gen. McDowell read the order and commented that it was an important order. He then gave them precise instructions as to where they could find Porter.

They found Porter's headquarters near the Bethlehem Church. Duffee estimated that it was about five miles from Pope's headquarters, and he estimated their time of arrival at about 5:30 P.M. At the time of their arrival, Gen. Porter was resting on the ground under the shade of a tree. Capt. Pope sat on the ground to talk to Porter, and Porter read the order with his head resting on one arm. Duffee estimated that they spent about twenty minutes with Porter before heading back.

On their way back, Duffee asked Pope's permission to leave him briefly to go to a well to get a drink of water. While at the well, an orderly approached Duffee and told him that Capt. Pope had been overtaken by a messenger and told to return to Porter's headquarters. Duffee rejoined Capt. Pope. When at Porter's headquarters the second time, Duffee did not recall seeing Gen. Porter. When they started back a second time, Duffee estimated that it was nearly 7 P.M. and stated that it was getting dark. They stopped at Gen. McDowell's headquarters on their way back for about twenty minutes, and when they reached Pope's headquarters, it was fully dark.

The Defense's Case

The first three defense witnesses were General Parke, Col. Clary, and Capt. Fifield. None of the three had any testimony relating to the five charges of this chapter. The fourth witness did. This was Capt. George Montieth, an aide-de-camp to Gen. Porter.

Capt. Montieth's testified that he was present when Gen. McDowell departed from Gen. Porter on the twenty-ninth. The two generals had been on a path in the woods, north of the Manassas Gap Railroad, about three quarters of a mile in front of Gen. Porter's troops. Gen. McDowell was alone when he departed.

Later, about sundown, a messenger arrived for Gen. Porter. The messenger was Capt. Pope. Montieth said he was not the man sent to bring Capt. Pope back after Pope had departed. However, Montieth knew that he had sighted Pope on Pope's first trip to Porter's headquarters, as he saw Pope and Porter together and he knew Porter was not at his headquarters when Pope returned.

Montieth slept on the ground near Porter that night. Porter awakened him during the night, told him he had received a message, and directed him to take the message to General Morell. Montieth knew that the message had been delivered to Porter between 3 and 4 A.M. on the thirtieth because he had talked to the courier. The courier told him that he had spent most of the night looking for Porter, having first gone to Manassas Junction.

Montieth delivered the message to Morell, who was at the front. Montieth did not know what the message said, but could see its impact. Morell immediately began withdrawing his troops from the front. Montieth returned to Porter's headquarters and, at that time or even earlier, Porter was directing his troops to march up the Sudley Springs road.

Montieth's testimony was important in a number of areas. First, Gen. Pope said that he read Porter's message between 7 and 8 P.M. on the twenty-ninth indicating Porter's intent to withdraw to Manassas Junction. It was upon reading the message that Pope decided to write his order ordering Porter to report to him. Pope must have assumed that Porter actually retreated, inasmuch as the courier first went to Manassas Junction to find him. According to Montieth, Porter had not withdrawn, since he went to the "front" at Porter's direction to deliver the order to Gen. Morell, and it was only after Morell received the order that he began to withdraw.

Montieth's testimony also implied that several hours elapsed between the time Pope issued his order and Porter received it, and that once Porter received it, he acted with alacrity.

Lieutenant Weld's Testimony

The next witness for the defense was another aide of Gen. Porter, Lt. Stephen Weld. Unlike so many other witnesses, Lt. Weld had a watch and occasionally looked at it. It was Weld who was entrusted with carrying a crucial message of Porter that was addressed to Generals King and McDowell but ended up in the hands of Pope.

Weld said that he was present when Porter and McDowell parted on the twenty-ninth. He estimated that he was within a hundred feet at the time and did not believe that anyone else was closer. Later that afternoon, Porter tasked Weld with delivering a message to Generals King and McDowell. He was to deliver the message both verbally and in written form. The verbal message, as Weld recalled, was that Gen. Morell would be strongly engaged; that there was a large force in front of Porter, that clouds of dust were seen there, etc. Weld glanced at the written message and it appeared to him to be substantially the same as the verbal, but with added details. Weld looked at his watch at the time he set out to deliver the message. As he recalled, it was either five minutes before 4 P.M. or five minutes after 4 P.M.

When Weld departed with the message, he was accompanied by an unstated number of orderlies. Weld said that, at the time of his departure, a part of Porter's corps was on the road between the junction of the Sudley Springs road and the road to Gainesville, and the other part was at the front (facing the enemy) in the direction of Gainesville.

While en route to deliver the message on the Sudley Springs road, Weld first met General Hatch of King's division. Hatch advised Weld that King was sick and that he was in command of King's division. Consequently, Weld gave Hatch the verbal message and handed him the written version. He then asked Hatch if he had any message for Gen. Porter. Hatch said, "Tell Porter that we have whipped the enemy and are driving them."[23] Just at that time, heavy musketry firing broke out in their front, and Weld asked Hatch if he should still send Hatch's message. Hatch said no, and then gave Weld a new message. He said, "Tell Porter we have driven the enemy into the woods."[24] Weld wrote this down and gave it to one of his orderlies and told him to take it to Gen. Porter. Weld then asked Gen. Hatch if he (Weld) should still take Porter's message to Gen. McDowell. Hatch answered that he should and pointed out where he had last seen McDowell.

Weld continued on in the direction indicated by Hatch and soon encountered Gen. McDowell in the vicinity of the intersection of the Warrenton pike and Sudley Springs road. Weld handed the written message to McDowell, who then pointed to Gen. Pope, who was standing nearby, and said: "I am not the man. There is the man."[25] Weld then gave both the verbal and written messages to Gen. Pope. Weld estimated the time of delivery to be "at least 5 o'clock."[26]

Weld asked Gen. Pope if he had anything for Gen. Porter. Pope replied: "Tell Porter that we are having a hard fight."[27] Pope put Porter's message in his vest pocket and then became preoccupied with an operational matter. Weld waited five minutes to see if Pope had anything more for Porter. Pope did not, so Weld wrote down the message and handed it to one of his orderlies for delivery to Porter.

Weld set out to return to Porter shortly after the orderly had left. While en route, Weld encountered the orderly, who said that he had been unable to find Porter to deliver Pope's message. Weld took the message back and said that he would deliver it to Porter himself. When Weld had initially departed from Porter, Porter had told him that, on Weld's return, he could find him at the front. In consequence, Weld headed directly for the front. Failing to find Porter at the front, he returned to Porter's headquarters, where he did find him. Because of Weld's false start in looking for Porter, Weld estimated that he spent at least one and a half hours on his return trip from Pope. Weld estimated that he finally found Porter at about 6:45 P.M. At that time, Weld said it was not yet dark, but dusk—that is, between sunset and dark.

About fifteen minutes after Weld returned to Porter (i.e., 7 P.M.), he said that a courier arrived from Pope's bearing a message. The courier was an officer, but Weld said that he did not know him. By the time the courier delivered his message, it was getting dark, and Weld said that, because of the darkness, he had to show the courier where the road back was.

Weld was confident that he observed the courier's initial arrival, and that he was not observing a return of the courier from an earlier arrival. He gave as his reason for thinking so that he observed Porter reading something (presumably the delivered message), writing something, and getting on his horse and heading for the front. Weld then said that he was not present if and when the courier returned.

Both Generals McDowell and Pope were recalled as witnesses. Each had some testimony relating to Weld's testimony. McDowell acknowledged that he met Pope on the twenty-ninth in the vicinity of the intersection of the Warrenton pike and the Sudley Springs road. McDowell put the time as "about sunset."[28] Pope put the time as about 5:30 or between 5:30 and 6 P.M. They were together but briefly. McDowell made no mention of having encountered a courier from Porter while they were together. Pope specifically stated that he had no recollection of encountering a courier from Porter, or of receiving anything from Porter, or of sending anything verbally to Porter at or around 5 P.M. Weld had testified that he encountered McDowell and Pope together in the vicinity of the intersection of the Warrenton pike and Sudley Springs road at about 5 P.M. on the twenty-ninth, that he showed his message from Porter to McDowell, that McDowell waved him on to Pope, who was standing nearby, that Pope read the message, and that Pope gave him a verbal message for Porter. Weld could not possibly have known that McDowell and Pope were together at that location and at that time unless he were there. Consequently, there is a strong presumption that Weld's account of the meeting is correct.

It is obvious that the message that Weld carried and handed to Pope at around 5 P.M. was different from the one that Pope said he read between 7 and 8 P.M. Both were addressed to McDowell and King. However, Weld said that his message said something about Morell being strongly engaged and a large force in front of Porter, and nothing about retiring to Manassas. Pope said that the message he read between 7 and 8 P.M. stated that Porter intended to retire to Manassas. The trial record reveals only a single message from Porter to McDowell and King on the twenty-ninth, the one about retiring to Manassas. From the Weld testimony, it is clear that there was greater contact from Porter to McDowell and King after they separated.

Pope had testified that he had become so upset with Porter for not attacking Jackson that, at 4:30 P.M., he sent a peremptory order to Porter to attack. Yet, here at about 5 P.M., we have Weld, a staff officer of Porter's, standing before Pope asking Pope if he had any instructions for Porter. Weld said that Pope simply told him, "Tell Porter that we are having a hard fight."[29] Pope claimed that he had no recollection of seeing Weld that afternoon, much less giving him any message for Porter.

There is yet another even greater enigma in Weld's testimony. He said that about 7 P.M., after he had returned to Porter's headquarters, a messenger arrived with a message for Porter from Pope. According to Pope, the only message he sent to Porter that afternoon was his 4:30 order to attack Jackson's flank immediately. We know that this message was carried by Capt. Douglas Pope, who said he delivered it to Porter at about 5 P.M. Did Weld observe Douglas Pope arriving two hours later than Pope testified? If not, who was the 7 P.M. courier from Pope, and what was he carrying?

Lieutenant Colonel Frederick T. Locke

The next defense witness who had information bearing on the five charges was Porter's chief of staff, Lt. Col. Frederick T. Locke. If some of Lt. Weld's testimony contradicted that of prosecution witnesses, essentially all of Locke's did. Here is what Locke originally testified, what prosecution rebuttal witnesses had to say, and what Locke said to the rebuttal witnesses.

It was between 12 and 1 P.M. when Locke first saw Gen. McDowell on August 29. At the time, the head of Porter's column was brought to a stop at Dawkins Creek because of contact with the enemy. Porter was in the process of deploying his troops in line of battle. Skirmishers were already deployed in front, and a battery was already unlimbered and set up.

Lt. Col. Locke and Capt. Martin, Porter's chief of artillery, were near Gen. Porter as Gen. McDowell approached. After McDowell and Porter exchanged amenities, Locke said he heard McDowell say: "Porter, you are out too far already; this is no place to fight a battle."[30] Porter and McDowell then engaged in some conversation that Locke could not hear, and then rode across the Manassas Gap railroad that ran near parallel to their road and on into some woods to their right.

Locke said that the woods were very dense, and that it would have been very difficult for organized infantry to pass through them. Artillery fire was audible through the woods. After a short time, McDowell departed. A little later, Porter sent for Locke and directed him to carry a message to Gen. King, whose division was on the road behind Porter's corps. Locke estimated that this occurred a half hour to forty-five minutes after McDowell departed. The message that Locke was to convey to King was that King was to remain where he was until he received further orders from Porter.

When Locke set off, he believed that King, although normally of McDowell's corps, was subordinate to Porter. He believed this because Porter's marching orders of that morning directed that he take King's division along with him. Locke said he found King near Bethlehem Church, which was at the intersection of the Gainesville–Manassas Junction road and the Sudley Springs road. Locke said that McDowell was with King. Locke passed Porter's message to King and then McDowell intervened. According to Locke, McDowell said: "Give my compliments to General Porter, and say to him that I am going to the right, and will take General King with me. I think he [General Porter] better remain where he is; but, if it is necessary for him to fall back, he can do so on my left."[31] Presumably, when McDowell said that he was going to the right, he meant up the Sudley Springs road towards Pope's position.

Locke said that he returned up the Gainesville–Manassas Junction road to Porter's position and gave Porter McDowell's message. Locke estimated that this occurred sometime later than 2:30 P.M. After Porter was given McDowell's message, Porter made some minor changes in the deployment of his troops. For one thing, he moved back the troops he had sent to his right a little bit so that they would be out of sight of the enemy and be protected from enemy fire. Locke did not consider these moves significant and did not consider them a retreat. After these moves, the troops at the front maintained their positions until the morning of the thirtieth.

Locke testified that there was some skirmishing and artillery fire on Porter's front during the day that inflicted some casualties, but no battle. He noted immense clouds of dust in their front, as if there was a massing of the enemy. He thought that the enemy was deploying into a line of battle within one and a half miles of Porter's front.

Locke said that a staff officer from Pope arrived at Porter's headquarters toward evening. He put the time at between sunset and dusk. Lt. Weld and Capt. Montieth were present with Porter at the time, as well as was Locke. Locke later learned that the staff officer was Capt. Douglas Pope and that he bore an order for Porter to attack Jackson's flank immediately. This would entail the troops at the front moving to their right, and Locke considered the woods and broken ground to be an obstacle to moving artillery.

Porter, after reading the message, ordered Locke to proceed up the road to Gen. Morell at the front and direct him to move forward and attack immediately. Porter stated that he would shortly follow.

The distance from Porter's headquarters to the front was about one and a half miles. When Locke gave Porter's order to Morell, Morell began at once moving up his troops for the attack, but stated that it was already too late in the day to accomplish anything. As Locke was leaving Morell, Porter was approaching. In the event, the attack was not made.

The prosecution called Gen. McDowell and Gen. King in rebuttal. The calling of Gen. King as a prosecution witness was unusual in the extreme, as he was a member of the court judging Gen. Porter.

Gen. McDowell picked up where he left off in his original testimony with his wordy answers that said nothing and his obfuscations punctuated with "don't knows" and "can't remembers." McDowell said he had no recollection of saying to Porter when they met, "Porter, you are too far out already," etc. He had no recollection of Lt. Col. Locke bearing an order approaching King and himself, and in fact, he could not even recall being with King that after-noon. Inasmuch as he did not even think he saw Locke that afternoon, he certainly could not have given Locke the order for Porter to stay where he was. Here are some of McDowell's answers verbatim as examples of his testimony:

> QUESTION: Have you, or not, any recollection of having said to General Porter, in your interview, when you first met him on the 29th of August, that this was no place to fight a battle; that he was too far in advance?
> ANSWER: I cannot recollect precisely what occurred between General Porter and myself, or what conversation or what words passed between us at that time. The subject of our conversation, as near as I can recall it to mind, was the order which each of us received from General Pope, and particularly that part of it which referred to our not going so far for-ward that we should not be able to get behind Bull Run that night or before morning. I cannot say what language I used, or how it may have been understood, whilst talking on that point. As to that particular spot or ground, so far as topography was concerned, not being a place for a battle, I have no recollection of having said anything that it was not a good place to fight on. It was about as good a place, so far as topog-raphy was concerned, as any other in that part of the country. I think our conversation was chiefly upon the subject of not putting ourselves in a position to be unable to fulfill the requirements of the order about retiring behind Bull Run, and about not going so far toward Gainesville, or going to Gainesville, that this could not be done. Without being able to say what was said by either him or me, I think, so far as my best rec-ollection goes, that the object and purpose of our conversation at that time was in relation to that point.[32]
> QUESTION: After the interview which you had on the 29th of August with General Porter, of which you have spoken heretofore in your testi-mony, you stated that you turned down toward or near Bethlehem Church. Will you state whether you have any recollection of a messen-ger—a staff officer—from General Porter, bearing a message, while you were there, and if you made any reply?
> ANSWER: I do not remember anything of the kind.
> QUESTION: Have you, or not, any recollection of having, after parting with

General Porter on the 29th of August, sent back to him a message like this: "Take my compliments to General Porter, and say to him that I think he better remain where he is," or words to that effect?

ANSWER: I have no recollection of sending any such message.[33]

The government now called Brigadier Gen. Rufus King as a rebuttal witness. Gen. King testified that he did not think that he had been with McDowell at any time on the twenty-ninth; that he did not recollect being approached by a staff officer with a message from Porter on that date; and, consequently, he certainly did not recollect McDowell giving any message to the staff officer for Porter. King's words were: "I do not remember any circumstances of that kind to have taken place on any day."[34]

The defense now recalled Lt. Col. Locke to rebut the rebuttal. Locke testified that he expected a battle on the twenty-ninth, and that he considered that his carrying Porter's order to King and McDowell's order to Porter to be of great importance. Consequently, the events of that day were indelibly imprinted in his mind. He said that, that very day, he told Colonel Warren, a

Brigadier General Rufus King of the Confederate States Volunteers. He was an officer of the court and was called to testify in the court-martial of Fitz-John Porter (courtesy the Massachusetts Commandery Military Order of the Loyal Legion and the U.S. Army Military History Institute).

brigade commander in Sykes's division, about McDowell's order to Porter. Furthermore, he said that he distinctly remembered the location at which he encountered King and McDowell and could walk to the spot today. He testified that he did not know King at the time he delivered Porter's order, but asked the general to whom he gave the message if he were King, to be sure he gave the message to the right person. Furthermore, he stated that when he arrived for the trial, he recognized King, who was a member of the court, as the man to whom he gave Porter's order.

In Gen. McDowell's original testimony on his conversation with Porter on the twenty-ninth, he said he told Porter: "You put your force in here and I will take mine up the Sudley Springs road, on the left of the troops engaged with the enemy"—or words to that effect. In McDowell's rebuttal testimony to Locke regarding the same conversation with Porter, he made no mention of making such a statement. Had he made such a statement, it is hard to believe that Porter, after McDowell left, would send Locke with an order to King telling King to remain where he was.

Lt. Col. Locke's testimony and Lt. Weld's testimony regarding Capt. Pope's arrival with Gen. Pope's 4:30 P.M. order to attack melded together nicely and tended to corroborate each other. Lt. Weld testified that he was with Porter when a courier arrived from Gen. Pope, but said he did not know who the courier was or what his message was. Lt. Col. Locke testified that he was present when Capt. Pope arrived with Gen. Pope's order to Porter to attack at once. He added that Lt. Weld was with Porter at the time. Thus, it is evident that both were present at Capt. Pope's arrival. Weld put the time at about 7 P.M. Locke estimated the time as at dusk. Thus, their estimates of Capt. Pope's time of arrival are compatible. Capt. Pope, in his testimony, said that he delivered the message to Porter at about 5 P.M. Pvt. Duffee, who had accompanied Capt. Pope, estimated their time of arrival at Porter's headquarters as about 5:30. Lt. Weld's and Lt. Col. Locke's estimates of the time of delivery of Pope's order do not even come close to matching the times claimed by Capt. Pope and Pvt. Duffee. However, Weld's and Locke's estimate of the time of arrival do match closely with Pope's and Duffee's estimate of the time of their second arrival. Could Weld and Locke actually have witnessed Capt. Pope's return rather than his initial arrival? It appears not, because both Locke and Weld said that Porter was present when they saw Capt. Pope arrive, and both Capt. Pope and Pvt. Duffee said that Porter was not present on their second arrival.

Who is wrong? Is somebody lying? This is a critical point for both the prosecution and the defense. If, in fact, Capt. Pope and Pvt. Duffee did not arrive the first time and deliver their message between 5 and 5:30, but actually arrived about 7 P.M., it probably would have been too late in the day for Porter to implement the order to attack. Gen. Porter's headquarters were near Bethlehem Church, which was about one and a half miles from Gen. Morell's position on the front. Before Porter could have even got an attack order to Morell, it would have been getting dark.

Next up for the defense was Capt. A. P. Martin, commander of division artillery in Gen. Morell's division. Martin also happened to be at the head of Porter's column when it was stopped at Dawkins Branch on the morning of the twenty-ninth of August. He testified that he was nearby when Gen. McDowell met Gen. Porter. He said that after they exchanged amenities, Gen. McDowell said "Porter, this is no place to fight a battle; you are out too far."[35] Martin said that he then walked off and heard no more. The only other person that he could recollect who was nearby at the time was Lt. Col. Locke. He put the time of the generals' meeting at "about 11 A.M."[36]

At the time, Martin said that skirmishers were already operating in front, and the troops were in the process of forming a line of battle. Martin then described the terrain. There was a ravine about a hundred and fifty yards in front of where the generals met (Dawkins Branch), then about three hundred yards of open plain, and then dense woods. The Gainesville–Manassas Junction road continued across the ravine, across the plain, and into the woods.

General Morell

The next defense witness was Maj. Gen. George W. Morell, one of Porter's two division commanders. It was Morell's division that was at the head of Porter's column when it encountered the enemy at Dawkins Branch on the Gainesville–Manassas Junction road that fateful morning of August 29. Morell's story was as follows.

The first order the corps received early that morning was to march from Bristoe to Centreville. Sykes's division was in the lead. When they had already passed the road from Manassas Junction to Gainesville, which radiated off to their left, they were ordered to proceed toward Gainesville. This necessitated countermarching, and now Morell's division was in the lead.

When they had proceeded about three miles up the road to Gainesville, Morell said he met a horseman coming the other way. The horseman said that he just left Gainesville (about three and a half miles farther up the road) and that there were four hundred Confederate skirmishers there, followed by the main body of the Confederate troops. Morell had proceeded a little farther when his skirmishers reported that they had encountered enemy skirmishers in their front. Porter, who was with Morell, ordered the column stopped, that a battery be placed on a hill they had just passed, and that the troops deploy. Morell estimated the time as about 10 or 11 A.M.

At a time that Morell estimated to be near the middle of the day, he saw Gen. Porter riding with Gen. McDowell. They passed off to the right, toward the railroad (the Manassas Gap railroad, which was to the right of and roughly parallel to the road) and into some woods.

In a short time, Porter returned alone. He then ordered Morell to move his command to the right, i.e., over the railroad. Morell succeeded in getting one of his three brigades over the railroad and to the edge of the woods when he got orders to return to his former position. At this point, they received a shot from enemy artillery directly in front and on the other side of the ravine. At this, Porter ordered the infantry back behind one of their batteries, where it sheltered behind a hill and some brush. Porter then posted Waterman's battery on the other side of the road, and they remained in this position for much of the remainder of the day.

The Sixty-second Pennsylvania Regiment was already in front as skirmishers and Morell now sent a second regiment to join it. This was the Thirteenth New York under Colonel Marshall, who now became the senior officer of the skirmishers. Marshall periodically sent back reports to Morell that the enemy was forming to their left in the woods.

Morell said that the ground in front of his position was open for one thousand to twelve hundred yards and, beyond that, there were woods. However, a point of woods protruded toward them along the road.

Cannon fire could be heard beyond the woods to their right periodically, but Morell thought it was far off. He considered the woods dense. He thought it difficult, if not impossible, to move artillery through the woods in daylight, and impossible at night. Near the close of the day, they could hear two or three volleys of musketry beyond the woods to their right, but that was the only musketry they heard, except for occasional shots in their front. Morell thought that the sounds of battle to their right were receding.

At just about sunset, Morell said that he received an order from Porter, written in pencil, to attack the enemy. The order was as follows:

> General Morell:
>
> I wish you to push up two regiments, supported by two others, preceded by skirmishers, the regiments at intervals of 200 yards, and attack the party with the section of the battery opposed to you. The battle works well on our right, and the enemy are said to be retiring up the pike. Give the enemy a good shelling when our troops advance.
>
> F. J. Porter
> Major General Commanding[37]

In view of the enemy in his front, Morell thought that Porter was in error about the enemy retiring. Consequently, he sent a message to Porter stating his opinion that he thought that Porter had issued his order under a misapprehension. However, as he did so, he continued his preparations for the attack as ordered.

About this time, Lt. Col. Locke arrived with verbal orders for Morell to attack. Morell assumed that the attack Locke ordered was the one originally ordered. However, it was now getting dark, and Morell advised Locke that he could not make the attack before darkness intervened. About this time, a new written order was handed to Morell. This one was for Morell to make dispositions to spend the night. Morell believed that this was tantamount to rescinding the attack order. At this point, Porter appeared in person and Morell proceeded with his preparations for the night. No attack was attempted.

Porter's order for Morell to prepare for the night was entered into evidence and was as follows: "Put your men in position to remain during the night, and have out your pickets. Put them so that they will be in line, and on rising will be in position to resist anything. I am about a mile from you. McDowell says all goes well, and we are getting the best of the fight. I wish you would send me a dozen men from the cavalry."[38]

The next defense witness was Col. George D. Ruggles. Ruggles was Pope's chief of staff and, hence, a strange witness for the defense. None of Ruggles's testimony related to the charges of this chapter; his testimony will be addressed later.

Brigadier General Charles Griffin

Brigadier General Charles Griffin was one of the three brigade commanders in Gen. Morell's division. On the day of the twenty-ninth, as the division set out on the Gainesville–Manassas Junction road, Griffin's brigade was in the lead. Here is his story.

On the morning of the twenty-ninth, the brigade marched from Bristoe to Manassas Junction. At this point, their orders were changed, and they were ordered to take the Gainesville–Manassas Junction road and march toward Gainesville. They left Manassas Junction at about 9 A.M. At this time, Morell's division was in the lead and Griffin's brigade was at the head of the division. They passed King's division, and after proceeding about two miles, met a cavalryman coming the other way. He reported that an enemy trooper had been captured ahead, but the enemy ahead consisted of only a few mounted men.

Griffin then halted his brigade and ordered four companies of the Sixty-second Pennsylvania to the front, with orders to keep about one half mile in front of the brigade, with skirmishers to the fore and flankers on either side of the road. The brigade then continued on a short distance until they came to a clear place (Dawkins Branch) where the skirmishers began exchanging fire with the enemy pickets. At this point, Gen. Porter rode up and ordered the column halted. Griffin then ordered the other eight companies of the Sixty-second Pennsylvania to the front as skirmishers. Beyond the open space in front, there were woods. At one point, the woods came to within six hundred yards of Griffin's front.

Gen. Porter then called Gen. Morell, Gen. Butterfield, and Gen. Griffin together, and they all got off their horses. Gen. Porter said that he had a communication to read to the group. Gen. Griffin assumed that the communication was an order from Gen. Pope. As Griffin recollected, the communication was to the effect that Porter's troops were to try to make a junction with Pope's at Gainesville, but that it might be necessary that night, or before morning, to fall back to Centreville on account of rations.

A battery was placed to the rear of the stop point, on a hill about three hundred yards distant. This was where the group heard the reading of the order. They were only there a short time when Gen. McDowell rode up. Griffin estimated the time as between 12 and 1 P.M. McDowell engaged in conversation with Gen. Porter. Griffin was not present at the conversation and did not know what they said. After the conversation, McDowell rode off to the right. Almost immediately afterward, Griffin received an order to move his brigade to the right. He moved about six hundred yards. The head of his column crossed the railroad and then ran into an obstruction they could not get through. The obstruction consisted of some thick pine bushes.

The next order Griffin got was to move back. The brigade moved back to the hill where the battery was and where the generals had met. As they were moving back, an enemy battery commenced firing at them. The brigade was then placed to the rear and the right of their battery on the hill. It was about 1 P.M. when the enemy battery opened up. Griffin considered that his was a good position to repel an attack.

Before the enemy battery opened up, Griffin's skirmishers captured three of the enemy. All three were cavalrymen. Griffin believed there was a large force of the enemy in front of them and, as he phrased it, "the larger part of Lee's army."[39] He based his estimate largely on the clouds of dust he observed emanating from what he assumed to be Thoroughfare Gap. His description of where the clouds of dust led from Thoroughfare Gap was confusing. Finally, he was asked to point out the position on a map. He pointed to Groveton. Griffin admitted that he never actually saw large bodies of enemy troops. He said that he only saw scattering groups of horsemen or of infantry and did not believe that he ever saw more than forty in a group.

Griffin testified that he could hear cannon fire in the distance during the day, but the only musketry he heard during the day consisted of occasional shots to the front. In the evening, a little after dark, he heard some very heavy volleys of musketry to his right, about two miles away.

Griffin said that Gen. Morell received orders to attack around sundown. The order was carried down the road by an orderly. At that time, Griffin's brigade was proceeding down the road in the direction of Manassas Junction. By this time, they had reached a point about one and a half miles from the position they had occupied earlier in the day. Col. Warren stopped the orderly and read the message. Griffin then faced his command about and immediately started back. He then rode ahead and met Gen. Morell, who by now had received and read the order. Griffin asked him if he was going to attack. He said Morell replied in substance that he was not, that it was too late, and that the order had been given under a wrong impression. The substance of the order was that the enemy was retreating and he should be pursued and attacked vigorously. Gen. Morell then allegedly said that, according to Col. Marshall, the enemy was not only not retiring, but was being reinforced. The command spent the night in the place they now occupied, or very near to it.

Brigadier Gen. John F. Reynolds

The next witness for the defense was Brigadier Gen. John F. Reynolds. Reynolds was a division commander. His division normally belonged to Porter's Fifth Corps. However, Reynolds's division reported in to Pope's Army of Virginia before Porter's other two divisions and, consequently, Pope temporarily assigned it to McDowell's corps. It was in this capacity that it served in the momentous events of August 29 and 30, 1862.

Reynolds's division passed through a portion of the triangle of land encompassed by the Warrenton pike, the Gainesville–Manassas Junction road, and the Sudley Springs road during the day of the twenty-eighth; he passed another portion on horseback during the night of August 28–29. Although the routes that Reynolds followed did not cover exactly the route Porter's troops would have had to take to cross over the triangle to Groveton, Reynolds's routes were close and indicative of the nature of the terrain. Reynolds's descriptions are as follows.

During the morning of the twenty-eighth, his division was tasked with proceeding from Gainesville toward Manassas. He started out following an overland route north of the Manassas Gap railroad. He put his three brigades in three parallel columns with his artillery in the intervals. After proceeding only about a mile or a mile and a quarter, the country became so broken, wooded, and obstructed that he moved his entire division over to the Gainesville–Manassas Junction road and continued on in that manner.

Later that evening, Reynolds proceeded on horseback from New Market (see map 15) to Groveton. He testified that the terrain was very broken by ravines and wooded, and he did not think it possible for a command to pass over it in proper order with its artillery in the face of an enemy.

Reynolds next testified to the position of his division at noon on the twenty-ninth. He said that Jackson's force at the time was entirely north of the Warrenton pike and that his division was at the extreme left end of Pope's forces that were facing Jackson. He testified that he had no knowledge of Porter's position at the time, but supposed that Porter was two and a half to three miles away across broken country.

Reynolds further testified that, although up to about 1 P.M. Jackson's right flank did not cross the Warrenton pike, troops coming down the pike began to form on Jackson's right and to extend it across the pike. Consequently, Reynolds was gradually obliged to change his front to face these troops. The prosecution then asked Reynolds his opinion as to what effect it would have had on the battle had ten thousand fresh troops attacked Jackson's extended flank at sunset. Reynolds replied: "A vigorous attack made there ought to have resulted favorably to our success; ought to have contributed greatly toward it, certainly."[40] Reynolds later added, "If there had been no troops in his [Porter's] front, I suppose he could have made the attack."[41]

Pope's order of the morning of August 29 to Porter and McDowell assumed that Reynolds's forces (on the far left of Pope's line) and Porter's forces, each moving on its own converging road toward Gainesville, would ultimately form a juncture. However, by noon on the twenty-ninth, both were stopped; and Reynolds, rather than being deployed perpendicular to the War-

Map 15—Reynolds's Routes

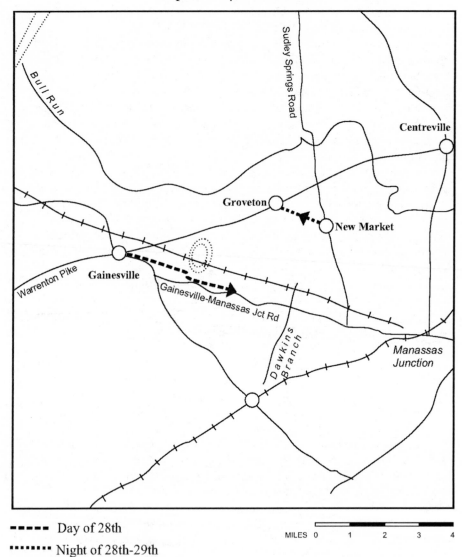

▬ ▬ ▬ ▬ Day of 28th

▪ ▪ ▪ ▪ ▪ ▪ ▪ Night of 28th-29th

MILES   0   1   2   3   4

renton pike and thus trending toward a juncture with Porter, was deployed more nearly parallel to the pike. Hence, Reynolds and Porter never came close to joining.

The next defense witness was Major George Hyland, Jr., major of the Thirteenth New York, the second regiment in the First Brigade of Morell's division. On the afternoon of the twenty-ninth, Hyland's regiment was employed as skirmishers while the corps was stopped at Dawkins Branch. He said that he was so employed from about 1 P.M. on the twenty-ninth until daylight on the thirtieth. The skirmishers were eight hundred to a thousand yards in front of Morell's division. He described the area in front of Morell's division as an open country, then a deep ravine with a stream running through it, and then, heavily timbered country. It was here that the skirmishers were located. The enemy commenced forming in front of Hyland's regiment between 2 and 3 P.M. Hyland believed that the forming was restricted to their front and right. He did not see any, or become aware of any, to their left.

Hyland believed the enemy force to be large—ten thousand or more, probably larger than their own. He based his estimate on the size of the force from the movements, from the commands he could hear, from the sounds of the movements of their artillery, from what he learned from other officers, and by observing the columns of dust rising from the direction of Thoroughfare Gap. Hyland reported what he learned to his superior, Col. Marshall.

In the evening, the Twenty-second Massachusetts and Berdan's Sharpshooters joined Hyland's regiment to their left as skirmishers.

More Testimony for the Defense

The next defense witness was Brigadier Gen. George Sykes, Porter's other division commander. Sykes had surprisingly little to say relative to the five charges of this chapter.

He testified that he was with Porter throughout the day of the twenty-ninth and the night of the twenty-ninth and thirtieth. He said that he and Porter were seated together near the Bethlehem Church when a messenger from Gen. Pope arrived with a dispatch for Porter. He estimated the time as about sunset, and said that he believed that this was the messenger's initial arrival and not his later return. Porter read the dispatch and sent off one of his aides. Sykes thought it was Capt. Montieth. Porter did not divulge the contents of the dispatch to Sykes. At this time, Sykes's troops were retiring down the road in the direction of Manassas Junction, but stopped in the vicinity of Bethlehem Church. Sykes did not elaborate on the reason for the stop and did not say whether or not it related to the dispatch.

The next three defense witnesses were generals. The first was Gen. Burnside. His testimony related entirely to Porter's attitude toward Pope and will be treated in Chapter 9. The next was Brigadier Gen. Daniel Butterfield. Butterfield was one of the three brigade commanders in Morell's division. He testified that on the morning of the twenty-ninth, his brigade first marched from Bristoe Station to Manassas Junction, and then out on the road to Gainesville to a point a little beyond Bethlehem Church. He said that as of 4:30 P.M. (the time Pope issued his attack order), he was with his brigade at the front. He said that he believed that the enemy was to his front and right, but could not see them because of the dense woods. Consequently, he did not know if they were in line of battle or not at that time.

Butterfield said that he had no idea of the size of the enemy he was facing when he arrived, but subsequently came to believe that they were considerable. When asked if Gen. Porter had sufficient force to push the enemy back, Butterfield stated that he could not say, inasmuch as he did not know the size of the enemy. Butterfield further testified that he was not present with Porter when Porter received Pope's 4:30 P.M. order to attack.

The third of the three generals to testify was Brigadier Gen. John Buford. Buford was chief of cavalry of the Second Corps of the Army of Virginia (Banks's corps). However, on the twenty-ninth, he was operating under the command of Gen. McDowell. Buford said that on that morning, he sighted a force of Longstreet's command proceeding along the road from Gainesville to Groveton (the Warrenton pike). He reported the sighting to Gen. McDowell sometime between 9 A.M. and 10 A.M. He sighted the force with his own eyes and reported it as seventeen regiments of infantry, one battery, and five hundred cavalry. He estimated the size of the infantry regiments at eight hundred men each, but did not include this in his report. Buford believed that this force was coming from Thoroughfare Gap. At the time of the sighting, the force had just cleared Gainesville.

Colonel E. G. Marshall

Perhaps the most important witness for the defense as regards the five charges of this chapter was Col. E. G. Marshall. Marshall was the senior man of Porter's corps who actually crossed over Dawkins Branch, entered the woods, and saw the Confederates with his own eyes and heard them with his own ears.

Col. Marshall was colonel of the Thirteenth New York Volunteers and a captain in the regular army. On the afternoon of August 29, while Porter's corps was stopped on the Gainesville–Manassas Junction road, Marshall was tasked with going forth with his regiment to serve as skirmishers in front of Porter's corps. Marshall testified:

> About 1 o'clock I was detailed by General Porter to go with my regiment across an open country and a ravine to some timber that was facing our line of battle, and deploy skirmishers to find out the position of the enemy, and anything else that I could find out concerning them.
>
> Immediately after going there, my skirmishers were fired on by a body of dragoons, and shortly afterward there was a section of artillery which opened fire upon General Porter's command. Soon after that, perhaps about 2 o'clock, the head of a large column came to my front. They deployed their skirmishers and met mine and about 3 o'clock drove my skirmishers into the edge of the timber. We were all on the left of the Manassas railroad, going toward Gainesville. This force continued to come

down all day, in fact, until 1 o'clock at night. It was a very large force, and they were drawn up in line of battle as they came down. I reported at different intervals to General Morell, my immediate commander, the position of the enemy. But at one time I deemed it so important that I did not dare to trust orderlies or others with messages, and I went myself, to him to confer concerning the enemy. This was about dusk. General Morell told me that he had just received orders from General Porter to attack the enemy—to commence the attack with four regiments. He seemed to be very much troubled concerning the order, and asked my advice, my opinion. I told him by all means not to attack; that it was certain destruction for us to do so; that I for one did not wish to go into that timber and attack the enemy. Their position was a very strong one, and they were certainly in force at that time twice as large as our own force—all of General Porter's corps. He had expressed to me the tenor of General Porter's order. I also deemed that we had executed the same with reference to the other part of the army—General Pope's army—by keeping this large body in force, and better than we would by attacking them, because if we had attacked them, I felt that it was certain destruction, as we would have had to move our line of battle across the ravine into this timber, and then, perhaps our line of retreat would have been entirely cut off from general Pope's army. I may say that this army that came down in our front was a separate and distinct army of the enemy from that which we saw General Pope's army fighting with.

About the same time, before I went in to General Morell, I could hear and judge of the result of the fighting between the force of the enemy and General Pope's army. I could see General Pope's left and the enemy's right during the greater part of the day, about 2 miles off, perhaps more, diagonally to our front and to the right. The enemy set up their cheering, and appeared to be charging and driving us, so that not a man of my command but what was certain that General Pope's army was being driven from the field. In the different battles I have been, I have learned that there is no mistaking the enemy's yell when they are successful. It is different from that of our own men. Our own men give three successive cheers, and in concert, but theirs is a cheering without any reference to regularity of form—a continued yelling.

Afterward, at dark, I was sent for by General Porter, and questioned very stringently with reference to the enemy; and my remarks to him were the same as I am now making, and as I made to General Morell. I also stated in conversation that I felt that our right was very weak, and that the pickets should be increased, for there was danger of our being cut off entirely from General Pope's army; and I was given one regiment under my command to go to the right of me, and four companies of another regiment to go to the left of me, as pickets; and General Griffin was also ordered to place a strong force on my right, and to connect with me.[42]

Additional questioning of Marshall by the defense, and questioning by the prosecution and court, brought out little additional information. Marshall's three main points were: (1) He believed that there were two separate and distinct bodies of Confederates with a considerable gap between them, i.e., the force facing Porter and Jackson's force facing Pope. (2) He believed that as of 4:30 P.M., when Pope issued his order for Porter to attack Jackson's flank, or later, it would have been impossible for Porter to do so without first defeating the force in his front, which he believed Porter could not do. (3) Upon arriving, at his estimate, on the size of the enemy facing Porter, Marshall put considerable weight on his observances of the clouds of dust leading to the front, but also on the fact that he could see parts of the enemy line from time to time through the dense forest.

More Defense Testimony

The next two defense witnesses were Maj. Gen. McClellan and Assistant Secretary of War John Tucker. Both testified only as to Porter's past activities and attitude. Following them, the next up was Lieutenant George T. Ingham. Ingham was aide-de-camp to Brig. Gen. Sykes. Sykes and Ingham were with Gen. Porter on the afternoon and evening of August twenty-ninth at Bethlehem Church when Capt. Douglas Pope arrive with Gen. Pope's 4:30 order for Porter to attack. Ingham said that it was past sunset when Capt. Pope arrived, and that Pope stayed with Gen. Porter about twenty minutes. After Capt. Pope departed, Porter decided that he had had something more for him and sent Ingham to bring him back. Ingham said that he overtook Capt. Pope one quarter to one half mile from Porter's corps. By this time, it was getting dark and, as Ingham phrased it, "I had to ride up close to Captain Pope to see who he was, it was so dark at the time."[43]

The next defense witness, Lieutenant James Stevenson, had an interesting tale to tell that was probably as useful to the prosecution as to the defense. Lieutenant Stevenson belonged to Col. Marshall's Thirteenth New York Volunteers that was deployed in front of Porter's command on the afternoon of the twenty-ninth as skirmishers. Stevenson, however, was not with the regiment at the time. He was with Gen. Pope's force on the Warrenton pike that was confronting Jackson, and was on a mail run.

Stevenson said that he set out on horseback from Pope's left flank to proceed directly overland to his regiment. He testified that the distance was about one and three quarters miles, that he met no Confederates en route, that he dismounted once or twice, that the trip required about one hour, and that he arrived at his regiment sometime between 1 and 4 P.M. on the twenty-ninth. Stevenson did not say how he knew that it was his regiment that was deployed beyond Dawkins Branch, or if it was just luck that he ran into his own regiment first. He described the terrain that he crossed between the commands as "rather a rough country, partly wooded, with a number of small ravines."[44] He thought that it was not country through which infantry could be marched in large masses.

Stevenson said that when he arrived at his regiment, he could see the enemy; he could see both infantry and artillery, and they were in formation. Stevenson estimated the number of the enemy to be twelve to fifteen thousand, and thought that they were being reinforced as evidenced by dust clouds in their rear. He estimated that the Confederates were about one half mile beyond the skirmishers of his own regiment, and about one mile from Gen. Porter's front on the other side of Dawkins Branch.

The defense's last witness, Lt. Col. Joseph P. Brinton, had no information relating the five charges of this chapter. Thus, Lieutenant Stevenson's testimony completed the defense to the five charges.

Guilty or Not Guilty

The evidence of the prosecution and defense has been presented. The testimony of the prosecution and defense may be synthesized into a single narrative for a picture of what really transpired on the Gainesville–Manassas Junction road on August 29, 1862.

When Porter marched out on the Warrenton Junction–Gainesville road toward Gainesville on the morning of August 29, he was marching in response to the following order: "Push forward with your corps and King's division, which you will take with you, upon Gainesville. I am following the enemy down the Warrenton Turnpike. Be expeditious or we will lose much."[45]

Porter had no sooner left than Pope received a note from Gen. McDowell, who had been out of touch, requesting that King's division be returned to his command. In response to this note, Pope issued his joint order to McDowell and Porter that is contained in charge 1, specification 1. This order stated, "You will please move forward with your joint commands toward Gainesville."[46] Among other things, it told McDowell to get a hold of Ricketts's division, the location of which Pope did not know, and to have it join the rest. Fortunately, Ricketts's division was nearby and McDowell added it to the end of the column proceeding toward Gainesville. Pope's joint order said nothing about King's division.

With Pope's joint order, what had started out as a straightforward command arrangement, with Porter in charge, now became a complex command morass. Inasmuch as Pope's joint order did not rescind the assignment of King's division to Porter, it would appear that as the column marched out, Morell's, Sykes's, and King's divisions were subordinate to Porter, and Ricketts's division was subordinate to McDowell. However, under the Articles of War, McDowell, being senior to Porter, could assume command of the whole if he so desired; as things turned out, he did so desire. Once McDowell started issuing orders, Porter lost his freedom of action.

When Porter's column stopped at Dawkins Branch some time around 11 A.M., McDowell rode to the head of the column to confer with Porter and to see what the problem was. Two defense witnesses swear that at this meeting they heard McDowell say, "Porter, you are out too far already. This is no place for a battle,"[47] or words to that effect. McDowell claimed that he had no rec-ollection of saying any such thing, but instead said he told Porter, "You put your forces in here, and I will take my troops up the Sudley Springs road, on the left of the troops engaged at that point,"[48] or words to that effect.

In any event, upon McDowell's departure from Porter, Porter must have thought that King's division was still subordinate to him, for he sent his chief of staff, Lt. Col. Locke, back down the line with an order for King. The order was for King to remain where he was until further ordered. Locke, how-ever, said he met McDowell, who gave him the following order for Porter: "Give my compliments to General Porter, and say to him that I am going to the right, and will take King's division with me. I think he [Porter] better remain where he was; but if it is necessary for him to fall back, he can do so on my left."[49] Locke was certain he gave this message to Porter. McDowell, how-ever, swore that he originated no such message and did not even see Locke that afternoon.

Whatever the truth of McDowell's and Locke's testimony, McDowell did take King's and Ricketts's divisions and march up the Sudley Springs road. At this point, Porter was left alone, with whatever force of the enemy was in front of him, to obey what he thought was McDowell's last order.

Just what was McDowell trying to do when he took his force from Porter? If we can believe what McDowell claimed he said to Porter, and if we can believe what Locke claimed McDowell said to him, McDowell was going to attempt to lessen the gap between Pope's force and Porter's by attaching his corps to Pope's left flank. Under Pope's joint order, Pope visualized Jackson retreating down the Warrenton pike toward Gainesville and him following. Porter, in the meantime, would be heading up the Gainesville–Manassas Junc-tion road toward Gainesville. As the two forces each got closer and closer to Gainesville, the distance between them would become less and less, until they inevitably joined hands. However, when McDowell left Porter, both Pope's and Porter's forces were stopped far from Gainesville, and the distance between them was over two miles.

McDowell never did succeed in attaching his corps to Pope's left flank and thus closing the distance between Pope and Porter. If Porter was waiting for this to happen, he waited in vain. He attempted to send scouts through the woods to establish contact with McDowell, but none succeeded. McDowell was not there, but Confederates were. The only messengers of Porter to ever reach McDowell were those that went back to the junction of the Manassas Junction–Gainesville road and Sudley Springs road, and thence up the Sudley Springs road.

Just what enemy force was in front of Porter when McDowell left? Both Porter and McDowell knew that Longstreet's five divisions intended to pass through Thoroughfare Gap and join Jackson. The gap was roughly eight miles distant from Porter's position at Dawkins Branch, and roughly the same distance from Jackson's and Pope's position at Groveton. Ricketts's division was assigned to defend the gap. However, both Porter and McDowell knew that on the night of the twenty-eighth, Ricketts had retreated from the gap all the way to Bristoe, and was now with McDowell. Thus, both knew that Longstreet was through the gap on the morning of the twenty-ninth. However, they had a paucity of knowledge as to just where he was. The only hard information they had that morning was the report they had received from Gen. Buford. Buford reported that, as of 9 A.M., he had sighted a force of seventeen infantry regiments, one battery, and five hundred cavalry clearing Gainesville on the Warrenton pike and heading toward Groveton. Just what was it that Buford sighted? In all probability, it was one of Longstreet's five divisions. Were any of Longstreet's troops in front of Porter when he first arrived at Dawkins Branch? Probably not.

In the testimony, it was revealed that Porter's skirmishers captured three Confederates that morning. All proved to be cavalrymen. Additionally, Col. Marshall, whose regiment had been deployed as skirmishers in front of Porter, testified that when his regiment took up position on the far side of Dawkins Branch at about 1 P.M., his men were immediately fired upon by enemy dragoons (dismounted cavalrymen). However, he further testified that, at about 2 P.M., a strong enemy column began to arrive and to deploy. Thus, it appears that from the time Porter arrived at Dawkins Branch at about 11 A.M. until 2 P.M., he was confronted only with Stuart's cavalry.

Thus, had Porter made a determined push any time before 2 P.M., he might have succeeded. Had he advanced but to the top of the other side of the ravine encompassing Dawkins Branch, he would have had an unobstructed view to his right of Pope's left flank and of Jackson's position. Had he succeeded but one mile farther, he would have reached a ridge containing the Monroe house that extended from the Gainesville–Manassas Junction road to the Warrenton pike. This ridge not only provided a magnificent view of the entire battlefield, but controlled both roads. In fact, within twenty-four hours, this ridge was to become Lee's headquarters when he defeated Pope's army.

These vital hours from 11 A.M. until 2 P.M. were precisely the hours when Porter's hands were tied because of McDowell's presence. However, we cannot entirely exonerate Porter for his activity or, rather, inactivity, from 11 A.M. until evening. Various of Porter's generals were heard to testify that they could hear the sounds of battle beyond the trees to their right, but none knew how far away the battle was. Yet, had they merely walked across the ravine in front of them, they could have seen. Col. Marshall, who was in charge of the skirmishers on the far side of the ravine, testified that he could see Pope's flank. Lieutenant Stevenson, who crossed over from Pope's flank to Marshall's position that afternoon, also said that he could see Pope's and Jackson's positions from Marshall's location. Yet, from the testimony of the defense, there is no evidence that Porter or any of the four other generals of his corps ever crossed over the ravine far enough to see with their own eyes where Pope's flank was. There was no evidence presented by the defense to indicate that, at any time that date, Porter made any determined effort to find out what exactly was in his front. He made no reconnaissance in force; he captured no more Confederate prisoners to ascertain their units' identity. He made no effort that we know of to determine how far to his left the Confederate force facing him extended. In fact, Gen. Sykes, who was in command of Porter's division in the rear, said that Porter spent the entire day of the twenty-ninth with him. When Capt. Pope arrived with Gen. Pope's 4:30 imperative order to attack, he found Porter with Sykes, resting on the ground at Bethlehem Church, one and a half miles from the front.

The time of delivery of Gen. Pope's "attack" order of 4:30 P.M. to Porter was a crucial element in the case. If it was 5 P.M., as Capt. Pope believed, Porter had ample time to make the attack before dark. If it was 7 P.M., as Lt. Weld believed, darkness would have intervened before Porter could have made the attack. Lt. Weld's estimate would seem to be the better of the two. Capt. Pope anchored his estimate of the time of delivery on the assumption that the time of his departure for delivery was the time written on the order. Weld based his estimate on the time of delivery on his watch. He looked at his watch at the time Porter gave him a message to deliver to Generals King and McDowell. The time was, as he recalled, either five minutes before or five minutes after 4:00 P.M. Weld then gave a detailed description of his movements from that time up to the time he witnessed Capt. Pope's arrival. From his description of his movements, it would appear that he could not have witnessed Capt. Pope's arrival much before 7 P.M. Furthermore, Capt. Montieth's and Lt. Col. Locke's testimony supported Weld's estimate of the time much better than Capt. Pope's estimate of the time.

The testimony indicates that Porter acted with alacrity upon receiving Pope's attack order. He immediately sent his chief of staff, Lt. Col. Locke, off to tell Gen. Morell to make the attack. Morell had testified that, late that afternoon, he had received an order written in pencil for him to attack. The order read:

General Morell:

I wish you to push up two regiments, supported by two others, preceded by skirmishers, the regiments at intervals of 200 yards, and attack the party with the battery opposed to you. The battle works well on our right, and the enemy are said to be retiring up the pike. Give the enemy a good shelling when our troops advance.

F. J. Porter
Major General, Commanding[50]

Porter, in summing up his defense, said that he sent this order to Morell just before he received Pope's order to attack. He said that he sent it because of the message that Gen. Hatch sent him via Lt. Weld. The message was: "Tell Porter that we have driven the enemy into the woods."[51] This indicated that the enemy was retreating. When Lt. Col. Locke arrived with Porter's verbal message to attack, Morell naturally believed that he was referring to the order of Porter.

Although Porter's order may have technically met Pope's directive to attack immediately, it certainly was not the kind of all-out attack on Jackson's flank that Pope had in mind. Porter's order was for a limited objective attack against a battery on his front and called for the participation of less than one third of his men. In any event, darkness intervened and no attack was made.

Porter's message to King and McDowell (that was delivered to Pope) said that Porter intended to retreat to Manassas junction. Gen. Pope, in his testimony, wove his reading of this message into a tight sequence as follows: (1) At 4:30 P.M., he sent his "attack immediately" message to Porter. (2) Between 7 and 8 P.M., he read Porter's "retreat to Manassas Junction" message. (3) At 8:50 P.M., in exasperation, he sent his "report immediately" message to Porter.

When Pope read Porter's retreat message, he probably assumed that Porter had written it after he received Pope's order to attack. More than enough time had ensued for this to have taken place. If Pope were correct, there was just cause for his anger. Porter would be in clear violation of Pope's order. But, Pope was wrong. His message to attack was delivered much later to Porter than he assumed, and Porter had written his message before receiving Pope's.

There is one question yet to address. Porter's message said that he intended to retreat to Manassas Junction. Did he do so? Did he take any action to do so? Brigadier Gen. Griffin, when testifying relative to Porter's aborted evening attack, said: "We had started back toward Manassas when this order came down the road. The order was carried by an orderly, who was stopped by Colonel Warren who read it. We faced our command about immediately and started back."[52]

It was never brought out in testimony if Griffin's movement toward Manassas was part of a retirement or just an adjustment in position. However, it was well established in testimony that, if it was the beginning of a retreat, the movement was slight. It was clear that at the end of the day, Porter's troops remained in approximately the same positions that they had occupied since noon.

At the end of the day, one big fact remained. Porter's potent force was located within about two miles of Pope's raging battle at Groveton throughout the day of the twenty-ninth and never participated.

Now to the guilt or innocence of each charge. The following "verdicts" are based on this author's analysis of the evidence. The court's verdicts are in a later chapter, after all of the evidence on all of the charges has been presented.

Charge 1, Specification 2: That Gen. Porter Disobeyed Gen. Pope's Joint Order to Generals McDowell and Porter

Pope's order to McDowell and Porter, like so many of Gen. Pope's orders, was poorly worded and confusing. (Refer to the beginning of this chapter for the full text of the order.) It did not tell Pope's subordinates what he was trying to do or what his objective was. Although the order contained many words, it only told Porter three things to do, and one of the three was only implied. The three are: (1) Move forward with your command toward Gainesville. (2) As soon as communication is established between your force and my force, halt. (3) The troops must occupy a position from which they can reach Bull Run tonight or tomorrow.

Porter indisputably complied with number 1 and 3. Number 2 visualized a situation that never came to pass. Pope visualized the two forces continuously moving on their respective roads toward the common junction at Gainesville, with the distance between the two forces continuously narrowing until they inevitably joined. Pope himself, in his testimony, stated that he visualized the joining near Gainesville. However, as we know, neither force got even half way to Gainesville. Pope's force was stopped at Groveton, and Porter's at Dawkins Branch—with the distance between them still over two miles. Even had Porter been able to continue on all the way to Gainesville, with Pope stopped at Groveton, they would have never joined.

Once the two forces were stopped, according to testimony, Porter attempted to establish cross-country contact with Pope's force, but was unsuccessful. A quote from Porter's "retire to Manassas" message that is part of the record helps prove this point: "I found it impossible to communicate by crossing the woods to Groveton.... I have attempted to communicate with McDowell and Sigel, but my messengers have run into the enemy."[53]

Author's verdict: Not guilty.

Charge 1, Specification 3: That Gen. Porter Disobeyed Gen. Pope's 4:30 Attack Order.

Gen. Pope's 4:30 attack order stated: "Your line of march brings you in on the enemy's right flank. I desire you to push forward into action at once on the enemy's flank, and if possible, on his rear, keeping your right in communication with General Reynolds...."[54]

Col. Marshall was one of only two witnesses who observed with his own eyes the enemy troops facing Porter and the location of Jackson's right flank. When asked if the enemy in Porter's front made a junction with the enemy in Gen. Pope's front, he testified: "I do not think they did. They would naturally have made a connection with their dragoons; but their line of battle was not a continuous line. Their line of battle in front of General Porter's command was separate and distinct from their line of battle in front of General Pope's command."[55]

Col. Marshall then judged the distance between the two Confederate lines of battle as two miles. To suggest that the Confederates in front of Porter were part of Jackson's command, as Gen. Pope did, was absurd. Jackson was fighting a desperate battle two miles away against a greatly superior force, and just barely managed to survive. It is all but certain that Porter was confronted with a separate and distinct enemy force, and to reach Jackson's flank, he would have had to march across the face of this force—a desperate undertaking with probably disastrous consequences.

In any event, it was so close to darkness when Porter received the attack message, and he was one and a half miles from the front when he did, it was a near impossibility to implement the attack before darkness intervened. In fact, the testimony indicated that not only could it not be done, but that he had tried.

Author's verdict: Not guilty.

Other Charges

The last three charges of this chapter are all against Article Fifty-two of the Articles of War, which states: "Any officer or soldier who shall misbehave himself before the enemy, run away, or shamefully abandon any fort, post or guard which he or they may be commanded to defend, or speak words inducing others to do the like, or shall cast away his arms and ammunition, or who shall quit his post or colors to plunder and pillage, every such offender, being duly convicted thereof, shall suffer death, or such other punishment as shall be ordered by the sentence of a general court-martial."[56]

Charge 2, Specification 1

The full text of charge 2, specification 1, is contained at the beginning of this chapter. It consisted of three elements: (1) Porter, within sight of the field of battle, and within hearing distance of the artillery, disobeyed Gen. Pope's 4:30 attack order. (2) He retreated from the enemy without any attempt to engage them. (3) He did not aid the troops who were already fighting greatly superior numbers and who were relying on his flank attack for victory.

As regards number 1, the response to the previous charge already demonstrates that Porter did not disobey Pope's 4:30 attack order. In fact, he could not obey it. As regards number 2, Porter did not retreat from the enemy, but remained in essentially the same place facing the enemy until recalled by Pope. Number 3 is redundant, harking back to the flank attack, which Porter could not make. Furthermore, number 3 contains false statements, in that Pope was not fighting superior numbers but, in fact, was greatly superior in numbers to Jackson, even without Porter. If anyone was facing superior numbers, it was Porter.

Author's verdict: Not guilty

Charge 2, Specification 2

The full text of charge 2, specification 2, is contained at the beginning of this chapter. It consisted of two elements: (1) Porter, being within the sound of the guns and knowing that an action of great consequence was being fought, and knowing that the aid of his corps was greatly needed, failed all day to bring it on the field of action. (2) He did "shamefully" fall back and retreat from the force of the enemy without any attempt to give battle and without knowing the forces from which he retreated.

Number 2 is easily refuted. Porter did not fall back until called off by order of Pope on the thirtieth. Number 1 is more controversial. Porter was first constrained by McDowell's presence, then by McDowell's last instructions, which presumably required him to maintain his position until McDowell formed on Reynolds' left. This, McDowell never did. All this time, the enemy force in front of Porter was obviously being built up, and those closest to the scene, such as Col. Marshall, considered that, by late afternoon, it was too formidable to attack. Porter could, of course, at any time, have retired and taken the Sudley Spring road to join Pope, as had McDowell. The tail of Sykes's division throughout the day was near Bethlehem Church, which was well under a two hour march to Pope's battle. However, had Porter done so, he would have violated Pope's order and absolutely precluded any "coup de grace" attack on Jackson's flank that so enamored Pope. When Porter finally did receive Pope's order to attack, he attempted to implement it with alacrity, but was overtaken by darkness. In the last analysis, the burden of proof rests with the prosecution.

Author's verdict: Not guilty.

Charge 2, Specification 3

The full text of charge 2, specification 3, is contained at the beginning of this chapter. The substance of this charge is that, while Porter visualized that Pope was being defeated and retreating, he did not come to his aid, but instead retreated to Manassas Junction.

This is a strange charge indeed. Inasmuch as Porter did not retreat to Manassas Junction, and Pope was not suffering a defeat and retreating, Porter is charged with committing a non-existing act in response to a non-existing situation. If Porter did, for a brief time, believe that Pope was being defeated and retiring, and that he would then be isolated and cut off from the main force and be subjected to destruction in detail, retreating to Manassas Junction may well have been an option worth considering. In any event, the sum and substance of this charge is the same as that of the previous charge, namely, that Porter knew that a battle was raging at nearby Groveton and did not get involved. If Porter was found not guilty for the last, he could not be guilty of this either.

Author's verdict: Not guilty.

6

Charge 1, Specifications 4 and 5

The first charge addressed related to activity on the twenty-seventh and twenty-eighth of August. The next five related to activity on August 29. The final three charges, presented as follows, related to activity on August 30. The three charges are:

Charge 1, Violation of the Ninth Article of War

Specification 4th.—In that the said Maj. Gen. Fitz-John Porter, being at or near Manassas Junction, on the night of the 29th of August, 1862, did receive from Maj. Gen. John Pope, his superior and commanding officer, a lawful order, in figures and words as follows, to wit:

Headquarters Army of Virginia
In the Field, near Bull Run, Aug. 29, 1862—8:50 P.M.

Maj. Gen. F. J. Porter:

General: Immediately upon receipt of this order, the precise hour of receiving which you will acknowledge, you will march your command to the field of battle of to-day, and report to me in person for orders. You are to understand that you are expected to comply strictly with this order, and to be present on the field within three hours of its reception, or after daybreak to-morrow morning.

John Pope
Maj. Gen., Commanding
[Referred to as the "Report Order"]

And the said Maj. Gen. Fitz-John Porter did then and there disobey the said order, and did permit one of the brigade of his command to march to Centreville—out of the way of the field of battle—and there to remain during the entire day of Saturday, the 30th of August. This at or near Manassas Station, in the State of Virginia on the 29th and 30th days of August, 1862.

Specification 5th.—In this that said Maj. Gen. Fitz-John Porter, being at or near Manassas Station, in the State of Virginia on the night of the 29th of August, 1862, and having received from his superior commanding

112

officer, Maj. Gen. John Pope, the lawful order set forth in specification fourth to this charge, did then and there disobey the same, and did permit one other brigade attached to his command—being the brigade commanded by Brig. Gen. A. S. Piatt—to march to Centreville, and did thereby greatly delay the arrival of the said General Piatt's brigade on the field of battle of Manassas, on Saturday, the 30th of August, 1862. This at or near Manassas, in the State of Virginia, on or about the 29th of August, 1862.

Charge 2, Violation of the Fifty-second of War

Specification 4th.—In this, that the said Maj. Gen. Fitz-John Porter, on the field of battle of Manassas, on Saturday, the 30th of August 1862, having received a lawful order from his superior officer and commanding general, Maj. Gen. John Pope, to engage the enemy's lines and to carry a position near their center, and to take an annoying battery there posted, did proceed in the execution of that order with unnecessary slowness, and by delays, give the enemy opportunities to watch and know his movements and to prepare to meet his attack; and did finally so feebly fall upon the enemy's lines as to make little or no impression on the same, and did fall back and draw away his forces unnecessarily and without making any of the great personal efforts to rally his troops or to keep their lines, or to inspire his troops to meet the sacrifices and to make the resistance demanded by the importance of his position, and the momentous consequences and disasters of a retreat at so critical a juncture of the day.[1]

Porter pled "not guilty" to all three charges.

The last charge appears almost nonsensical, and gives the appearance that the accuser was "piling on" in an attempt to destroy the accused. Mercifully, before the evidence phase of the trial, the judge advocate announced that he did not intend to offer any evidence relative to the third charge. This was tantamount to dropping the charge.

This left two charges, both relating to the failure of brigades of Porter to appear on the battlefield in a timely manner in response to Gen. Pope's order. These were the brigades of Generals Griffin and Piatt. Upon reading the two specifications, a logical question arises. Even if both specifications are proved, is Porter guilty? To be specific, if Porter, with five of his seven brigades, appeared on the field of battle as ordered, and two did not appear because they took the wrong road—is Porter guilty of disobeying the order? The key word appears to be "permit." Did he disobey the order because he "permitted" the brigades to take the wrong road? Was he guilty even though he did not know they were going to take the wrong road, or even know when they did?

Gen. Pope testified that, in response to his 8:50 P.M. order contained in the specification, Gen. Porter himself and a portion of his command appeared before him at the battlefield the following morning. However, two of his seven brigades were missing and, as reported by an aide, were at Centreville. These were the brigades of Piatt and Griffin. Pope acknowledged that Piatt's brigade, without orders, upon discovering its mistake, managed to make its way to the battlefield late in the day and participated in the final phases of the battle. Griffin's, however, never arrived and never participated. Pope thought that the absence of Piatt's brigade most of the day, and of Griffin's all of the day, had a major impact on the outcome of the battle. When Pope was specifically asked if he considered the absence of these two brigades a clear violation of his order, he replied, "Undoubtedly."[2]

The defense persisted and asked Pope in just what particular the accused failed to obey the 8:50 order. Pope answered: "I thought that he failed to obey the order entirely, because two brigades of his command were not only [not] brought up with him, but by some means had either straggled or been permitted to straggle from the command and were in Centreville."[3] The accused then asked: "Do you mean to say that, because two brigades referred to were in Centreville, the accused entirely neglected to obey the order?"[4] Pope responded: "I presume that is a matter for the court to decide. My own answer to that would be a mere opinion on the subject. That is exactly a question for the court to decide."[5]

The defense continued: "State in what, if to any extent, the accused did obey that order or carry it out."[6] Pope replied: "The accused appeared upon the field on Saturday morning, the 30th of August with his command, except, so far as I am informed, the two brigades specified."[7] The defense asked, "At what hour of the morning did he appear with his commands?"[8]

Pope responded: "I do not now at what hour of the morning precisely; but it was somewhere between 8 and 10 o'clock; perhaps earlier than 10 o'clock; perhaps 8 o'clock. I know I made no objections in consequence of the hour he arrived there."[9]

Brigadier Gen. Roberts of the prosecution was next and had little to offer relative to the charges. He said that he was familiar with the order, and that it was dispatched from Pope to Porter at about 8:30 P.M. by an aide. He did not know when Porter received it. He was not present when Porter arrived on the morning of the thirtieth and did not see Porter until about noon. He knew that Porter had arrived with part of his command earlier that morning, but did not know which part was missing.

Surgeon Robert Abbott, medical director of Porter's Fifth Corps, was a witness for the prosecution. Abbott's primary testimony was on matters related to charges other than the two charges of this chapter. However, the defense questioning of Abbott did elicit some information favorable to the defense of the two charges. Abbott testified as follows.

On the early morning of the thirtieth, he was proceeding toward Gainesville with a wagon load of medical supplies in an attempt to overtake his corps. However, he met Gen. Morell coming the other way. Morell told Abbott that the corps was now marching toward Centreville, and turned Abbott around. When Abbott reached Centreville, he realized that it was all a mistake. He then headed to his left toward the battle area looking for Porter. He found Porter and his men at the front—the extreme advance as he called it—in action. Abbott estimated the time as 8 A.M.

Lt. Col. Thomas C. H. Smith, aide to Gen. Pope, testified on being questioned by the accused that, on the thirtieth, Gen. Porter reported to Gen. Pope "quite early in the morning."[10]

This constituted the prosecution's full case onto the two charges. In effect, it rested solely on Gen. Pope's testimony that, although Porter showed up as ordered, he was minus two brigades that constituted almost a third of his command. The defense now opened its case.

The first defense witness was Capt. George Montieth, aide-de-camp to Gen. Porter. Montieth testified that he was sleeping on the ground near Gen. Porter when the courier arrived with Pope's message for Porter to report to him. He said that Porter woke him up and gave him a message to take to Gen. Morell, whose troops were at the front. Montieth estimated the time of the courier's arrival as between 3 and 4 A.M. on the morning of the thirtieth. Although he was asleep when the courier arrived, he knew the time because, once awakened, he talked to the courier. The courier told him that he had great trouble finding Porter, that he spent most of the night searching for him, and that he first looked in Manassas Junction.

Montieth delivered his message to Gen. Morell. He said that although he did not know the message's content, he noted that Morell, upon reading it, immediately began withdrawing his troops from the front. Montieth then rode directly back to Gen. Porter. By the time he got there, or immediately thereafter, Porter's troops were taking to the road. Montieth estimated the time of his return to Porter as 4:30 to 5 A.M. Porter's troops then marched up the Sudley Springs road to the battle area.

The fact that the courier went first to Manassas Junction looking for Porter firmly establishes that Pope believed that Porter actually retreated, as he had indicated he intended to do in his note to King and McDowell.

The next witness was Lt. Stephen Weld, acting aide-de-camp to Gen. Porter. Weld testified that he was also present when the courier brought Pope's "report" message to Gen. Porter. He estimated the time of the courier's arrival as between 3 and 3:30 A.M. on the morning of the thirtieth. Weld said he thought the courier was an officer, and his message caused an immediate flurry of activity. Gen. Porter ordered Lieutenant Chamberlain of Gen. Sykes's staff off with a message to some of Sykes's troops, and an officer of his own staff off with a message to the front. He also ordered Weld to show Captain Smead of Smead's battery the route to where Weld had found Gen. Pope on the previous evening. Weld said that Lieutenant Chamberlain and the other officer departed on their missions immediately, but that he waited a half hour to forty-five minutes until it got lighter to show Smead the route.

Next up for the defense was Lt. Col. Frederick T. Locke, Porter's chief of staff. Locke testified that Pope's order to report to him was delivered at about 3:30 A.M. on the thirtieth. Gen. Porter immediately sent an officer to Gen. Morell with a message for Morell to bring in his pickets and to prepare to join the rest of the command on the march. Gen. Sykes was also ordered to immediately get under arms and to prepare to march. Lt. Col. Locke, however, had no recollection of any message being sent by Porter to Gen. Sturgis.

Piatt's brigade was part of the reserve corps at Washington commanded by Gen. Sturgis. When Piatt's brigade was shipped down the Orange and Alexandria railroad to reinforce Pope, it was accompanied by Sturgis. Pope assigned the brigade to Porter's corps. However, inasmuch as Sturgis was the senior officer present, it was he rather than Piatt who was actually in command. Thus, Porter's apparent failure to inform Sturgis of the move to report to Pope proved to be significant.

The next defense witness was Major Gen. George Morell, the central figure in the two charges. Morell testified that, shortly before daylight on the thirtieth, he received an order from Gen. Porter, the original of which was then admitted into evidence. The order was as follows:

> General Morell:
>
> Lose not a moment in withdrawing and coming down the road to me. The wagons which went up, send down at once, and have the road cleared; and send me word when you have all in motion.
>
> F. J. Porter
> Major-General, Commanding
> Your command must follow Sykes.'[11]

The order bore the endorsement: "Received a few minutes before daylight Aug 30, 1862."[12]

Morell said that, in response to the order, he immediately issued commands to his three brigade commanders and his artillery commander to retire. Butterfield was to move first, then Barnes, and then Griffin, who was to bring up the rear and cover the retreat. Morell also ordered Hazlitt's battery, which consisted of ten-pound Parrott guns, to be replaced by Martin's battery of twelve-pound smooth bores to cover the withdrawal.

By the time Griffin called in his skirmishers and was ready to move, it was already daylight, and the rest of the command was out of sight. Morell and his staff rode on ahead of Griffin, hoping to overtake the troops on the road ahead. Failing to do so, Morell ordered a staff member to ride on ahead until he overtook the command, and then return and act as a guide for Griffin. After some time, the staff member returned and said that he had ridden all the way to Manassas Junction and back and failed to find the rest of the command. The rest had turned off on the Sudley Springs road. (See map 16.)

Porter's order to Morell did not say what the destination of Morell's com-

Map 16—Griffin's March of August 30

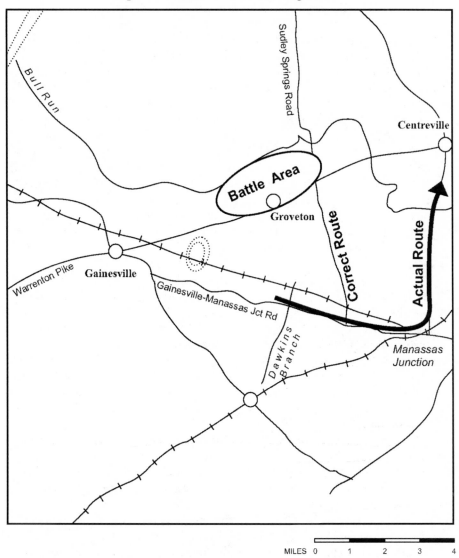

mand was. It merely directed him to follow Sykes. Morell testified that the last order he had seen indicating a destination for the corps was the order of the previous day directing it to Centreville. He thus concluded that Centreville was probably still the desired destination and directed the brigade to continue to Centreville.

Upon arriving at Centreville, Morell said that he went to the location of

Pope's old headquarters expecting to find Pope there. Here he met Col. Clary of Pope's staff, who told him of his error. He told Morell that Pope and, presumably, Porter were on the battlefield. Morell immediately sent off a note to Porter, advising Porter that both he and Griffin were at Centreville and would join him as soon as possible. Morell then rode over to Griffin and found Griffin's men being issued rations. Morell directed Griffin to hurry up and get to the battlefield as soon as possible. Morell then rode on ahead with his staff to the battlefield. Lastly, Morell said he knew nothing of Piatt's (Sturgis's) movements beyond the fact that he was sure that Piatt was not on the road ahead of him.

After Gen. Morell's testimony as to Griffin's movements, Brigadier Gen. Griffin presented his story. He testified that the brigade spent the night essentially where it was at dark. Movement began at daylight. Griffin was ordered to follow Sykes but was also ordered to cover the rear. Thus, he had to send out pickets to replace those of the other brigades. By the time he called in his pickets and was ready to march, the other brigades had a half hour start on him and were out of sight. Gen. Morell, the division commander, accompanied the brigade.

When Griffin reached the intersection of the Gainesville–Manassas Junction and Sudley Springs road, there was a man without a hat and coat standing there. The man said to Griffin that "the regulars—Martindale's and Butterfield's brigades—went up this road,"[13] pointing to the Sudley Springs road. Griffin, however, said that he felt that even though some of the division may have taken a different road, the intention was for the corps to assemble at Centreville. In any event, Gen. Morell, who was senior, was directing the route of the brigade, and Morell was not present when Griffin talked to the stranger at the intersection. The brigade continued on the Manassas Junction road en route to Centreville.

Near Manassas Junction, Griffin said that his brigade passed Gen. Sturgis with Piatt's brigade. Sturgis said that he had been directed to follow Sykes and asked which way Sykes had gone. Griffin, in his testimony, did not elaborate further on his exchange with Sturgis, nor say what Sturgis decided to do. (Actually, Sturgis followed Griffin's brigade.)

Griffin said that he did not hear the guns of battle until after they arrived at Centreville. He did begin to hear them at about 4 P.M. Griffin's brigade departed Centreville and headed for the battlefield at about 5 P.M. However, he said that the road was blocked up by wagons and stragglers coming toward Centreville, and the bridge at Cub Run was broken through, so that it was impossible to get past it.

Griffin's testimony completed the substantive testimony relating to the two charges of this chapter. Strangely, neither Gen. Sturgis nor General Piatt, nor anyone else from Piatt's brigade, was called to testify. Having heard all the evidence, one thing is evident—Porter's performance was abysmal in that he managed to lose almost a third of his force when less than five miles from the battlefield and within sound of the guns. Neither Griffin nor Sturgis was ever told where he was supposed to go. Both were merely told to follow Sykes, and Sykes was not in sight of either when they began to move. There was only one crossroads where they could have gone wrong, and both managed to do just that. A careful corps commander would have posted a staff officer, known to both Griffin and Sturgis, at the crossroads to ensure that each took the right road. However, the charge was not incompetence. And, if incompetence were to be the charge for the events of August 29 and 30, 1862, far better cases could have been made against Generals Pope and McDowell; Pope for refusing to believe, despite all evidence, that Longstreet was on the field, and McDowell for getting lost when he was needed most and injecting himself into Porter's command when he was needed least.

The charge, however, was not incompetence, but disobedience of an order. Porter made every effort to obey. He appeared before Pope with most of his command as ordered, at a time acceptable to Pope, and he presumed that he had ordered his two missing brigades to do likewise. Consequently, this author casts his vote as "not guilty" to both charges.

7

Pope, Porter, and McDowell

Major General John Pope

John Pope was forty years old in 1862. He was not academically a stupid man. He had graduated from West Point seventeenth in a class of fifty-six in 1842. He was assigned to the topographic engineers. This was an elite group accessible only to those who graduated near the top of their class. Article Sixty-three of the Articles of War recognized their elevated status: "The functions of engineers being generally confined to the most elevated branch of military science, they are not to assume, nor are they subject to be ordered on any duty beyond the line of their immediate profession, except by order of the President of the United States; but they are to receive every mark of respect to which their rank in the army may entitle them, etc."[1]

The engineers were not just concerned with army matters. They were involved in all surveying and construction that involved the federal government. This may have provided a satisfying and rewarding career. However, it had a downside for an army officer. It provided little opportunity for gaining experience in troop command. In his capacity as an engineer, Pope was involved in surveying roads along the Canadian border, in determining the navigability of the Red River, and, as chief engineer of the department of New Mexico, surveying the route for the railway to the Pacific. Pope served honorably during the Mexican War and was awarded two brevets. The beginning of the Civil War found him as a captain.

Pope was well connected politically. He was from Illinois, as was Lincoln. His father, a prominent Illinois judge, was a close friend of Lincoln. When Lincoln was elected president, Pope was one of four junior officers selected to accompany the president-elect to Washington.

In May 1861, Pope, with a number of other junior officers in the regular army, was commissioned a brigadier general in the United States Volunteers. For his first assignment, he was ordered to the Department of the West, headquartered in St. Louis and commanded by Major General John Fremont, already a prominent figure known nationally, if not internationally. He had participated in the exploration and mapping of the west, for which he was

known then and now as "the Path-
finder." Fremont also ran against
Buchanan for president in 1856.
Pope was among those who con-
spired against Fremont behind the
scenes and managed to get him
removed from office.

Fremont's replacement was
Henry Halleck, who was later to
become general-in-chief of all the
armies. Halleck was impressed with
Pope and appointed him commanding general of the newly organized
25,000-man Army of the Mississippi. Its function was to open up
the northern Mississippi to Union
navigation. Pope set to his task with
energy. He first captured the Confederate base at New Madrid. He
next set out to remove the cork in
the bottle, so-called Island Number
Ten. This island was manned by
twelve thousand Confederates and
fifty-eight cannon. However, by a
clever campaign, Pope succeeded in
capturing it. On this basis, he was
promoted to major general and
again came to the attention of Lin-

**Major General John Pope of the United
States Volunteers, the accuser in the court-
martial of Fitz-John Porter (courtesy the
Massachusetts Commandery Military
Order of the Loyal Legion and the U.S.
Army Military History Institute).**

coln, who was always on the lookout for successful and aggressive generals.

On June 26, 1862, Pope took command of the Army of Virginia. On July
14, he issued his first proclamation to his new command. It managed to alienate just about every officer in the east. It contrasted the glorious future under
his leadership with the shameful past under the presumably hapless boobs of
the east. The proclamation is as follows:

Washington, D. C., July 14, 1862

To the Officers and Soldiers of the Army of Virginia:

By special assignment of the President of the United States I have assumed
command of this army. I have spent two weeks in learning of your where-
abouts, your condition, and your wants, in preparing you for active operations, and in placing you in positions from which you can act promptly
and to the purpose. These labors are nearly completed, and I am about to
join you in the field.

Let us understand each other. I have come to you from the West, where we have always seen the backs of our enemies; from an army whose business it has been to seek the adversary and to beat him when he was found; whose policy has been attack and not defense. In but one instance has the enemy been able to place our Western armies in defensive attitude. I presume that I have been called here to pursue the same system and to lead you against the enemy. It is my purpose to do so, and that speedily. I am sure you long for an opportunity to win the distinction you are capable of achieving. That opportunity I shall endeavor to give you. Meantime I desire you to dismiss from your minds certain phrases, which I am sorry to find so much in vogue amongst you. I hear constantly of "taking strong positions and holding them," of "lines of retreat," and of "bases of supply." Let us discard such ideas. The strongest position a soldier should desire to occupy is one from which he can most easily advance against the enemy. Let us study the probable lines of retreat of our opponents, and leave our own to take care of themselves. Let us look before us and not behind. Success and glory are in the advance, disaster and shame lurk in the rear. Let us act on this understanding; and it is safe to predict that your banners shall be inscribed with many a glorious deeds and that your names will be dear to your countrymen forever.

John Pope
Major General, Commanding[2]

Pope followed this up with dispatches signed "Headquarters in the saddle." This caused the story to quickly percolate through the ranks that Pope's headquarters were in his hind quarters. Pope was now pitted against Robert E. Lee. Worse yet, he was now pitted against the Lee-Longstreet-Jackson-Stuart team. Pope alone, among Lee's opponents, was personally disliked by Lee. That was not unusual. Many people disliked Pope. In fact, he had more than his share of unlikable characteristics. Among other things, he was a braggart who tended to cross the line between exaggeration and lie in the magnifying of his accomplishments. He once told journalists that he had taken ten thousand prisoners in his mopping-up operations after Corinth—when the actual number was about one thousand.

If there is one group of people that normally likes a general, it is his staff. A general's staff is his official family, his family away from home. He usually eats with them, lives with them, and sometimes dies with them. They take care of him and he takes care of them. Pope's own staff did not like him. This is illustrated in the sworn testimony of his chief of staff, Col. Ruggles, at the Porter court-martial:

QUESTION: Are your feelings toward General Pope kind and friendly?
RUGGLES: I can hardly say they are, from the treatment I received while upon his staff.
QUESTION: Can you not answer the question more distinctly, and say

whether, at this time, your feelings are friendly or hostile to General Pope?

RUGGLES: I am on speaking terms with General Pope, but I would not like to serve with him as a staff officer. I would call upon him as a matter of respect, if he were in the city.

QUESTION: Have you, or not, entertained the impression that you were badly treated by him in your official relations to him or otherwise?

RUGGLES: I entertain, and I have entertained, the opinion that I was badly treated by him in both official and social relations. To explain that, I will say that there was considerable trouble between General Pope and several of his staff officers, and I was one of those. I thought several times that I was not treated as a gentleman should have been treated.[3]

A few others who knew Pope had expressed similar sentiments. Assistant Secretary of the Navy Gustavus Fox wrote in a letter to Admiral S. P. Lee: "Pope is a lying braggart, without brains of any kind...."[4] Colonel Thomas Brodhead of the First Michigan Cavalry wrote to his sibling while dying from a wound acquired at second Manassas: "I am one of the victims of Pope's imbecility and McDowell's treason. Tell the President would he save the country, he must not give our hallowed flag to such hands."[5] Postmaster Montgomery Blair wrote: "Old John Pope, his father was a flatterer, a deceiver, a liar and a trickster, all the Popes are so."[6] Blair went on to say that Pope was a blower and liar and ought never have been trusted with such a command. Maj. Gen. Samuel D. Sturgis said, "I don't care for John Pope one pinch of owl dung."[7]

The Lee team knew Pope and knew him well. Gen. Longstreet had been a four year classmate of Pope at West Point. General Anderson, a division commander under Longstreet, had also been a four year classmate.

The audacity of Lee's operation against Pope boggles the imagination. It violates just about every military maxim. First, Lee divides his army almost in half in the face of an already greatly superior enemy. Second, he sends Jackson's half completely around Pope's army and more than a day's march away from Longstreet's half. Now, Pope's entire army is closer to Jackson than Longstreet. Third, Lee has no potential reinforcements, but Pope has massive reinforcements at nearby Alexandria waiting to join him. Jackson is now alone between Pope's entire army to his south and west, and the massive reinforcements one day to his north. Fifth, Jackson has no supply line, while Pope is sitting on his, albeit momentarily cut. Sixth, Jackson does not retreat toward the oncoming Longstreet, but takes a defensive position to await Longstreet's arrival. The two unite to destroy Pope. When one looks at Lee's entire operation, one must conclude that, either he was insane, or he gauged Pope to be a complete fool. We know from later events that he was not insane.

After the debacle of second Manassas, there was extended correspondence between Gen. Pope and Gen. Halleck. This correspondence does not reflect well on the character of Pope. Although the country was now in desperate circumstances, the correspondence implied that the main effort of the War Department should be directed to the resurrection of the reputation of John Pope.

And yet, after second Manassas, Pope went on to new assignments where he served his country well. Thus, Pope's three month sojourn in the east in June, July, and August 1862 was a small blip in an otherwise long and successful military career.

Major General Fitz-John Porter

Porter and Pope had much in common. Both had come from upper middle class families. Pope's father was a judge and Porter's a naval captain. Both had attended West Point and graduated near the top of their class; Pope, seventeenth of fifty-six in the class of 1842; Porter, eighth in a class of forty-one in the class of 1845. Each won two brevets in the Mexican War. Both were promoted to brigadier general of U.S. Volunteers in 1861. Lastly, each was forty years old in 1862. But here the similarity ends. Porter was handsome, gentlemanly, and well liked by his peers and subordinates. Despite the fact that Pope and Porter overlapped one year at West Point, they did not know each other up to the time Porter reported to Pope on August 27, 1862.

Porter was very much a McClellan man. In fact, this is what was to cause his downfall. Their association extended back to their West Point days. McClellan, like Porter a good student, was to graduate second in the class of 46, one year after Porter.

In April, 1861, McClellan, then major general of Ohio Volunteers, requested Porter's services as adjutant, but was refused. However, when McClellan became commanding general of the Army of the Potomac, he again asked for Porter and was now too powerful to be refused. Porter quickly advanced in responsibility under McClellan, rising from division commander to commanding officer of the Fifth Corps. McClellan closeted himself with Porter for discussion and advice more than with any other subordinate. He did so even though he had subordinate corps commanders who were a half generation older and more experienced.

When McClellan arrived before the first Confederate obstacle on his Peninsula Campaign, the Confederate fortifications at Yorktown, he decided upon a siege and put Porter in charge of the siege. This was Porter's first opportunity in the war to come front and center; and come front and center he did. Porter was, in the immortal words of Sir William Gilbert, the "very model of a modern major general." Porter quickly became a favorite of the press, which avidly reported each of his moves. Porter naturally adopted the most advanced technology, which, in the eyes of many, consisted of Professor Lowe's observation balloons. The gallant Porter, however, was not content to listen to reports of other observers. He went up himself. While hundreds or even thousands watched, his balloon became un-tethered and drifted over the Confederate lines at Yorktown. The Confederates began taking pot shots at him. It seemed he was a goner for sure. However, the wind then changed direction, and Porter drifted back over his own lines and emerged unscathed—to countless cheers. The Confederate defenses of Yorktown proved to be a sham and the siege a farce. This, however, did not hurt Porter's fame. He then went on to greater feats.

As McClellan's army moved ponderously down the peninsula and approached Richmond, it crossed the Chickahominy River. Porter's Fifth Corps ended up on the north side, and the remainder of McClellan's army on the south side. Lee recognized this as an opportunity to isolate and destroy Porter's corps. Thus began the battles of Mechanicsburg and Gaines' Mill. Porter, by obstinate resistance and clever maneuvering, managed to extricate his corps and thus deprive Lee of a smashing victory. Furthermore, in both battles, Porter's corps inflicted more casualties than it took. Porter was now riding high, but there was more to come.

As McClellan retired across the peninsula to his new base on the James River, Porter brought up the rear and covered the retirement. The Confederates overtook him at a place called Malvern Hill. The Confederates attacked Porter's near impregnable position with wave after wave of troops. Porter, after inflicting frightful casualties on the Confederates, successfully withdrew. He had given them a real bloody nose. In fact, this may have been the Union's biggest success in the east to date.

Porter was now second in popularity to his boss within the Army of the Potomac, and undoubtedly more popular within many circles of the government. This was to be the pinnacle of his fame. Some correspondence lends an idea of the esteem in which Porter was held:

Headquarters Army of the Potomac,
Camp near Harrison's Bar, July 9, 1862

Hon. E. M. Stanton,
Secretary of War:

Sir: The energy, ability, gallantry, and good conduct displayed throughout the eventful period of this campaign, through which we have just passed, by Brig. Gen. F. J. Porter, deserves the marked notice of the Executive and of the nation. From the very commencement, his unwearied assiduity in his various duties, the intelligent and efficacious assistance which he has rendered me under all circumstances, his skillful management of his command on the march, in the siege, or on the field of battle, and his chivalric and soldierly bearing under fire, have combined to render him conspicuous among the many faithful and gallant spirits of this army. I respectfully, therefore, recommend that Brig. Gen. Fitz-John Porter receive the brevet of brigadier-general in the Regular Army for Hanover

Court-House, May 27, and the brevet of major-general in the Regular Army for the battle of Gaines' Mill, June 27.

I have the honor to be sir, very respectfully, your obedient servant,

Geo. B. McClellan,
Major-General, Commanding.

P. S.—If there were another grade to add, I would ask it for the battle of Malvern. The latter eclipses in its result any other engagement in the campaign, and too much credit cannot be given to General Porter for his skill, gallantry, and conduct on that occasion. If there be any vacancy among the general officers in the Regular Army, I ask one for him. I saw myself the dispositions he made and the gallantry he displayed. I do not speak from hearsay, but from personal observation. Would that the country had more general officers like him.

Geo. B. McClellan
Major-General, Commanding.[8]

In 1863, after the Porter trial, the assistant secretary to Lincoln, John Hay, wrote to the secretary to Lincoln, John Nicolay: "Porter was the most magnificent soldier in the Army of the Potomac, ruined by his devotion to McClellan."[9]

We now come to Halleck's termination of McClellan's Peninsula Campaign and the order to withdraw all McClellan's troops from the peninsula to the Washington area. Initially, Porter was all for it. He did not realize that he, along with his corps, was going to be transferred to Pope's Army of Virginia. When this realization came, it came as a shock. He would no longer be working for his friend and mentor, for one who fully appreciated him, relied upon him above all others for his judgment, consulted with him. He was going to be transferred to a known blowhard and braggart, to a man who was widely disliked and whom he did not know. To add to that, all three of Pope's corps commanders were senior to Porter. He would be low man on the totem pole. It is easy to imagine some resentment on Porter's part. He was only human.

When Porter debarked with his corps at Aquia, he was in Burnside territory, and Burnside territory was friendly territory. Burnside was senior to Porter. Burnside, however, like Porter, was a McClellan man; and Burnside, like McClellan, was a friend of Porter. Porter would remain under Burnside's command as he marched up the Rappahannock until he reported to Pope.

As Porter marched up the Rappahannock, telegraph wires were strung up behind him, keeping him in contact with Burnside's headquarters, and Burnside's headquarters was connected by telegraph with the War Department in Washington. As Porter got closer and closer to Pope's theatre of operations, he got more and more information on what was happening there. He sent periodic status reports back to Burnside, reporting all he knew. These reports, however, were laced with personal comments, often disparaging to Pope and

Pope's abilities. They also clearly reflected that Porter's loyalties lay with McClellan; he even asked if "Mac" could get him out of this. Porter, of course, assumed and intended that his messages were going no farther than Burnside.

As we know, Jackson suddenly appeared in Pope's rear on the night of August 26 and cut both Pope's rail and telegraphic communications with Washington. The War Department building was located immediately adjacent to the White House in Washington, and Lincoln had the habit of walking over to the telegraph office in the War Department during the evening to see how things were going. Suddenly, all communications with Pope were cut off. Lincoln heard nothing and was desperate for information. The only telegraph line to the Rappahannock still open was the one to Burnside's headquarters. Lincoln ordered that any information to Burnside's headquarters concerning Pope should be passed on to Washington. Consequently, all of Porter's messages, unknown to him, were automatically passed on to Washington. Here, they were read by Halleck and Lincoln, and probably Stanton. They were also read by someone who passed on their contents to Pope.

By the time Porter reported in to Pope on the morning of August 27, the two men already had good reason not to like each other. Here are excerpts from Porter's messages to Burnside:

> We are working now to get behind Bull Run, and, I presume will be there in a few days, if strategy don't use us up. The strategy is magnificent, and tactics in the inverse proportion.... I was informed today, by the best authority, that, in opposition to General Pope's views, this army was pushed out to save the Army of the Potomac—an army that could take the best care of itself.... Most of this is private, but if you can get me away, please do so.[10]

> Please hasten back the wagons I sent down, and inform McClellan, that I may know that I am doing right....[11]

> All that talk about bagging Jackson etc. was bosh. That enormous gap—Manassas—was left open, and the enemy jumped through, and the story of McDowell having cut off Longstreet had no good foundation. The enemy destroyed an immense amount of property at Manassas—cars and supplies.... I expect the next thing will be a raid on our own rear by Longstreet, *who was cut off*.[12]

> I hope for the best. My lucky star is always up about my birthday, the 31st, and I hope Mac's is up also. You will hear of us soon by way of Alexandria....[13]

This reference to Alexandria is sarcasm. This is Pope's supply base outside Washington, to whence he would retreat if defeated.

> Heintzelman and Reno are at Centreville where they marched yesterday. Pope went to Centreville with the last two as a bodyguard, at the time not

knowing where was the enemy, and when Sigel was fighting within 8 miles of him and in sight. Comment is unnecessary. I hope Mac's at work, and we will soon get ordered out of this. It would seem, from proper statements of the enemy, that he was wandering around loose, but I expect they know what they are doing, which is more than anyone here or anywhere knows.[14]

(Refer to Appendix 4 for the full text of Porter's messages to Burnside.)

The very incidents that brought Porter fame on the peninsula may well have influenced his decision-making on August 28 and 29. When Porter was stopped at Dawkins Branch on August 29 and considered sending his men down the ravine in his front, up the other side, and across the open space, against the Confederate line of battle hidden in the trees beyond, he may well have thought back to the slaughter of the Confederate troops at Malvern Hill, who were thrown against a near impregnable position. When he considered his isolated position on August 29, he may well have thought back to Mechanicsburg and Gaines' Mill, when the Confederates recognized that he was separated from the main force and attempted to destroy him in detail.

Major General Irvin McDowell

Gen. McDowell was forty-four years old in 1862, four years older than Pope and Porter. He graduated from West Point in 1838, four years before Pope and seven years before Porter. McDowell was unusual for a West Pointer at the time. He was from a well-to-do family, and resided and was educated in France up to the time he entered West Point. McDowell had a good record in the Mexican War, and then spent most of his pre–Civil War career close to the center of power. Accordingly, by the war's beginning, he had friends and patrons in high places. These included the senior general of the army, old Gen. Winfield Scott, and Secretary of the Treasury Salmon Chase.

Partly because of his connections, McDowell was promoted three grades and given the top field position in the east. This was to organize the predecessor of the Army of the Potomac and to lead it into battle. This McDowell did. He led it straight into the Union's first disaster, the first battle of Bull Run (or Manassas) that took place July 21, 1861. It was then and now widely proclaimed that it was not McDowell's fault; that political pressures forced him into action before he was ready. This was undoubtedly true. On the other hand, the Confederates that defeated him weren't ready either.

After the battle of Manassas, McDowell was reduced to division and then corps commander, and served first under McClellan and then under Pope. McDowell was not a charismatic leader and was not popular with his troops. He also had an abrasive personality. He did, however, have some admirable qualities. Unlike many other generals, he appeared able to put the cause above personal considerations. He appeared able to serve faithfully and with good grace under individuals who were not only junior to him, but had previously served under him. When assigned to Pope and Pope's Army of Virginia, he was senior to Pope. Pope, however, claimed that McDowell always faithfully, fully, and cordially subordinated himself to him. These qualities were also appreciated by the civil authorities in Washington. Even after the second battle of Manassas, Secretary of War Chase, Secretary of War Stanton, and President Lincoln all considered that McDowell was a first rate, loyal officer who never sulked, talked loose, or played a part in military politics.

It's difficult to place the full blame for the Union defeat at the second battle of Manassas on the shoulders of any one general. However, among those who contributed most to the loss, Gen. McDowell would certainly be a leading candidate. During the evening of August 28, the two divisions of McDowell alone stood between Jackson and Thoroughfare Gap—Ricketts at the gap, and King moving along the Warrenton pike toward Groveton. Where was McDowell at this critical time? Miles away at Manassas looking for Gen. Pope, and completely out of contact with either of his divisions.

During McDowell's absence, both of his divisions entered into action. Ricketts retreated all the way to Bristoe, and King all the way to Manassas Junction. This was done by the decision of the two division commanders without input or knowledge by McDowell. When Pope awoke on the morning of the twenty-ninth, he found to his great surprise and disappointment that he had no one between Jackson and the gap.

McDowell, thus being absent when and where he was most needed, now re-appeared and intervened when and where he was least needed. On the morning of the twenty-ninth, Pope had ordered Porter to take his own corps and King's division and march out on the road to Gainesville until his force merged with Pope's troops that were moving along the Warrenton pike. As Porter's force moved out, it had one objective, one order, and one leader. Then McDowell re-appeared. He requested that Pope re-assign King to him, and he then accompanied Porter's column.

When Porter confronted the enemy at Dawkins Branch, he stopped, deployed his lead division in line of battle, and prepared for action. At this point McDowell rode up, took charge, and issued confusing orders. He then took King away from Porter, reducing Porter's force by one third. Thus, he created a paralyzing delay as the Confederate force built up in front of Porter. What was possible for Porter at 11 A.M. with the support of King became no longer possible by 2 P.M. without King. The culprit was McDowell.

By the time of completion of the second battle of Manassas, the clamor against McDowell was so great among the rank and file that he could no longer effectively lead troops unless something were done to restore confidence in him. Lincoln suggested to Salmon Chase that this might be accomplished by McDowell requesting a court of inquiry, and this be conducted in public. When Chase suggested this to McDowell, McDowell responded that this would be difficult because no one charged him with anything. Chase responded by stating that he had seen a letter written by a colonel of the First Michigan Cavalry. The letter was addressed to the colonel's siblings and was written by the colonel as he lay dying from wounds acquired during the battle. The colonel charged that he was dying because of "Pope's imbecility ... [and] McDowell's treachery."[15] Chase suggested that this letter might serve as a basis for McDowell requesting a court of inquiry. Even though the letter consisted of a comment and not a formal charge, McDowell agreed that the letter could serve as a basis for his requesting a court of inquiry. McDowell then prepared a letter to President Lincoln, requesting the court of inquiry using the colonel's comment as a basis. This request was almost unprecedented. Seeing that the colonel's letter did not say specifically what McDowell had done to deserve the treachery charge, McDowell's letter requested an overall examination of his conduct as a general. (Refer to Appendix 5 for the full text of McDowell's request for a court of inquiry.)

A court of inquiry is not a trial. As the name indicates, it is a fact-finding body, but uses court procedures. Witnesses can be summoned and are examined under oath. Under Article Ninety-one of the Articles of War, a court of inquiry shall consist of one or more officers, not to exceed three, and a recorder.

The court was convened by an order of General-in-Chief Halleck, dated November 21, 1862. The designated members were Major General George Cadwalader, U.S. Volunteers (president); Brigadier General John H. Martindale, U.S. Volunteers; and Brigadier General James H. Van Alen, U.S. Volunteers. Colonel H. Pelouze was designated recorder. McDowell offered no objection to any of the appointments.

Cadwalader was fifty-eight years old and a lawyer by profession. However, he had served in the Mexican War as a brigadier general of volunteers. At the outset of the Civil War, he was appointed major general of state volunteers by the governor of Pennsylvania. After a short stint in the field in 1861, Cadwalader served on various boards and committees in Washington.

Forty-seven year old Brigadier Gen. Martindale was an 1853 graduate of West Point. However, shortly after graduation, he left the service to pursue a career in the law. At the outset of the Civil War, he was commissioned a brigadier general of volunteers. Martindale participated in McClellan's Peninsula Campaign with great distinction, but ran afoul of general Porter. During McClellan's retreat across the peninsula to the James River, Martindale stated that he would rather surrender to the Confederates than abandon his wounded. For this, Porter filed charges against him. Martindale, however, was fully exonerated. At the time of selection of the members of the court, Martindale was military governor of Washington.

Brig. Gen. Van Alen was not a career officer, but a wealthy New York merchant. At the outset of the war, he recruited a cavalry regiment, offered his services, and was made its colonel.

The selection of the court members, like the Porter court-martial members, thus seems to have been based in large part, if not fully, on their availability.

The court members were perplexed when they found that they had no charge to investigate. They were then presented with McDowell's letter to the President to serve as a basis for their inquiry. This entailed practically an investigation of McDowell's overall performance. The court divided their investigation into five areas as follows:

(1) Gen. McDowell as a division or corps commander under Gen. McClellan

(2) The separation of Gen. McDowell's corps from the Army of the Potomac and formation of the Department of the Rappahannock

(3) Gen. McDowell as commander of the Department of the Rappahannock

(4) The correspondence of Gen. McDowell with the enemy's commanders or with anyone within the enemy's line

(5) Gen. McDowell as a commander in the Army of Virginia under Gen. Pope

The court met for the first time on November 21, 1862, and rendered its report on February 14, 1863. It must have been particularly galling to Gen. Porter to have to testify at a court, the purpose of which was to restore McDowell's reputation, while McDowell appeared as a chief accuser at a court intended to destroy Porter's reputation.

McDowell's court of inquiry not only extended far longer than Porter's court-martial, but called far more witnesses. In all, forty-seven witnesses testified, including seventeen generals. As stated earlier, Secretary of War Stanton sent a letter to the Porter court directing it to speed up its proceedings and come to a quick termination. No such admonition was sent to the McDowell court.

As might be expected, the court found McDowell's performance in four of the five areas investigated not only blameless, but meritorious. It was only in the matter of the second battle of Manassas that it found criticism. It criticized precisely the matter previously noted—McDowell's absence from his corps the critical night of August 28–29.

Whatever moral capital McDowell had accumulated by his pre-court reputation of putting duty above self, he squandered by requesting the court. Here, in the midst of the greatest crisis in the history of his country, while fellow citizens were being maimed, crippled, blinded, killed, and made widows and orphans, he was prepared to subject the country to this huge diversion of resources solely for his reputation. The court not only consumed the full time of the three generals who were members, but also consumed the time, travel, and talent of the seventeen generals who were called to testify.

McDowell was to play no further part in the Civil War.

8

The Motivation Question

The preceding chapter shows that Porter sent a number of dispatches to Burnside that contained comments hugely critical, one might even say contemptuous, of Pope and his capabilities, and that these messages fell into the hands of the prosecution. It is just possible to imagine that if Porter were contemptuous of Pope's capabilities, it might be pleasing to Porter to see the outcome of Pope's campaign vindicate his judgment. To extend this reasoning further, it might even incline Porter to give less than his best effort to facilitate such outcome. If this were the case, it would be a motive for Porter's performance. This line of reasoning was not lost on the prosecution. As a starter, the prosecution introduced into evidence Porter's messages to Burnside. These are contained in Appendix 4.

The next testimony was from Gen. Roberts, Pope's inspector general. It was Roberts who signed the charges against Porter. Cross-examination by the defense yielded the following:

> QUESTION: Did it occur that the witness at any time, on or about the 27th, 28th, or 29th of August, made statements to General Pope touching the probability that General Porter would fail, or touching the fidelity of General Porter to his duty as an officer?
>
> ANSWER: After General Porter failed to march at 1 o'clock on the morning of the 28th of August, in compliance with General Pope's orders, it occurred to me that General Porter might fail General Pope, for the reason that I had never conceived that an officer who failed to obey so plain an order would do his duty. And when General Porter failed to attack on Friday, the 29th, when I expected he would attack, and when I know General Pope expected he would attack, that impression of mine was made still stronger that he would not do his duty. I may have suggested to General Pope my impression that he better not rely on General Porter; but I do not now recollect that I did state that to him.
>
> QUESTION: Is it true, in any event, that prior to action taken by General Porter under the order of the 27th of August, the witness made any such statements touching the fidelity of General Porter to General Pope?
>
> ANSWER: I made none prior to that time, and prior to that time I had felt convinced that General Porter would not only do his duty, but I was

of the impression that he would do it as well as any officer in the army could do it.

QUESTION: Then the grounds, and all the grounds, of any such unfavorable suggestions made by the witness, if any were made, are simply the judgment formed by the witness of the events with which General Porter was connected on the 27th and 28th of August?

ANSWER: They were not the only grounds, as, on the 28th, while at Manassas Junction, an officer of the army, a major-general, whose name it is not necessary for me to mention, in a conversation that I had with him, in which I mentioned General Porter and the high estimation in which I had held him, told me that I did not know him, and told me that he would fail General Pope. The disobedience of the orders, and this conversation, led me up to the opinion that General Porter was not doing his duty in good faith to General Pope.

QUESTION: Had you heard such unfavorable surmise or report concerning General Porter prior to the 28th of August?

ANSWER: I had not.[1]

The court directed Roberts to divulge the name of the major general. It was Maj. Gen. Phil Kearny, division commander in Heintzelman's corps.[2] No one could be produced who heard the conversation between Roberts and Kearny, and Kearny was dead, having been killed in the battle of Chantilly on September 1, 1862. Pope's testimony reveals that Roberts told him of his conversation with Kearny:

QUESTION: By whom were you told or cautioned that the accused would fail you and when were you told?

POPE: I think on the 27th of August, and again on the 28th of August, by General Roberts, and on the night of the 28th by Lieutenant Colonel Smith.

QUESTION: Were these the only two officers from whom you got this information?

POPE: These are the only two officers that I remember distinctly. I heard much talk of that kind from many others, but I do not remember who they are. I heard it on several occasions.[3]

Lt. Col. Thomas C.H. Smith was aide-de-camp to Gen. Pope and testified for the prosecution. Smith said that on the afternoon of August 28, he was sent back to the ammunition train at Bristoe and charged with its distribution. After the work was well in progress, he set out to return to Gen. Pope's headquarters, but found that he had moved. He then stopped at Gen. Porter's tent to enquire if he knew where Pope had gone. This resulted in a ten minute conversation with Porter that Smith described as follows:

After asking him about the road, I told General Porter the amount of ammunition that I had sent forward to him, and also that the balance would come immediately forward. I asked him if he had received it, or made some remark; I cannot remember the exact expression. General Porter said that he had not; that was the substance of his reply—either in

reply to some question of mine or to some remark, or of himself, he said
that he had no officers to take charge of it and distribute it, or look it up,
or something of that kind. I remarked that he could hardly expect us at
headquarters to be able to send officers to distribute it in his corps; that
it had been sent forward on the road, in the direction where his corps was.
He replied that it was going where it belonged; that it was on the road to
Alexandria, where we were all going. I do not know as it is evidence to give
the spirit in which this was said—the way it impressed me. Those remarks
were made in a sneering manner, and appeared to me to express a great
indifference. There was then a pause for a moment. General Porter then
spoke in regard to the removal of the sick and wounded from the field of
Kettle Run. He said it would hurt Pope, leaving the wounded behind. I
told him that they were not to be left behind. That I knew that a positive
order—an imperative order—had been given to General Banks to bring
all the wounded with him, and for that purpose to throw property out of
the wagons if necessary. To this General Porter made no reply in words;
but his manner to me expressed the same feeling that I had noticed before.
This conversation, from General Porter's manner and look, made a strong
impression on my mind.

I left him, as I have said, after an interview of about ten minutes, and
rode on, arriving at our headquarters on Bull Run just as we entered them
and pitched our tents for the night. After my tent was pitched, and I had
had something to eat, I went over to General Pope, and reported to him
briefly what I had done in regard to the ammunition. I then said to him,
"General, I saw General Porter on my way here." Said he, "Well, sir." I
said, "General, he will fail you." "Fail me," said he; "what do you mean?
What did he say?" Said I, "It is not so much what he said, though he said
enough; he is going to fail you." These expressions I repeat. I think I
remember them with exactness, for I was excited at the time from the
impression that had been made upon me. Said General Pope, "How can
he fail me? He will fight where I put him; he will fight where I put him;"
or, "He must fight where I put him; he must fight where I put him"—one
of those expressions. This General Pope said with a great deal of feeling,
and impetuously and perhaps overbearingly, and in an excited manner. I
replied in the same way, saying that I was so certain that Fitz-John Porter
was a traitor, that I would shoot him that night, so far as any crime before
God was concerned, if the law would allow me to do it. I speak of this to
show the conviction that I received from General Porter's manner and
expressions in that interview. I have only to add that my prepossessions
of him were favorable, as it was at headquarters, up to that time. I never
had entertained any impression against him until that conversation. I knew
nothing with regard to his orders to move up to Kettle Run, and I knew
nothing of any failure on his part to comply with any orders.

QUESTION: State more distinctly the point where you saw General Porter
    on the 28th of August.
ANSWER: He was encamped at Manassas water station, between Bristoe

and the junction. The water station was a short distance from his head-quarters. [The witness indicated upon the map before the court where he thought the place to be.] I do not think the water station is more than one-third the distance from Bristoe to Manassas Junction. That is my impression; I cannot speak positively about it.

QUESTION: In the conversation to which you refer, did or did not, General Porter manifest any anxiety to get possession of, and have distributed in his corps, the ammunition of which you speak?

ANSWER: No, sir; I thought he showed an utter indifference upon the subject; showed it very plainly.

QUESTION: At what hour of the day did this conversation between you and General Porter take place?

ANSWER: I think it must have been about 4 o'clock in the afternoon; half-past 3 or 4 o'clock.

QUESTION: In anything that was said in that conversation or in the manner of General Porter, was there evidenced any desire or any willingness on his part to support General Pope in the military operations in which he was then engaged?

ANSWER: Quite the contrary to that.

QUESTION: Can you state whether the disinclination to support General Pope, which you thought he manifested, was the result of disgust with the immediate service in which he was then engaged, or of hostility to the commanding general, or upon what did it seem to rest?

ANSWER: It seemed to me to rest on hostility. But I do not know that I could analyze the impression that was made upon me. I conveyed it to General Pope in the words that I have stated. I had one of those clear convictions that a man has a few times, perhaps, in his life, as to the character and purposes of a person whom he sees for the first time. No man can express altogether how such an impression is gained from looks and manner, but it is clear.[4]

The defense questioning of Smith made a number of points. Smith's total military service at the time of his meeting with Porter had been one year and three days. He had never met Porter before and did not know what his normal mannerisms were. In his meeting, Porter was not rude or unfriendly. To the contrary, he was gentlemanly and courteous and was only "sneering" in the matters alluded to. Smith could not describe Porter's "sneering" manner, but said he instinctively knew it when he encountered it.

The defense took a double barreled approach to defuse the prosecution's attack. First, it asked each general if he heard Porter say anything inimical to Pope, or do any less than his best to support Pope. Second, the defense attempted to show that Pope was actually satisfied with Porter's performance shortly after the battle, and that it was only later, when the rank and file, press and public began to blame Pope that Pope attempted to shift the blame to Porter.

As regards the first approach, these questions were put to the various generals:

To Sykes:

Did you ever see in him [Porter] any slackness to do his duty; any evidence of a disposition to fail his commanding general or country?[5]

To Butterfield:

Did you see anything he did, or in anything he said, after he marched from Aquia Creek, or when it was understood that you were to come under the command of General Pope, any evidence of an indisposition upon his [Porter's] part to be faithful to General Pope and his country?[6]

To Griffin:

Did you or not, hear General Porter, at any time during the 27th, 28th, 29th or 30th of August, criticize General Pope's military conduct, or his capacity for generalship, unfavorably? If so, will you state the substance of such criticism?[7]

To Morell:

Please state when where and how, if at all, to the best of your knowledge and judgment, the accused ever failed during that period to exhibit all proper zeal and energy, first, to make junction, when ordered to do so, with the command of General Pope; and second, to cooperate with that command in faithful duty against the enemy.[8]

To Burnside:

From the knowledge that you had of the accused, both before and while he was going to join Pope's command, derived from his acts and conversations, have you any reason to believe, that he would fail in obedience to General Pope, or performing, to the best of his ability, the duty which he might be under after joining General Pope's command?[9]

To McClellan:

Had you any reason, at any time, after he [Porter] received notice that he was to go to the assistance of General Pope to believe that he would fail General Pope, or the country in the discharge of his duty?[10]

All generals responded firmly in the negative.

In regard to the defense's second approach, namely that Pope had no criticism of Porter at the time, the defense zeroed in on two conversations between Pope and Porter. The first occurred on the morning of August 28, after Porter's belated arrival at Bristoe. No one else was present at this conversation, but the testimony generally concurred that Pope did not censure Porter at this time.

The second conversation occurred at Fairfax Court House on September 2, after the second battle of Manassas. The defense contended that at this conversation, Pope stated that he was satisfied with Porter's explanations and that he had no criticism of Porter's performance. Pope had no recollection of making such statements and recalled that he did criticize Porter. Col. Ruggles, Pope's chief of staff, testified that he overheard snatches of the conversation, and that what he heard partially supported Porter's version. Ruggles testified that he heard Pope say that he had no criticism of Porter beyond the fact that Griffin and his brigade failed to participate in the battle of the thirtieth.

9

Summation and Verdict

On January 19, 1862, Judge-Advocate Holt summed up the case for President Lincoln. (Although the summation was written after the verdict was rendered, I shall present it first.)

Review of the Judge-Advocate
Judge-Advocate-General's Office,
January 19, 1863

Sir: In compliance with your written instructions, under date of the 13th [12th] instant—

To revise the proceedings of the court-martial in the case of Maj. Gen. Fitz-John Porter, and to report fully upon any legal questions that may have arisen in them, and upon the bearing of the testimony in reference to the charges and specifications exhibited against the accused, and upon which he was tried—

I have the honor to submit the following report:

As the animus of the accused toward his commanding general, in pursuing the line of conduct alleged against him, must largely affect the question of his criminality, and may furnish a safe and reliable light for your guidance in determining points otherwise left doubtful by the evidence, it is proper that it should, if possible, be ascertained before entering at large upon the review of the case, which you have instructed me to make.

General Porter, with his command, belonged to the Army of the Potomac, which had closed its disastrous campaign on the Peninsula just before the moment at which the narrative of the events set forth in the record before you is taken up by the witnesses who have deposed. General McClellan and Assistant Secretary of War Tucker state that he displayed great energy and zeal in debarking his troops and hastening their departure for Aquia Creek. The former, however, adds that it was not then known to the accused that he was to be placed under the immediate command of General Pope, the question of the command not having at that time been decided. It should likewise be borne in mind that the transfer of the Army of the Potomac, once begun, was a movement of extreme peril, and that extraordinary efforts on the part of all engaged in it were prompted, not only by those high considerations of patriotism which must be supposed to have been present, but also by the equally urgent instincts of self-preservation. The order of General Halleck, directing the junction of the command of the accused with that of General Pope, seems to have reached him at Aquia Creek. From this he proceeded, in obedience to the order, to effect the junction, and at that time, as we learn from General Burnside, lacked confidence in General Pope, and shared the distrust, alleged by the witness to have been entertained by many officers, of his capacity to conduct the campaign in which the Army of Virginia was then engaged. He reported to General Pope by note on the 26th, and in person on the morning of the 27th of August, 1862, at Warrenton Junction. In the brief conference which ensued between them in the forenoon of that day, he must have acquired all the information he then possessed as to the plan of the campaign and as to the disposition of the forces of the contending armies. After this conference, at 4 o'clock P.M. of that day, he sent to General Burnside the dispatch first referred to in the testimony. In that dispatch, interspersed amid various items of military intelligence, are found the following expressions:

> We are working now to get behind Bull Run, and I presume will be there in a few days, if strategy don't use us up. The strategy is magnificent and tactics in the inverse proportion. I was informed to-day, by the best authority, that, in opposition to General Pope's views, this army was pushed out to save the Army of the Potomac—an army that could take care of itself.
>
> Most of this is private, but if you can get me away, do so.

Again, at 2 P.M. of the 28th, he dispatches:

> All that talk about bagging Jackson, &c., was bosh. That enormous gap—Manassas—was left open, and the enemy jumped through, and the story

Major General Ambrose Burnside of the United States Volunteers was Ninth Corps commander and a friend of Porter's (courtesy the Massachusetts Commandery Military Order of the Loyal Legion and the U.S. Army Military History Institute).

of McDowell having cut off Longstreet had no good foundation. The enemy destroyed an immense amount of property at Manassas—cars and supplies. I expect the next thing will be a raid on our rear by Longstreet, who was cut off.

Another dispatch to same, dated Bristoe, August 28, 1862, 9:30 A.M., and introduced by the accused, concludes as follows:

I hope for the best. My lucky star is always up about my birthday, the 31st, and I hope Mac's is up also. You will hear of us soon by way of Alexandria.

To the same officer, from Bristoe, 6 A.M., 29th, he telegraphs:

Heintzelman and Reno are at Centreville, where they marched yesterday. Pope went to Centreville with the last two as a body guard, at the time not knowing where was the enemy, and when Sigel was fighting within 8 miles of him and in sight. Comment is unnecessary. I hope Mac's at work, and we will soon get ordered out of this. It would seem, from proper statements of the enemy, that he was wandering around loose, but I expect they know what they are doing, which is more than any one here or anywhere knows.

The precise import of these remarkable words, in their connection, cannot be mistaken, nor can it fail to be observed how harshly they jar upon the proprieties of military life. It may be safely affirmed that they express, on the part of the accused, an intense scorn and contempt for the strategy and movements of the Army of Virginia, a weariness and disgust for his association with it, added to a bitter fling at his commanding general, as found in the extraordinary declaration that he had taken two divisions of his army as a "body guard" to Centreville. The words, as quoted, disclose also a looking by the accused, not to General Pope, but to General McClellan as his guide, and a reliance upon his exertions and influence to relieve him from his connection with the Army of Virginia, and in expectation, if not a hope, that they would all soon arrive at Alexandria. This, it is true, would involve the discomfiture of that army, but it would also involve the discredit of its commander, and would restore the accused to his former position under General McClellan. Such must have been the anticipation, and such certainly was the result.

In explanation of these dispatches, and with a view to relieve the mind of the impression they tend to make, it was alleged in the defense, and was proved by General Burnside, that they were official in their character, and that the accused had been requested to furnish him information in reference to current military events occurring in connection with the army with which he was serving. So far as the purpose for which they were offered by the Government is concerned, it is wholly immaterial under whose prompting, or for what end, they were written. If the words make it manifest that the accused entertained feelings of contempt and hostility toward the Army of Virginia and its commander, it matters not whether they were spoken in private and confidential or in an official communication. The fact, however, that such words are found in a grave and formal official correspondence must serve to show how strong these feelings were, and how difficult it was to repress their utterance.

In reply to what must be regarded as the prevailing sentiment of the language quoted, there was read in the defense a dispatch from the accused to General McClellan—which was not sent—dated September 2, 1862. It is full of fervent patriotism and of professions of devotion to his duty in connection with the Army of Virginia and its commander. The court undoubtedly gave to this paper the consideration it deserved. Unhappily it came too late. The Army of Virginia had suffered, in the way of disaster, all that the enemy and the inaction of the accused could inflict upon it; and at the very moment this dispatch was written, the field for the "cordial co-operation and constant support" which it promised was being swept away by the order issued that morning for the Army of Virginia to fall back within the entrenchments of Washington, and, of course, under the command of General McClellan.

The testimony furnishes yet other indications of the animus of the accused. General Pope was warned by General Roberts and Lieutenant-Colonel Smith, and by others, that the accused "would fail him." In his frank and unsuspecting nature, he seems to have flung the imputation from him. He had not, then, the light which the pages of the record before you now furnish. When, afterward, on his arrival at Washington, he was informed of the dispatches sent by the accused to General Burnside, his mind appears to have been very differently impressed.

In the afternoon of the 28th of August, General Roberts became satisfied that the accused was not doing his duty in good faith to General Pope. He arrived at this conclusion, as well from his alleged disobedience of the order to march at 1 A.M. of that morning as from the declaration of General Kearny. General Roberts had previously held the accused in high estimation, and when mentioning this to General Kearny, the latter said that "he (General Roberts) did not know him, and that he would fail General Pope."

Lieut. Col. Thomas C. H. Smith, an aide-de-camp on the staff of General Pope, called on the accused in the afternoon of the 28th of August. He had not heard of his disobedience of any orders, and had, like General Roberts, the most favorable opinion of his character and conduct as an officer; yet, such was the impression made upon him by his manner and conversation, that at the close of their interview, he left him, fully satisfied that he would fail General Pope, and would withhold from him his support in the then pending operations of the Army of Virginia. Soon thereafter he arrived at the headquarters of General Pope, and said to him that he had just seen General Porter on his way there, and that he would fail him, and added:

> So certain am I that Fitz-John Porter is a traitor, that I would shoot him to-night, so far as any crime before God is concerned, if the law would allow me to do it.

The impression thus expressed he still retains, and reiterated in his testimony. This evidence is of a most striking character, and should be closely examined with a view to the ascertainment of the weight to which the opinion of the witness is entitled. It has been stigmatized in the defense of the accused as "ravings" and as "wild fantasies," which "encumber the record" as "rubbish." Such epithets were not warranted either by the language or manner of the witness. While expressing himself thus forcibly, it was evident that he was a man of fine intelligence, and equally evident that his conscientiousness rendered him careful and guarded in his statements. Certainly the particular impression referred to was deposed to with a depth and solemnity of conviction rarely paralleled in judicial proceedings. Under the pressure of the severe cross-examination to which he was subjected, he endeavored to lay bare the foundations on which his belief of the accused's meditated treachery rested. The task, however, was a difficult one, and he may not have been entirely successful. In reference to a large quantity of ammunition ordered by and forwarded to the accused, but which had not been received, he manifested utter indifference, stating that "it was going where it belonged; that it was on the road to Alexandria, where we are all going"—a favorite thought, as appears from his dispatches. His manner was sneering throughout, whenever allusion was made to matters connected with General Pope; and—"His look was that of a man having a crime on his mind."

It was physically impossible for the witness to reproduce the manner, the tone of voice, and the expression of the eye, and the play of the features, which may have so much influenced his judgment; yet these often afford a language more to be relied on than that of the lips. He could not hold up before the court, for its inspection and appreciation, the sneer of which he spoke; and yet we know that a sneer is as palpable to the mental as a smile is to the natural vision. It is a life-long experience that souls reach each other, and that there are intercommunings of spirits, through instrumentalities which, while defying all human analysis, nevertheless completely command the homage of human faith. Great crimes, too, like great virtues, often reveal themselves to close observers of character and conduct as unmistakably as a flower garden announces it presence by the odors it breathes upon the air. The witness may have misconceived this "look," but from the calamities likely to follow such an act of treachery, if indeed, it was then contemplated, it must be admitted as altogether probable that the shadow of such a crime struggling into being would have made itself manifest. In view of the fearful perils which then menaced the Army of Virginia, to which they owed a common duty, is it not passing strange that during this interview the accused uttered not to the witness one word of kindness or cordiality, or encouragement or determination in reference to the sanguinary conflict in which the morrow was to involve them with a common enemy?

With this exhibition of the disposition of the accused toward the service in which he was engaged, I will proceed to review, as briefly as possible, the testimony in its bearing upon the charges and specifications of the record.

The order of General Pope, set forth in the first specification of the first charge, directed the accused, then at Warrenton Junction, to start at 1 o'clock on the morning of the 28th of August, and to march with his whole corps so as to be at Bristoe Station, distant 9 miles, at daylight. It recited that General Hooker had "had a very severe action with the enemy, with a loss of about 300 killed and wounded"; that the enemy were retiring along the railroad, and that it was necessary to drive them from Manassas and clear the country between that place and Gainesville. The urgency of the necessity under which the order was issued was further expressed in these words: "It is necessary, on all accounts, that you should be here [Bristoe Station] by daylight. I send an officer with this dispatch, who will conduct you to this place."

The order was delivered by the officer referred to (Capt. Drake DeKay), at between half-past 9 and 10 o'clock of the evening of the 27th. On delivering it, he stated to the accused: "The last thing General Pope said to me, on leaving Bristoe Station, was, that I should remain with General Porter and guide the column to Bristoe Station, leaving at 1 o'clock, and that General Pope expected him certainly to be there by daylight."

General Hooker's command was out of ammunition, and an attack from the combined forces of Jackson and Ewell was expected early on the morning of the 28th, and hence the urgency with which this prompt and vigorous movement was pressed upon the accused. The order was not obeyed.

The march, according to several of the witnesses, did not begin until daylight. Captain DeKay, who acted as guide, and moved at the head of the column, states that he was waked up just at dawn, and that he breakfasted before the march began. Captain Monteith, called by the accused, when asked if, in point of fact, the march commenced before daylight, replied: "I think it was about dawn of day."

General Sykes, also a witness of the accused, deposed that his division led on that morning; that he generally allowed from one and a half to two hours between reveille and the advance; that on the morning of the 28th, the reveille was beaten from ¼ to ½ past 2 o'clock, and that the advance was sounded as soon as they could distinguish the road, thereby evidently referring to the dawn of day. General Pope, having been asked whether, on the receipt of certain messages from the accused, the latter was on his march in obedience to the order of the 27th of August, answered: "I do not know that he was. On the contrary, from a note I received from him, I did not understand that he would march until daylight in the morning."

While the weight of the testimony is to the effect that the troops did not move forward until daylight, none of the witnesses represent them as having done so earlier than 3 o'clock, and the arrival at Bristoe Station took place, not at daylight, as directed by the order, but at twenty minutes past 10 of the forenoon of the 28th. If our army—a large part of it without ammunition—had not, in the meanwhile, been fallen upon and beaten, it was not because of any exertions made by the accused to prevent such a catastrophe, but simply because the enemy had not thought proper to make the anticipated attack.

The violation of this peremptory order is sought to be excused, or rather fully justified, by the accused on three grounds: First, the fatigue of his troops; second, the darkness of the night; third, the obstructions on the road growing out of breaks and difficult places in it, and the presence of wagon trains in motion.

A part of the troops had marched on the 27th from 17 to 19 miles; the remainder not so far. The command of General Sykes had marched but from 12 to 14 miles. A portion of them did not arrive at their encampment at Warrenton Junction until about sundown—half past 6 o'clock; the others arrived earlier; some of them as early as 10 o'clock in the morning. The generals who advised and participated in the determination not to move at 1 o'clock, deposed that their troops were very much exhausted. Had the order been obeyed, the troops reaching their encampment earliest would have had fifteen hours, while those arriving latest would have had six hours and a half for rest. Would not this have been sufficient to prepare them for a march of only 9 miles? Had they reached Bristoe Station at daylight, the march for none of them would have exceeded 28 miles in twenty-four hours, while for a large part of the command it would have been less. Does not the military history of the world show that in great emergencies such forced marches often occur, and that soldiers are fully capable of enduring them?

The early part of the night was starlit, and not unusually dark. At about 11 o'clock the sky became overcast, and the night grew very, or as some of the witnesses express it, "extremely dark," and so continued until morning. It was a darkness, however, not complicated with cold, or rain, or storm. It is a noticeable fact, also, that the determination not to move at 1 o'clock, in obedience to the order, was not occasioned by this extreme darkness, but had been taken before Captain DeKay lay down, which was at 11 o'clock.

The first answer to the position taken in the defense, that in consequence of this darkness it was impossible to obey the order, is found in the testimony of Capt. Duryea, who deposes that on the night of the 27th of August he marched with his command from Warrenton, and did not halt until about midnight, and that he did not experience any unusual difficulties growing out of the night.

Maj. S. F. Barstow was also on the march that night until 9 o'clock, and was up the following morning before daylight, and says: "I have no vivid recollection of that night beyond other nights. It seemed to me to be very much like other nights on which we moved." He adds that no difficulty was experienced in marching the troops up to the hour at which they encamped.

Lieutenant-Colonel Myers, who, as chief quartermaster to General McDowell, had charge of the trains passing over this road on the night of the 27th, states that he was up nearly all that night. He was asked the following question: "In view of the condition of the road, as you have described it, and also the character of the night, was or was not the movement of troops along that road practicable that night?" He replied: "I do not know of anything to hinder troops marching along the railroad there. There was a road running each side of the railroad. I should think it would have been easy for troops to move along there, although I may be mistaken in that."

General Reynolds, called by the accused, and who entertained a very strong estimate of the embarrassments in the way of the march of troops on the night of the 27th over the road to Bristoe Station, admitted on cross-examination, that dark as was the night, troops could have marched, provided they had had a road and a guide to conduct them—both of which the command of General Porter had. General Heintzelman testifies that it was not impossible for troops to have marched over that road on the night of the 27th, but that there would have been a great many stragglers, of which, he said, there are more or less on all night marches. He describes the road as narrow, but "in tolerable good condition."

General Pope was asked this question: "If there were any obstacles in the way of such a march as your order contemplated, either growing out of the night or the character of the road, will you please state them?" He answered:

There was no difficulty in marching, so far as the night was concerned. I have several times made marches with a larger force than General Porter had, during the night. There was some obstruction on the road, in a wagon train that was stretched along the road, marching toward the Manassas Junction, in rear of Hooker's division, not sufficient, in my judgment, to have delayed for any considerable length of time the passage of artillery. But even had the roads been entirely blocked up, the railroad track was clear, and along that track had passed the larger portion of General Hooker's infantry. There was no obstruction to the advance of infantry.

There were a very few breaks in the road, but its general condition is shown to have been good. General Pope made the following statement on this point:

> Along the road between Warrenton Junction to Kettle Run, which is perhaps 3 miles west from Bristoe Station, the track had been torn up in places; but during the day of the 27th of August, I directed Captain Merrill, of the Engineers, with a considerable force, to repair the track up to the bridge over Kettle Run, which had been burned. He reported to me on the night of the 27th that he had done so; so that from Warrenton Junction to the bridge over Kettle Run there was no obstruction on the railroad of any description. The bridge of Kettle Run had been burned, but a hundred yards above the bridge the road crossed the creek by a ford; and from there toward Bristoe Station, the most of the country, in fact, nearly the whole of it, was open country; that is, as I remember the country, riding along on the afternoon of the 27th of August.

General Roberts, who passed from Warrenton Junction to Bristoe Station on the 27th, says: "The condition of the road was good generally;" and in another part of his testimony General Pope used this language: "The road was in good condition everywhere. At most places it was a double road on each side of the railroad track. I am not sure it was a double road all the way; a part of the way I know it was." Captain DeKay states that "the road was good;" and Lt. Brooks, who was well acquainted with it, that it was "very good." Lieutenant-Colonel Myers was asked: "Question. What was the condition of the road between Warrenton Junction and Bristoe Station at that time (27th), so far as regards the passage of wagons, artillery, &c.?

Answer. It was in excellent condition at that time."

The chief obstructions upon the road, however, and those most elaborately presented by the evidence and argument of the accused, were wagon trains. Captain DeKay thinks that, had the march begun at 1 o'clock, the greater part of these wagons would probably have been in camp, and would thus have been avoided. A part of them are shown to have been on the road throughout the night, and between 2 and 3 o'clock. Colonel Clary found them so jammed as to constitute a serious obstruction for some 3 miles. But even here the railway track was alongside of the road, and could easily have been used by the infantry. For the first 3 miles from Warrenton Junction, it was in proof that the road was wholly unobstructed.

Captain Fifield, a witness of the accused, deposed that with 100 men he could have prevented the jam of the wagons, and that with 150 he could have kept the road entirely clear. Why did not the accused detail this force, and at once remove the obstacles which are now relied on to excuse him for his alleged disobedience of orders? The testimony leaves no doubt but that he could have done so, and that every wagon might thus have been taken out of the way of his troops by 1 o'clock. The subject does not appear to have been discussed, or even thought of. It is true that at 12 o'clock on the night of the 27th, Lieutenant Colonel Brinton came from Catletts Station to Warrenton Junction, and on having an interview with the accused, he spoke to him of the wagons on the road; whereupon accused directed him on his return to have the road cleared. On his arrival at Catletts Station, he told the adjutant "to send out some men to get these wagons out of the way." He does not know that the direction he gave was complied with. This was at 1 o'clock, the hour at which the troops should have been in motion. All the circumstances surrounding this direction on the part of the accused leave the impression that he could not have anticipated from it the removal of the obstacles in his way. It was accidental, and was without vigor or precision, and given at an hour that showed the subject had not been with him one of any solicitude. It is observable, also, that even this feeble and inefficient provision looked to clearing the road, not for a march at 1 o'clock (for all thought of that had been abandoned), but at daylight, or at earliest, at 3 o'clock.

On the consultation which took place between the accused and his generals, when the order was received, the opinion was expressed by the latter (and it has been repeated in their testimony) that nothing would be gained in the way of time by starting at 1 o'clock instead of a later hour—say 3 or 4. As starting at 3 would require a night march of one hour, and starting at 1 a night march of three hours, this opinion imports a declaration that the troops could march no farther in three hours than they could in one hour, the darkness for the whole period of time being the same. If the opinion referred to a starting at daylight, then it carries with it the assumption that during the three hours, from 1 to 4 o'clock, the troops would have been unable to make any progress whatever, and this, notwithstanding the first 3 miles of the road from their encampment is shown to have been entirely unobstructed. Surely these opinions have not been well considered.

There are certain other facts disclosed in the testimony <u>which go far to indicate a settled purpose on the part of the accused to disregard this order</u> of his commanding general. It was couched in terms as strong as a military man could employ in addressing a subordinate; and yet its urgent language was not commented upon, and does not seem to have attracted any attention, as appears from the conversation that ensued between the accused and his generals after its receipt. The accused, as we learn from Captain DeKay, handed it to one of his generals present, saying—"There is something for you to sleep on"—Not something that you are to prepare to execute—not something which announces that the army with which we are connected is threatened by great perils, which we must make extraordinary efforts to meet, but "something for you to sleep on." The whole tone of that conversation was to the last degree saddening and discouraging for those who believe that in the prosecution of the war much vigor is much wisdom.

Again, General Griffin, called by the accused, testified that, after having marched about a mile with his brigade, he came to a halt, and remained there until two hours after daylight, and the remainder of the forces, no doubt, did the same. This explains why the arrival at Bristoe Station was not until twenty minutes past 10. No reason that deserves a moment's consideration is given for this long delay. It is true that General Griffin says: "I know the artillery which followed the brigade—that is, a carriage or two of the artillery which followed the brigade—got stuck in the mud, or in a little creek, and had trouble getting out." When more closely questioned as to the cause of the halt, he said: "I halted because I found, when I got to the point where I did halt, that I had only a portion of my brigade with me. In the darkness, by some accident or other, we had become separated, and I halted to get my brigade together. And the artillery, I presume, is what detained us there until we started again. That is my impression. I do not know that positively. General Morell was in command of the division."

This may explain the halt, but not the delay until the late hour mentioned. It was in summer and a season of drought, as appears from the clouds of dust which are continually brought to our notice by the testimony; and we cannot be misled as to the amount of obstacle the mud in such a stream, at such a season, would offer to the onward march of soldiers determined to do their duty.

Again. When the forces were in motion, there was no haste or vigor displayed. Captain DeKay says: "The march was at the rate at which troops would move if there was no necessity for a rapid movement." And he adds: "They could have moved faster than they did."

General Pope deposed: "I sent back several officers to try and see General Porter, and request him to hurry up and report to me where his troops were, as I was very apprehensive that after day had dawned we should have an attack upon us from the enemy. I think they all returned. The report made to me was, that General Porter was coming along very slowly, and was pushing the wagons out of the road."

Whatever may be thought of the difficulties in the way of the night march required by this order, it was the manifest duty of the accused to make a sincere and determined endeavor to overcome them. If, after having promptly and vigorously made this effort, and started as ordered, he had failed to arrive at Bristoe Station at daylight, either from the exhaustion of his troops, the darkness of the night, or the character of the road, the responsibility of the failure would not have been charged upon him. The contemptuous and unfriendly feelings disclosed in the dispatch to General Burnside—which was written about five hours and a half before this order was received—will probably furnish a more satisfactory solution of the question why this effort was not made than can be found in the nature of the obstacles themselves.

Nor is it believed that the conduct of the accused finds any shelter in the Napoleonic maxim quoted in the argument for the defense. The discretion it allows to a subordinate, separated from superior officer, is understood to relate to the means, and not the end, of an order. When the accused determined that, instead of starting at 1 o'clock, he would start at 3 or 4, he did not resolve that he would arrive at Bristoe Station by daylight, in a different manner from that indicated by his commanding general, but that he would not arrive there by daylight at all. In regard to this—the end of the order—he had no discretion.

The order set forth in the second specification to first charge was addressed to Generals McDowell and Porter, jointly, and a copy, or, rather, duplicate, of it was delivered to each of them, it may be inferred from all the evidence on the point, at about 10 o'clock in the morning of the 29th of August. Previously to this they had met with their forces, and, under the Sixty-second Article of War, General McDowell had assumed the command. The order directed them to move with their joint command toward Gainesville until they should effect a communication with the forces of Heintzelman, Sigel, and Reno, and then to halt, taking care to occupy such a position that they could reach Bull Run that night or by the morning of the following day. The order contained these further words: "If any considerable advantages are to be gained by departing from this order, it will not be strictly carried out."

At the time this order reached Generals McDowell and Porter, they were on the road between Manassas Junction and Bethlehem church, and were proceeding in the direction of Gainesville, as the order contemplated. The order being issued to them jointly, showed that it was the purpose of General Pope that they should act independently of each other, and each in direct subordination to himself; and he testified that such was his intention. Under these circumstances, it may be well questioned whether, under the Sixty-second Article of War, General McDowell could continue the command which he had assumed over their joint forces. That article excludes the idea of the presence of an officer superior in rank to those commanding the different corps of which it speaks. In this case, General Pope was absent but a few miles—was, in fact, occupying the same field of military operations with Generals McDowell and Porter, and claimed to decide the question (which it certainly belonged to him to determine) that these generals were so far in his presence that he might command them directly, and not through each other.

Their forces continued their march—those of the accused being in the advance—until the front of his column had reached some 3 miles beyond Bethlehem church, and until a small part of General McDowell's command had passed that point. General McDowell then rode forward to the head of the column of the accused, where an interview and conference took place between them, to which reference is frequently made in the testimony. They discussed the joint order, and General McDowell determined, for himself, that there were—"considerable advantages to be gained by departing from it," and by moving his forces along the Sudley Springs road toward the field of a battle then being fought by the main army of General Pope, at the distance of 3 or 4 miles. His purpose was to throw himself on the enemy's center, and he wished the accused to attack his right flank. He therefore said to him: "You put your force in here, and I will take mine up the Sudley Springs road, on the left of the troops engaged at that point with the enemy."

And he left him, at about 12 o'clock, with the belief and understanding that he would put in his force at that point. Why this expectation was doomed to disappointment may possibly be gathered from the following extract from General McDowell's testimony as to what occurred during his conversation with the accused:

> QUESTION: You have said that the accused made an observation to you which showed that he was satisfied that the enemy was in his immediate front; will you state what that observation was?
> ANSWER: I do not know that I can repeat it exactly, and I do not know that the accused meant exactly what the remark might seem to imply. The observation was to this effect [putting his hand in the direction of the dust rising above the tops of the trees], "We cannot go in there anywhere without getting into a fight."
> QUESTION: What reply did you make to that remark?
> ANSWER: I think to this effect: "That is what we came here for."

These words will certainly stand in memorable contrast with the sad utterance to which they were a reply.

General McDowell, on parting with the accused, ceased to exercise any authority over his command, and he was thus left untrammeled, and in possession of the joint order, still in full force. Soon after General Griffin's brigade—a part of the corps of the accused—was ordered to move to the right, as if for the purpose of advancing on the enemy, as directed by General McDowell. It had proceeded, however, only about 600 yards, when, coming into "some small pine bushes," and somebody saying there were obstacles ahead, a retreat was ordered, and they fell back to their original position. General Griffin saw no obstacles himself, and he made no reconnaissance. This was all that was done toward carrying into effect the stirring and soldierly direction of General McDowell.

Some time after this faint demonstration—it may have been an hour or more, General McDowell having left at about 12—a rebel battery threw three or four shot at the head of the accused's column. It was at once replied to and silenced, and then came the order to fall back, of which Colonel

B. F. Smith, who witnessed the artillery firing, speaks so distinctly. The note of the accused to Generals McDowell and King, which was read in evidence and is without date, must have been written immediately after this artillery firing, and after the order to retreat which followed it. It is in the following words:

Generals McDowell and King:

I found it impossible to communicate by crossing the roads to Groveton. The enemy are in strong force on this road, and, as they appear to have driven our forces back, the firing of the enemy having advanced and ours retired, I have determined to withdraw to Manassas. I have attempted to communicate with McDowell and Sigel, but my messengers have run into the enemy. They have gathered artillery and cavalry and infantry, and the advancing masses of dust show the enemy coming in force. I am now going to the head of the column, to see what is passing and how affairs are going. Had you not better send your train back? I will communicate with you.

F. J. Porter
Major-General

This note appears to have been written for the purpose of explaining why the accused had not "put his force in" at the place which General McDowell had pointed out. It announces most energetically a determination "to withdraw"—i.e., retreat—to Manassas, because of the approach of the enemy, and because the battle seemed to be going against the Federal forces. That this purpose was promptly carried out, substantially, if not to the letter, is made evident from the fact that, at between 5 and 6 o'clock, the accused was found at or near Bethlehem church, surrounded by his troops, whose arms were stacked. It is further proved by Col. B. F. Smith, who was in the front at the time of the artillery firing, and alleges that he and the troops of his command then fell back, under orders, to within a mile or two of Manassas, where they passed the night, having arrived there in the afternoon. It is yet further shown by General Griffin, examined by the accused, who says his brigade retreated from a mile and a half to two miles. This retrograde movement might have been excused had it been made in good faith for the purpose of reaching Bull Run that night; but no such purpose was entertained, nor has it been insisted that it was, either by the testimony or the argument. General McDowell says the accused might have attacked the enemy and would have still had ample time for falling back on Bull Run. Indeed, as appears from the map, such an attack would have been an advance in the direction of Bull Run. He might have found justification, too, for this step, had it been taken from a conviction that, in the sense of the order, "considerable advantages" were to be gained by departing from its terms. No such position, however, could be successfully taken in the defense. The only "advantages" which the retreat promised were the personal safety of the accused and staff, and the exemption of his troops from any participation in the sanguinary battle then being fought immediately to his right. Surely such advantages as these, purchased, as they were, at the imminent hazard of the sacrifice of the whole army, were not those contemplated by the order. The advance of the accused, either along the Gainesville road or to the right, would have brought him into conflict with the enemy. The court concluded, and justly, that his falling back, under the circumstances and for the purpose mentioned in his note to Generals McDowell and King, was a violation of the joint order to himself and General McDowell.

It would seem, also, to have been a manifest violation of the duty resting on him as a soldier, in the position in which he was placed, without reference to any specific order or direction leading or directing him to engage the enemy. In forward, aggressive movements, it is an established principle of military science that the column shall be so held in their advance as to be ready to afford mutual assistance in time of need. Another elementary principle of such movements is, that in the absence of positive, restraining orders, the march shall always be toward the sound of the guns, thus confirming the sentiment of the words of General McDowell, that it is the soldier's mission to fight. Both these fundamental rules of the military profession were disregarded in the retreat of the accused. He fell back precisely at the moment that obligation to co-operate which was pressing upon him required him to advance, and his march was not toward, but from, the sound of the enemy's cannon.

The order of 4.30 P.M., August 29, directed the accused "to push forward into action at once on the enemy's right flank, and, if possible, on his rear." It was not obeyed, nor was any attempt made to obey it.

It was claimed in the defense that the accused should not be condemned for disobedience; first, because the order was received too late to be obeyed, and, secondly, because obedience to it was impracticable in consequence of the presence of the enemy in overwhelming force, and in consequence of the character of the country over which the movement would have had to be made.

There is a decided conflict in the testimony as to the hour at which the order was received. It bears date 4.30 P.M., and Captain Pope, the staff officer who bore it, says that he proceeded direct from General Pope to the accused, and delivered it—"as early as 5 o'clock, or probably three or four minutes after 5."

Charles Duffee, the orderly who accompanied him, testifies that they left General Pope at about half-past 4, and went on to the headquarters of the accused at a pace—"about as fast as they thought their horses could travel." He thinks about an hour was occupied on the road, and that the order reached the accused at about half-past 5. These statements are corroborated by the evidence of General McDowell as to the time and place at which he met them and read the order. General Pope says: "I know that an aide-de-camp, riding rapidly, could go from the field of battle to Manassas Junction, or to any point west of Manassas Junction, on the Gainesville road, if he found General Porter in advance of Manassas Junction, within an hour, by going at speed." General Roberts, who was present when the order was issued, expressed the opinion that it should have been delivered— "in half an hour, or less, as orders are generally carried on such occasions."

Adopting the latest estimate—that of General Pope and the orderly— this would give the accused two hours of daylight within which to make the attack.

On the other hand, there are five witnesses introduced by the accused, three of them being his staff officers, viz: General Sykes, Lieutenant-Colonel Locke, Captain Monteith, Lieutenant Weld, and Lieutenant Ingham, who depose that the order was not received until about sundown.ONE OF THEM, INDEED, THOUGH HE IS NOT SUPPORTED BY THE OTHERS, FIXES THE HOUR MUCH LATER. If, in ascertaining the value of testimony, witnesses were counted, and not weighed, the question would be at once settled by the relative numbers as given. Such, however, is not the rule of law, and it may be that, after carefully considering all the circumstances, the court felt that the explicit and intelligent statements of Captain Pope and his orderly, fortified by the corroborative evidence of Generals Pope, McDowell, and Roberts, were not overcome by the opinions of the five officers named. There was, outside of the positive testimony, a consideration strongly supporting this view, and it is this: THERE IS NO QUESTION AS TO THE TIME AT WHICH CAPTAIN POPE LEFT WITH THE ORDER; it was at 4½ o'clock; he rode as fast as his horse could carry him, and had but about 5 miles to travel; and yet, according to the theory of the defense—that he did not arrive until sunset, or half-past six—he was two hours on the way. Is it credible that a staff officer, bearing an important order, in the midst of a fiercely contested battle, would have traveled at this rate, and this, too, when he was conducted by an orderly acquainted with the road, and encountered no obstacle to his progress? Is it not much more probable that but a single hour was occupied, and that, in point of fact, he arrived at half-past 5?

CONCEDING, however, for the sake of argument, the position taken by the defense, THAT THE ORDER WAS NOT RECEIVED UNTIL SUNSET, THIS WOULD HAVE LEFT THE ACCUSED AN HOUR OF DAYLIGHT WITHIN WHICH TO MAKE THE MOVEMENT. The enemy had been so far encouraged in their advance by the inaction of the forces of the accused, and by their falling back, that at this late moment the front of his column was not separated from the advance of the rebels by more than a mile or a mile and a half. But little time, therefore, was required to make the attack. It is admitted that it was not made, but was there any earnest or vigorous effort on the part of the accused to obey the order? Colonel Locke states that, soon after the receipt of the order from General Pope, he bore one from the accused to General Morell, directing him to engage the enemy, which, as appears from statement of Colonel Marshall, was to be done with but four regiments; but General Morell testified that before there was time to carry this order into execution—say, within about half an hour after its receipt—it was countermanded by another, directing him to pass the night with his troops where he was. This was all that was done toward attacking the enemy, and yet General McDowell testified that an attack even at this late hour—indeed, at any hour before the battle closed, which was at dark—would have resulted in a victory for our arms.

There is one fact—probably the most remarkable one disclosed by the record—which must have impressed the court as going far to manifest the true spirit of the conduct of the accused on this occasion. The forces of General Morell were in the front, and those of General Sykes were immediately in their rear, and supporting them. In the progress of any determined movement against the enemy, therefore, the command of General Sykes would be necessarily involved, and the presence of that general would be required; yet General Sykes states that he was with General Porter when the order from General Pope was received and when that to General Morell was sent; that he remained with him all the evening and night; and that he never heard that an order to attack the enemy had been received from General Pope, or had been forwarded to General Morell.*

(*The troops of General Sykes extended along the road from those of General Morell toward, and maybe, to where General Porter was. It is not, therefore, intended to intimate that, in being with General Porter at the moment, he was out of place, but to say that had it been General Porter's purpose that his order to General Morell to engage the enemy should be vigorously carried out, he would, from General Sykes' necessary relation to the movement, have advised him of it, and have directed him to go forward and prepare for performing his part in its execution.) What conclusion is necessarily drawn from this? If the accused had seriously determined that the order to General Morell should be executed, would he not have apprised General Sykes of its character, and directed him to proceed at once to his command? When we add to this the feebleness of the attack directed—being but with four regiments—and the further fact that the order was revoked before it was possible to make the movement, can we escape a painful impression that the order itself was issued without any expectation that it would, or any purpose that it should, be obeyed?

There is yet one other fact presented in connection with this order which deserves a passing notice. Captain Pope found the accused with his troops halted, and the arms of some of them stacked. After delivering the order, and during his stay of fifteen or twenty minutes, he did—"not observe any orders given, or any indication of preparation for a movement in the direction of the battle-field."

On his return, nearly an hour afterward, the same condition of things existed. The following extract from the testimony of Mr. Duffee, who accompanied Captain Pope, will yet further illustrate the absence of all anxiety, if not of all interest on the part of the accused:

> QUESTION: Did you see the order delivered into the hands of General Porter?
> ANSWER: Yes, sir; I saw him take the order from Captain Pope.
> QUESTION: Was he in his tent or out of doors?
> ANSWER: He was lying down under a shade tree when he took the order.
> QUESTION: Did he change his position on reading the order, or did he continue to lie down?
> ANSWER: I cannot state positively whether he rose to his feet or not; but at the time he was reading the order, I noticed that he was lying in this position on the ground [describing him as resting on his elbow, his head upon his hand].
> QUESTION: Did you leave him lying down on the ground when you came away?
> Answer: Yes, sir.

The accused had, for between five and six hours, been listening to the sounds of the battle raging immediately to his right. Its dust and smoke were before his eyes, and the reverberation of its artillery was in his ears. He must have known the exhaustion and carnage consequent upon this prolonged conflict, and he had reason to believe, as shown by his note to Generals McDowell and King, that our army was giving way before the heavy re-enforcements of the enemy. He had a command of some <u>13,000 fresh and well-appointed troops</u>, who had marched but a few miles, and had not fought at all on that day. Under these circumstances, should not an order to charge the enemy have electrified him as a soldier, and have brought him not only to his feet and to his saddle, but have awakened the sounds of eager preparation throughout his camp? But the bugle-note of this order seems to have fallen unheeded, and after reading it, and at the close of an interview of from 15 to 20 minutes, the messenger who bore it turned away leaving the accused still—"lying on the ground."

There is some contrariety in the evidence as to the force of the enemy by which the accused was opposed. The weight of the testimony is that it was small, decidedly so in the early part of the afternoon, when the attack directed by General McDowell should have been made. General Roberts thinks there was only a cavalry force, with some light artillery. Col. B. F. Smith, who was at the head of the column at the time the rebel battery was silenced, and who fell back with his command half an hour afterward, noticed clouds of dust beyond the trees, but whether there were troops advancing or moving in another direction, he could not tell. He saw nothing to induce him to believe that they were retreating before the enemy, but supposed that they had been making a reconnaissance in force, and having completed it, were falling back for some other duty. General Griffin, a witness for the accused, who was also at the front, and enjoyed every opportunity of observation, having been asked as to the position of the enemy in relation to General Porter's corps between 5 and 7 o'clock of the 29th, replied: "It is a hard question to answer. I do not know much about the enemy; I only know that during the day large clouds of dust were going to our front and to our left from a point stated to us then to be Thoroughfare Gap. The batteries which opened upon us at 1 o'clock were within 1,200 or 1,500 yards of us. We saw no force at all; we saw scattering groups of horsemen, or of infantry. I do not believe we saw in any one group over 40 men."

Major Hyland, who belonged to Colonel Marshall's regiment of skirmishers, and was some 800 or 1,000 yards in advance of General Morell, says the enemy began to form in his front and to the right between 2 and 3 o'clock. He saw none to the left. Thinks the force was very large, and although unable to give even a proximate estimate of their numbers, believes they were strong enough to have resisted an attack of General Porter's corps. Second Lieutenant Stevenson supposed the enemy's forces to consist of from 12,000 to 15,000; but he was a young man, with limited experience, and when he stated that the enemy's line of battle was but a mile long, it was sufficiently evident that a large abatement was to be made from his estimate. Colonel Marshall set the enemy's troops down at twice the number of the corps of the accused. It is obvious, however, that he was largely influenced in forming this opinion from the clouds of dust, which may have arisen as much from the movement of ambulances and wagons as from the march of troops. He states that they came from toward Thoroughfare Gap, and separated into two columns, one of which proceeded in the direction of the battlefield at Groveton, and the other came down on the Gainesville and Manassas road. Now, we learn from General Buford that the enemy's forces passing through Gainesville that day from Thoroughfare Gap, and counted by himself, did not exceed 14,000 men, and dividing these into two columns, it is believed that at no time on the 29th could the accused have been confronted by a rebel force exceeding 7,000, a little more than half the strength of his own corps. The strong probability is, that the force was not so large; but supposing the enemy to have had quite as large a force as his own, was that a reason why he should not make the attack, seeing that a severely contested battle was then pending?

The course of the inquiry on the part of the defense would seem to imply an impression that the accused could not attack the right flank because he found an enemy in his front, and could not attack the front because the order was to engage the right. A dead-lock, however, in military movements could scarcely be suffered to be produced by such a process as this. General McDowell solves this question by saying that if the enemy's forces were posted in the front of the accused in the manner indicated by the witnesses, they must have constituted his right flank, so that a movement in that direction would have been a literal compliance with the order.

A conclusive reply to the suggestion that the ground between the enemy and the accused was impracticable for military movements, is found in the testimony of Lieutenant-Colonel Smith. He says: "I infer that the corps of the accused could have moved up, its right wing joining with the forces engaged, and have flanked the enemy. This is not all an inference merely from the general character of the country. It is based, also, on the fact that a portion of the country over which, as I understand it, the corps of the accused would have moved upon the enemy, was sufficiently practicable to enable the enemy, as they did, to make a similar movement on our left on the next day."

Some of the witnesses of the accused declared that artillery could not have passed over this ground, while others testified that infantry could not have been marched through the woods in any order. Under a cross-examination, however, the obstacles on which these opinions were based were much reduced in the attempt to enumerate them. The general description of the country given is that it is open, with fields and woods and occasional ravines, but not remarkable for its ruggedness. There were no impassable streams, or morasses, or precipices. General McDowell deposed that he did not consider that there were any insuperable obstacles—"in the way of the advance on the part of General Porter's command upon the flank of the enemy."

And he proved the sincerity of this opinion by directing him to make the movement. After reciting in detail certain facts leading to this belief, he thus concludes: "These movements by these two divisions of my corps, my own movements, and the movements of the enemy, give me the belief that troops could move through the country comprised between the Warrenton turnpike and the Sudley Springs road and the road from Bethlehem church to Gainesville. I will mention, further, that that country is a mixture of woods, cleared ground, and hills, and that it is easy for troops to march without being seen or seeing the enemy."

A glance at the map which accompanies the record will show that the ground in question is embraced by this boundary and description.

It may be admitted—and perhaps the testimony requires the admission to be made—that in falling upon the enemy on the afternoon of the 29th, the accused would have encountered both difficulty and danger; but difficulty and danger, in time of war, are daily and hourly in the category of the soldier's life. Their presence should be for him not a discouragement, but an inspiration. To grapple with them should be his ambition; to overcome them, his glory.

That a vigorous attack upon the enemy by the accused, at any time between 12 o'clock, when the battle began, and dark, when it closed, would have secured a triumph for our arms, and not only the overthrow of the rebel forces, but probably the destruction or capture of Jackson's army, the record fully justifies us in maintaining. This opinion, in effect, is emphatically expressed by Generals Pope, McDowell, and Roberts, and by Lieutenant-Colonel Smith, all of whom participated in the engagement, and were well qualified to judge. General Roberts, who was on the field throughout the day, says: "I do not doubt at all that it would have resulted in the defeat, it not in the capture, of the main army of the Confederates that were in the field at that time." To the same effect is the following explicit language of General Pope: "Late in the afternoon of the 29th—perhaps toward half-past 5 or 6 o'clock—about the time that I hoped General Porter would be in his position and assaulting the enemy on the flank, and when General McDowell had himself arrived with his corps on the field of battle, I directed an attack to be made on the left of the enemy lines, which was handsomely done by Heintzelman's and Reno's corps. The enemy was driven back in all directions, and left a large part of the ground, with his dead and wounded upon it, in our possession. Had General Porter fallen upon the flank of the enemy, as it was hoped, at any time up to 8 o'clock that night, it is my firm conviction that we should have destroyed the army of Jackson."

Even had the attack itself failed, General McDowell states that the number of troops which would have been withdrawn from the main battle by the enemy to effect this result would have so far relieved our center as to render our victory complete. When we recall the calamities already suffered by our country, and contemplate the untold grief to the homes and hearts of its people which may yet follow from the escape of that army on that day, we can appreciate with some approach to accuracy the responsibilities incurred by a line of conduct which so certainly and so fatally led to that disaster.

The first, second, and third specifications of the second charge arraign the conduct of the accused on the 29th, under the Fifty-second Articles of War, as "misbehavior before the enemy." If a soldier disobeys the order of his superior officer before the enemy, he commits a double crime, by violating both the Ninth and Fifty-second Articles of War, and he may be prosecuted and convicted of either or both offenses. So any other breach of duty, connected with military movements and occurring in the presence of the enemy, has assigned to it by the Articles of War a depth of criminality which would not belong to it under other and ordinary circumstances. This results from the increased disaster likely to follow from misconduct in such a conjuncture, and from the fact that insensibility to duty is doubly criminal when displayed in the midst of those dangers which ever inspire the true soldier with renewed devotion to the honor and interests of the flag. The accused is shown to have been, with his command, in the presence of the enemy from the beginning to the end of the battle of the 29th—a period of at least seven and a half or eight hours. His troops were fresh and well equipped; and that from his position he was bound to have taken part in the engagement, and that his failure to do so was to the last degree culpable, cannot be denied, unless it can be made to appear that he was restrained by some uncontrollable physical necessity or by some positive order of his commanding general. The attempt has been made to justify his conduct on both grounds. The examination already made of the testimony warrants the conviction that the material obstacles in his way, growing out of the proximity and strength of the enemy and the nature of the country, were not sufficient to excuse his inaction. His chief of staff, however, Lieutenant-Colonel Locke, called by the defense, deposed that in the afternoon of the 29th he bore a message from the accused to General King, whom he found near Bethlehem church with General McDowell; that General McDowell sent back by him to the accused a reply in the following words: "Give my compliments to General Porter, and say to him that I am going to the right, and will take General King with me. I think he (General Porter) had better remain where he is; but, if it is necessary for him to fall back, he can do so upon my left." And the witness testified that he regarded this as an order, and communicated it to the accused, and this, it is insisted, restrained him from attacking the enemy.

In the first place, it is to be remarked that this language does not import an order, but simply a suggestion and counsel from one companion in arms to another. Again, General McDowell was not then in a condition to command the accused, and this both he and the accused must have well known. They were separated from each other, and were not, in the terms of the Sixty-second Article of War, "joined or doing duty together." General McDowell was proceeding at the moment, with his forces, upon an entirely distinct service from that in which the accused was engaged. But the whole of Lieutenant-Colonel Locke's statement in regard to this message was swept away by the evidence of Generals McDowell and King. The witness had stated that the message was given to him in the presence of General King, and was heard by him. General King, however, testified that he was not with General McDowell at all after the morning of the 29th, and that he heard no such message; while General McDowell declared that none such was sent by him. It is further urged in the defense that, although the evidence may thus fail to show that such a message was sent, yet that it was delivered to the accused and he was justified in obeying it. This position is assumed in disregard of the maxim "falsus in uno, falsus in omnibus." The same witness who deposed to the receipt of the message from General McDowell deposed to its delivery to the accused, and in neither point was he supported by the testimony of others. Having been discredited as laboring under a complete misapprehension in regard to the first, this discredit necessarily attaches to the second, and, under the maxim quoted, his entire statement falls to the ground. But even if it had been established, that this message had been sent and received, and that it was in form an order, and given by proper authority, still it is not claimed that it reached the accused before about 3 o'clock. This would leave his inaction, from 12 to 3 o'clock, in the presence of the enemy, and in the midst of a battle, unexplained, and therefore unpalliated in its culpability by anything that is contained in the record.

Although that portion of the defense which would justify the inaction of the accused, because of the enemy and of the difficult nature of the ground in his front and to his right, has been commented on, <u>it may not be inappropriate to add that history shows these obstacles to be insignificant as contrasted with those which have been often in great emergencies overcome by military commanders</u>. The battle of Hohenlinden furnishes an illustration, and in one respect bears a striking analogy, while in another offering a remarkable contrast to the events of the 29th August. A few extracts from Thiers' history of the Consulate and the Empire, vol. 1, pp. 217, 218, 219, Lippincott & Co.'s edition of 1861, will suffice to show the appositeness of the reference.

Moreau, with 60,000 French troops, was met by an Austrian army 70,000 strong. "Richepanse and Decaen's divisions," says the historian,

> were sent by Moreau an order, somewhat vaguely expressed, but positive, to throw themselves from the right-hand to the left-hand road, to get into the latter, into the environs of Maltenboet, and there surprise the Austrian army, entangled in the forest. He neither indicated the route to be pursued nor provided against accidents which might occur. He left everything that was to be done to the intelligence of Richepanse.... At length, as the battle progressed, a wavering was observed in the Austrian troops of the center, which proved to be Richepanse falling on their rear.... He had started without waiting for Decaen, and daringly penetrated into that tract of thickets and ravines, which separated the two roads, and marching while the fight was going on at Hohenlinden, and making incredible efforts to drag with him over that inundated ground six pieces of small caliber.
>
> Richepanse, reckoning upon Decaen to extricate Dronet's brigade, had marched without losing a moment for Maltenboet, for his military instinct told him that was the decisive point. Though he had left but two demi-brigades of infantry (the Eight and Forty-eighth), a single regiment of cavalry (the First Chasseurs), and six pieces of cannon, with about 6,000 men, he had continued his march, dragging his artillery by hand, almost always through the quagmire.... He then fell to the left, and took the bold resolution of falling on the Austrian rear in the defile of the forest.
>
> Marching, sword in hand, amidst his grenadiers, he penetrated into the forest, sustained, without flinching, a violent discharge of grapeshot, then fell in

with two Hungarian battalions, which hastened to bar up his passage. Richepanse would have inspirited his brave soldiers with words and gestures, but they had no need of them. 'Those fellows are our prisoners,' cried they, 'let us charge!' They charged accordingly, and completely routed the Hungarian battalions. Presently they came to masses of baggage, artillery, infantry, accumulated pell-mell at this spot. Richepanse struck inexpressible terror into this multitude, and threw it into frightful disorder. At the same moment he heard confused shouts at the other extremity of the defile. It was Ney, who, advancing from Hohenlinden, had penetrated by the head of the defile, and pushed before him the Austrian column which Richepanse was driving the other way by attacking it in the rear.

A complete rout of the Austrian army ensued. Its loss was some 20,000 men, with nearly all its artillery and baggage, and "what," as the historian observes, "was of still greater importance, its moral courage." "This battle," continues M. Thiers, "is the most brilliant that Moreau ever fought, and certainly <u>one of the greatest in the present century, which has beheld such extraordinary conflicts.</u>"

What were the difficulties that appalled the accused on the 29th as compared with those surmounted by Richepanse with but 6,000 men? <u>This example is an impressive proof of what a general can and will achieve when his heart is in his work</u>, and when he finds himself in the presence of the enemies of his country. General McDowell, as a soldier and a commander, deposed that it was the duty of the accused to have attacked the enemy on the 29th, and it would seem this duty was so manifest and so clearly the result of his position that no order could have added much, if anything, to its force and urgency. What General McDowell prescribed for his associate in arms he unhesitatingly accepted for himself. He had no summons to arouse him, and no guide to conduct him but the sound of the cannon, following which, he with his command, found his way to the battle-field, where his instincts as a soldier told him both his duty and his honor required him to be. And it is, no doubt, to this timely arrival and active participation in the conflict that we are largely indebted for General Roberts' declaration that at the close of the day, the advantages were decidedly on the side of the Federal troops. Had the accused, obeying the same impulse that carried General McDowell up the Sudley Springs road, made a movement upon the enemy with the vigor and heroism which the occasion demanded, it is altogether probable that the glory of Richepanse would have been his, and the fate of the Austrians that of the rebel army. After carefully considering all the impediments which have been so elaborately arrayed as in the way of the accused on the night of the 27th, and throughout the day of the 29th, <u>we cannot but realize that they shrink away and are scarcely to be named beside those obstacles of darkness, and tempest, and snow, and morass, and Alpine precipices, and frowning batteries which the warriors</u>

of other times and lands have unhesitatingly confronted and bravely overcome.

But there is one feature of the inaction of the accused on the 29th which
it is especially sorrowful to contemplate. How, unrestrained as he was, and
with the cannonade of the battle in his ears, and its smoke and the dust of
the gathering before his eyes, he could, for seven and a half or eight hours,
resist the temptation to plunge into the combat, it is difficult to conceive.
But this alone is not the saddest aspect in which his conduct presents itself.
This aspect is distinctly set forth in the third specification of the second
charge. Colonel Marshall states that from the cheerings and peculiar yells
of the enemy heard on the evening of the 29th, he and every man of his command believed that General Pope's army was being driven from the field.
General Morell also says that from the sound of the artillery the battle
seemed to be receding, which indicated that it was going against the Federal forces. The accused, in his note to Generals McDowell and King, speaking of the enemy, says: "As they appear to have driven our forces back, the
firing of the enemy having advanced and ours retired, I have determined to
withdraw to Manassas"; and, in further justification of this step, he adds:
"They have gathered artillery and cavalry and infantry, and the advancing
masses of dust show the enemy coming in force."

In the afternoon, then, of the 29th, it is clear that the conviction was
entertained by the accused and his officers that our forces were being driven
before the enemy—a conviction which, in tones above even the roar of the
artillery, should have appealed to his soldier's heart to rush to the rescue.
But, heedless of the summons, he turned, not toward, but away from his
struggling companions in arms, in the direction of Manassas.

Must we seek an explanation of this want of sympathy with the brave
men who were doing battle that day in the feelings, as shown by his dispatches, which unhappily possessed him in reference to the Army of Virginia and its commanding general? That army, as he seems to have been
aware, was sent forth not to capture Richmond or to occupy the South, but
simply to harass and baffle the march of the advancing masses of the enemy,
while the Army of the Potomac was being extricated from the perils that
surrounded it on the Peninsula—a service which should not have provoked
a sneer from the accused. It cannot be improper to add, what the record
will sustain me in saying, that so far as light is shed upon the subject by the
testimony, the Army of Virginia appears to have nobly performed the ardu-
ous and perilous work committed to its hands. Its campaign was brief, but
marked by signal vigor and ability, and animated by a spirit which, shrink-
ing from neither toil nor exposure nor danger, bravely struck the enemy
whenever and wherever he could be found.

The accused presents two general grounds of defense, which apply to
all the accusations against him. They are, first, his general reputation for

zeal and loyalty; and, secondly, the expression of satisfaction with his conduct which General Pope is alleged to have made at Fairfax Court-House on the 2d of September.

In reference to the first, the testimony is full and earnest as to his former services and character for faithfulness and efficiency as an officer. The law admits such proof in criminal prosecutions, because a presumption of innocence arises from former good conduct, as evidenced by general reputation. The presumption, however, is held to be entitled to little weight except in doubtful cases. Where it comes into conflict with evidence that is both positive and reliable, it at once gives way.

In regard to the second, Colonel Ruggles testified that at the close of a conversation on the 2d September, at Fairfax Court-House, between General Pope and the accused, the general expressed himself satisfied with his conduct, referring, as the witness believed, to the transactions on which the present charges are based. Colonel Ruggles admits, however, that he was not a party to the conversation; that he heard it only in scraps, and endeavored not to hear it at all. General Pope, on the other hand, deposed that he was not satisfied, and could not have been, and that the expression heard by Colonel Ruggles related to explanations made by the accused as to certain disparaging telegrams which he was understood to have sent to General Burnside. In view of the relation of these two officers to the conversation, the court, of course, could not hesitate to accept the version of General Pope as the true one. Even if General Pope had declared himself satisfied, it would not have affected the status of the accused before the law. His responsibility was to his Government and country, and not to the commanding general. Nor can any presumption arise against this proceeding from the failure of General Pope to prefer charges against the accused. It was his privilege to prefer them, but he was not bound to do so. He discharged his whole duty when, in his official report, he laid these transactions before his Government for its consideration.

This case has been most patiently investigated. If, in war, and in the midst of active hostilities, any Government has ever devoted so long a period of time—some forty-five days—to the examination of a military charge, it has not come to my knowledge. The court was not only patient and just, but liberal, and in the end everything was received in evidence which could possibly tend to place the conduct of the accused in its true light. It is not believed that there remains upon the record a single ruling of the court to which exception could be seriously taken.

The case is important, not only because of the gravity of the charges and the dignity of the officer arraigned, but also because of the fact that it involves a principle which lies at the very foundation of all discipline and of all efficiency in military operations—the principle of military obedience. A standard author, treating on this branch of jurisprudence, says: "Hesitancy in the execution of a military order is clearly, under most circumstances, a serious offense, and would subject one to severe penalties; but actual disobedience is a crime which the law has stigmatized as of the highest degree, and against which is denounced the extreme punishment of death. (DeHart, p. 165)"

The same author continues: "In every case, then, in which an order is not clearly in derogation of some right or obligation created by law, the command of a superior must meet with unhesitating and instant obedience."

So vital to the military system is this subordination of will and action deemed, that it is secured by the most solemn of human sanctions. Each officer and soldier before entering the service swears that he "will observe and obey the orders of the officers appointed over him:" and it is from this, probably, that the offense of disobedience derives much of the depth and darkness of the criminality with which it is stamped by the Articles of War. Obedience, indeed, is the very jewel of the soldier's life. It adorns him more, even, than laurels, which are so often plucked by unholy hands. The soldier who has given to the order of his superior officer a prompt, an earnest, a heartfelt support, has triumphed in the field of duty, even though he may have fallen on the field of arms.

The offenses for which the pleadings and testimony arraign the accused are the very gravest that a soldier can possibly commit, being neither more nor less than the willful violation of the orders of his commanding general in the midst of momentous and perilous military movements, and the shameful abandonment of a struggling army which it was his solemn duty to support, in the very presence of the enemy, and under the very sound of his artillery. The court was careful to give to the accused the benefit of all well-founded doubts that arose in their minds, in reference either to the fact of disobedience or in reference to the measure of criminality that prompted it, and hence they found him not guilty of the fourth and fifth specifications of first charge; and, in the same spirit, the fourth specification of second charge was withdrawn. While, however, the court felt that of crimes such as these no officer should be convicted but upon the clearest and most convincing proof of his guilt, they must also have felt that the honor of the profession of arms and the most enduring interests of our common Government and country imperatively demanded that there should be no acquittal when that proof had been made.

J. Holt,
Judge-Advocate-General[1]

In Holt's report to Lincoln, two questions are addressed. What did Lincoln ask of Holt, and what was it that Holt provided to Lincoln? Lincoln's task to Holt was as follows:

War Department
Washington City, January 12, 1862

The Judge-Advocate-General is instructed to revise the proceedings of the court-martial in the case of Maj. Gen. Fitz-John Porter, and to report fully upon any legal questions that may have arisen in them, and upon the bearing of the testimony in reference to the charges and specifications exhibited against the accused and upon which he was tried.

Abraham Lincoln[2]

Confusing? Yes. Holt, in response to Lincoln's directive, referred to his report as the "Review of the Judge Advocate." In fact, Holt's report was a prosecutor's closing argument.

In most cases, if a person heard only the prosecutor's closing argument, he would conclude that the accused was a guilty, dastardly villain. Conversely, if he heard only the defense's closing argument, he would conclude that the defendant was a persecuted, innocent victim. Let us hope that Lincoln did not base his decision on approving Porter's sentence solely on Holt's report.

The Verdict

The court rendered its verdict on January 10, 1863. It was as follows:

On the first specification of the first charge (disobeyed order to be at Bristoe at daylight on August 28): Guilty

On the second specification of the first charge (disobeyed the order addressed jointly to Porter and McDowell to take road to Gainesville until they joined with Pope's force): Guilty

On the third specification of the first charge (disobeyed the 4:30 P.M. order to attack Jackson's flank and rear): Guilty

On the fourth specification of the first charge (disobeyed the order to report to Pope in person with command after daybreak on the thirtieth in that Griffin's brigade was absent): Not Guilty

On the fifth specification of the first charge (permitted Piatt's brigade to take the wrong road, and thus failed to bring it to the battlefield on the morning of the thirtieth in accordance with Pope's order of specification four): Not Guilty

On the first specification of the second charge (failed to attack the enemy and instead shamefully retreated): Guilty, except so much of the specification as implies that he, the accused, "did retreat from the advancing forces of the enemy"[3] after the receipt of the order set forth in the specification.

On the second specification of the second charge (within the sound of guns, etc., and knowing that the aid of his corps was needed, did shamefully retreat, etc): Guilty

On the third specification of the second charge (in the belief that Pope was suffering a defeat, did shamefully fail to go to his aid, etc): Guilty, except the words "to the Manassas Junction."[4]

On the first charge (disobedience of an order): Guilty

On the second charge (shameful conduct in the face of an enemy): Guilty

Here is a comparison of the court's verdict on each specification to the author's verdict:

	The Court	The Author
Charge 1	Guilty	Guilty
Specification 1	Guilty	Guilty
Specification 2	Guilty	Not Guilty
Specification 3	Guilty	Not Guilty
Specification 4	Guilty	Not Guilty
Specification 5	Not Guilty	Not Guilty
Charge 2	Guilty	Not Guilty
Specification 1	Guilty	Not Guilty
Specification 2	Guilty	Not Guilty
Specification 3	Guilty	Not Guilty

The Sentence

The sentence read: "And the court do therefore sentence him, Maj. Gen. Fitz-John Porter, of the United States Volunteers, to be cashiered, and to be forever disqualified from holding any office of trust or profit under the Government of the United States."[5]

The verdict and sentence must have been devastating to Porter. As of January 1863, it had been almost twenty-two years since he first entered the army as a cadet at West Point. The military had been his adult life. He knew no other. Now, at forty-one, in middle age, with a wife and four children, he was shut off from his only profession forever.

He had risen to the very pinnacle of his profession. The country watched his each and every move. He had gone from honor to honor. Now he was disgraced. He walked in a general and now he was to walk out less than a private. If he volunteered as a private, he could never rise to corporal or sergeant, as these were positions of trust.

The country was now in the midst of its greatest crisis. The outcome was still very much uncertain. Porter had been playing a leading role. Now he could not play at all. He must watch from the sidelines as a disgraced observer. The shame and humiliation would be enough to destroy many a man. Did it destroy Fitz-John Porter?

He still had one ray of hope. The nightmare might still pass. The sentence could not be implemented unless and until approved by Lincoln, and Lincoln was notoriously charitable. Lincoln could approve the sentence, or he could reduce or waive any or all of it. It was still just possible that Porter could get off with as little as a reprimand, or even no punishment at all.

The Porter file was handed to Lincoln on January 12, 1862. It was at this point that Lincoln requested Holt's "review." From this date, Porter must have spent anxious days and sleepless nights while he awaited the President's decision. The President was busy these days and the days dragged on. No one knows how much time Lincoln actually spent with the file, if any. Did he rely solely on Holt's review?

On January 21, 1863, the big day finally arrived. Lincoln promulgated his decision. It was:

> The foregoing proceedings, findings and sentence in the foregoing case of Maj. Gen. Fitz-John Porter are approved and confirmed; and it is ordered that the said Fitz-John Porter be, and he hereby is cashiered and dismissed from the service of the United States as a major general of volunteers, and as colonel and brevet brigadier general in the regular service of the United States, and forever disqualified from holding any office of trust or profit under the Government of the United States.
>
> Abraham Lincoln[6]

Porter's nightmare thus, this date, became a reality.

10

The Rehearing

Porter believed that he had been done a great injustice and spent much of the remainder of his life trying to right it. He petitioned each successive president. He had, of course, no luck with Lincoln, who had read Porter's messages to Burnside and considered him guilty. Then, in April 1865, a little more than two years after Porter's trial, Lincoln was assassinated and replaced by Andrew Johnson. Johnson had his own problems. He was beleaguered throughout much of his presidency and barely survived impeachment. Johnson completed Lincoln's second term in 1868 and was then followed by three successive Civil War generals, all of whom were familiar with the Porter case.

The first of the Civil War generals after Johnson was Ulysses Grant. Grant served two terms, through 1876. Although Grant and Porter were major-generals of volunteers at the same time, they never served in a common campaign. Grant served in the west, while Porter served in the east; Grant was only transferred to the east after Porter's court-martial. Grant, like Lincoln, believed that Porter had received a fair trial and just punishment, and did not respond to Porter's entreaties.

Grant was followed in 1877 by Rutherford B. Hayes. Hayes, like Porter, had risen to the rank of major general of volunteers during the war. Hayes, unlike Grant, had also participated in a common campaign with Porter. Both participated in the Maryland Campaign that immediately followed the second battle of Manassas and culminated in the battle of Antietam. In the campaign, Porter was in command of the Fifth Corps, and Hayes was colonel in command of the Twenty-third Ohio Infantry in the Kanawa Division. Hayes, however, did not see the culmination of the campaign, as he was severely wounded at the battle of South Mountain. Porter looked upon Hayes as his first good opportunity to redress his wrong. On March 9, 1878, Porter wrote Hayes the following letter from New York City:

> To His Excellency Rutherford B. Hayes,
> President of the United States:
>
> Sir: I most respectfully, but most urgently, renew my oft-repeated appeal to have you review my case. I ask it as a matter of long-delayed justice to myself. I renew it upon the ground heretofore stated, that public justice

cannot be satisfied so long as my appeal remains unheard. My sentence is a continuing sentence, and made to follow my daily life. For this reason, if for no other, my case is ever within the reach of executive as well as legislative interference.

I beg to present copies of papers heretofore presented, bearing upon my case, and trust that you will deem it a proper one for your prompt and favorable consideration.

If I do not make it plain that I have been wronged, I alone am the sufferer. If I do not make it plain that great injustice has been done me, then I am sure that you, and all others who love truth and justice, will be glad that the opportunity for my vindication has not been denied.

Very respectfully, yours
Fitz-John Porter[1]

Time was passing Porter by. He was already fifty-five. This time though, his letter brought prompt action. President Hayes ordered General-in-Chief William T. Sherman to activate a board of officers to review Porter's case. This Sherman promptly did. The activating letter designated Major General J. M. Schofield, Brigadier General A. H. Terry, and Colonel G. W. Getty as members and Major Asa B. Gardner as judge advocate-recorder. The board was ordered to convene at West Point, New York, on the twentieth day of June 1878.

The board was, of course, not a court-martial, and its proceedings not a trial. Its function was fact finding. It was to review old evidence and examine new. The board was expected to arrive at conclusions and to make recommendations. Although the board could not reverse Porter's verdict or remit his punishment, Congress and the President could, and it could recommend that they do so and submit the necessary justification.

The board operated in the manner of a court but lacked a court's powers. It could not compel the attendance of a witness. It could issue subpoenas, but lacked the legal means to force compliance. Lying before the board did not constitute perjury under the then federal perjury laws. However, the board was not quite as impotent as might appear. It was constituted by order of the commander-in-chief of the armed forces via the commanding general of the army, and it members were senior army officers. If one happened to be in the army at the time, and many or most of the witnesses were, the army had other means to ensure their presence and ensure that they spoke the truth.

The board had certain advantages over the original court-martial in arriving at the truth and producing justice. First and foremost, its proceedings would not be conducted in a time of crisis and would not be conducted at a forced pace. It had unlimited time. Second, it now had available the Confederate official reports submitted by the participants of the battle, and it could summon and question key Confederate players. Third, it now had accurate maps of the battlefield that were not available in 1863. And last, it could summon witnesses who could not be produced in 1863 because of war considerations.

However, the board would also labor under certain disadvantages when compared to the original court-martial. Although time available would be an advantage, time elapsed would prove a disadvantage. Almost sixteen years had passed since the events in question had taken place. Memories had begun to dim and were likely to be contaminated by the great publicity afforded to the case. Of even greater importance, many of the key players were dead. On the Confederate side, Lee, Jackson, and Stuart were all dead, as were two of Jackson's three division commanders. On the defense side, Generals Reynolds and Griffin were dead, and on the prosecution side, Generals King and Buford were dead. Perhaps most important of all, the man who had brought the charges against Porter, Gen. Roberts, was dead.

The three members of the board constituted a most illustrious group. Schofield, the president of the board, was born in 1831 and graduated from West Point in the class of 1853. He then had a most impressive career in both war and peace. During the Civil War, he was promoted to brigadier general at age thirty-one and major general at thirty-three. In this capacity, he was designated commanding general of the Army of the Ohio, thus becoming the youngest Union army commander.

Schofield was awarded the congressional medal of honor for gallantry in the battle of Wilson's Creek in 1861, and in 1864 was in command of the Union forces at the battle of Franklin when they so reduced Hood's Confederate Army of Tennessee that this constituted the beginning of the total collapse of the Confederacy in the west.

Major General J.M. Schofield of the United States Volunteers, president of Porter's re-hearing (courtesy the Massachusetts Commandery Military Order of the Loyal Legion and the U.S. Army Military History Institute).

In the post-war era, Schofield served as the secretary of war in the Johnson administration, replacing Edward Stanton. Schofield then returned to active military duty. At the time of his appointment to the board, he was superintendent of the military academy at West Point. In 1888, Schofield was appointed commanding general of the entire army and held this position until his retirement in 1895.

During the war, Schofield never served in the same theater as Porter at the same time and never participated in any common campaigns. Schofield, however, did know Porter. Porter had been an instructor at the military academy at the time Schofield was a cadet.

The second member of the board, Brig. Gen. Alfred Terry, was considered one of the finest non–West Point generals of the war. General Grant's assessment of Terry was this:

> General Alfred H. Terry came into the army as a volunteer without a military education. His way was won without political influence up to an important separate command—the expedition against Fort Fisher, in January, 1865. His success there was most brilliant, and won for him the rank of brigadier-general in the regular army and major-general of Volunteers. He is a man who makes friends of those under him by his consideration of their wants and their dues. As a commander, he won their confidence by his coolness in action and by his clearness of perception in taking in the situation under which he was placed at any given time.[2]

Unfortunately, Terry is largely remembered today as the general in charge of the ill-fated 1876 expedition against the Sioux Indians, during which the infamous "Custer's Last Stand" took place. Although this was clearly Custer's fault and not Terry's, Terry never tried to defend his reputation. Terry never served in the same theater as Porter and never participated in any common campaigns. As far as is known, he did not know Porter prior to the convening of the board.

The last member of the board was Col. G. W. Getty (G. W. stands for George Washington). Getty, like Schofield and Porter, was a West Point graduate. However, Getty graduated way back in 1840, thirteen years before Schofield and five years before Porter.

Getty, unlike Schofield, had much pre–Civil War combat experience. He participated prominently in both the Mexican War and the Seminole Indian War. Getty saw about as much combat during the Civil War as any Union general, and rose to the rank of major general in the Volunteers. During the early phases of the war, he participated in all of the battles and campaigns that Porter did. These included the Peninsula Campaign, the Second Bull Run Campaign, and the Maryland Campaign. In fact, Getty was a participant, subordinate to Porter, in the three battles that made Porter famous. These were Mechanicsville, Gaines' Mill, and Malvern Hill.

Porter was referred to as the "petitioner" by the board rather than as the defendant. Under the rules, he was entitled to be represented by counsel and, in fact, chose three prominent attorneys: Joseph H. Choate, Anson Maltby, and John C. Bullitt.

The board opened its proceedings at West Point on June 25, 1878. It heard the petitioner's case at West Point through September 12, and then, after a lengthy recess, reconvened at New York City to hear the government's case.

The opening at West Point was probably a concession to Gen. Schofield, who was superintendent of the military academy at the time. Many of the witnesses called to testify, both Confederate and Union, were graduates of the military academy. It must have been a nostalgic experience to them to return to their alma mater after four desperate years of rebellion and thirteen additional years; to visit their old rooms, walk through their old classrooms, the chapel, and the parade grounds. Then too, both Confederate and Union may have met old classmates and friends also called to testify. As they intermingled, Confederate and Union generals were indistinguishable, except that the Confederate generals were now sometimes addressed by the board as "mister."

The legal expertise for the government resided in the position of the judge advocate-recorder, which was occupied by Major Gardner. Gardner was a lawyer; the three members of the board were not. It was Gardner's job to summon witnesses, to interrogate them, and to prepare the record. Even though Gardner was the government's legal expert on the case, under the existing law, the president of the board reigned supreme and could overrule Gardner, even on points of law. This put Gardner and Gen. Schofield on a collision course almost from the outset; it was ultimately to erupt when it came to the question whether Gen. Pope was going to be required to testify. But, more about this later.

Gardner's position was really more difficult than that of the petitioner. Porter had over fifteen years to prepare his case and to identify and select witnesses. He could be expected to produce witnesses who would provide only his side of the story. Furthermore, Porter was represented by three high-powered attorneys, while Gardner stood alone.

Gardner's job was not to prosecute Porter, but to see that all sides of the story were presented so that the board could arrive at the truth. However, inasmuch as Porter could be expected to present only his side of the story, Gardner had to provide the other. Thus, in actuality, Gardner's task was little distinguished from that of prosecutor.

The proceedings of the Schofield Board described here come from two sources. First of all, there was the official transcript prepared by the court reporter. In addition, however, there was a second and perhaps even more valuable resource. The proceedings were of great public interest and each session was attended by a contingent of newspaper reporters. Reporters of the *New York Times* attended every session, and extensive reporting appeared in each issue. Here then, was not only a lifeless, verbatim account of the testimony, but the impression each day's testimony made on a presumably neutral but professional observer who actually witnessed the proceedings with all of the nuances and mannerisms of its performers. Each days *Times* article was considered in this description and evaluation of the proceedings.

Anson Maltby opened the case for the petitioner. He said that new evidence would be introduced to strengthen the point that Porter's exhausted command better carried out the spirit of Pope's order the night of August 27–28 to march to Bristoe by marching at 3 A.M. than they would have done by marching at 1 A.M.; that the charge of disobedience of this order was only a make-weight to the more serious charges as to later conduct; that other generals had failed to carry out the letter of similar orders issued that night without comment; that no bad effect was claimed to have followed the alleged disobedience; that the joint order to Porter and McDowell on the twenty-ninth was executed fully and completely; and that Porter's halt was enforced by the spirit of the joint order, and by McDowell taking King away and leaving Porter with nine thousand men to hold in check and prevent the throwing on Pope of twenty thousand men under Longstreet; that Pope did not know of Longstreet's presence; that new evidence would be produced to show that Porter did not know that Pope was involved in any battle on the twenty-ninth, beyond an artillery duel until nearly dark; that Porter could not go cross country to Pope because of the presence of the enemy and the nature of the country; that Porter did not retreat as charged; and that Porter did not receive Pope's 4:30 order to attack until 6:30. Maltby concluded by stating that Porter's actions of the day were the most meritorious of all, because without loss of blood, he pinned down Longstreet's twenty thousand men and prevented him from joining Jackson against Pope.

Maj. Asa Gardner opened the case for the government. He spoke for almost five hours. He thoroughly reviewed the original trial and concluded that its verdict was just and its punishment was not cruel. He chided Porter for publicly claiming that he was improperly convicted and that his sentence was unjust. He referred to Porter's attacks against the court in 1863, 1867, and 1869 as libelous. He pointed out that most members of the court were old friends or old acquaintances of Porter; that Porter was given the opportunity to object to any member—and objected to none.

He mentioned that Porter later claimed that key witnesses were unavailable, but at the time, stated that he was ready for trial. Now Porter claimed that the verdict should be reversed on the basis of "newly discovered evidence." Gardner said that he proposed to show that the so-called "newly discovered evidence" was not really newly discovered evidence that would have entitled it to consideration in any court of justice having appellate authority. He further proposed to show that this evidence was quite without value in any determination as to the charges on which the petitioner was tried.

For clarity and simplicity purposes, this chapter will treat the charges in the order levied, concentrating on the salient evidence that relates to Porter's guilt or innocence and passing lightly over testimony that was either inconsequential or redundant. Testimony that is at variance with that introduced in the original court-martial, and irreconcilable differences between testimony introduced by the petitioner and the government, will be discussed.

Charge 1, Specification 1

In brief, this charge constituted the disobedience of an order. On the night of August 27–28, Porter was ordered to depart with his corps from Warrenton Junction at 1 A.M. and to arrive at Bristoe Station by daylight on the twenty-eighth.

The uncontested facts of the case were that Porter received the order between 9:30 and 10 P.M. on the twenty-seventh, did not depart until 3 A.M. on the twenty-eighth at the earliest, and the head of his column did not arrive at Bristoe Station until after 10 A.M. on the twenty-eighth.

Porter's defense against charge 1, specification 1 was largely a replay of his trial in 1862. He again trotted out Fifth Corps Generals Morrell, Sykes, and Butterfield, and staffers Locke, Montieth, and Weld, as well as some new witnesses. He undoubtedly would have also produced Gen. Griffin had he still been alive. Porter's witnesses testified that the night was "very dark," "intensely dark," "pitch dark," "the darkest night ever known," "could not see your hand before your face," etc. Porter's witnesses also testified to the fatigue of his troops and to the blockage of the road by Pope's wagon train.

If there was anything new in Porter's case, it was the testimony of Col. Ruggles, Pope's chief of staff, who appeared as a petitioner's witness. Ruggles testified that it was impossible to march at 1 A.M. because of the intense darkness, and the road was blocked with stumps and Pope's wagon train. In fact, he testified that he himself became lost that night while looking for his mess wagon. Few, if any, of Porter's witnesses were actually on the road between Warrenton Junction and Bristoe between 1 A.M. and dawn.

Maj. Gardner called over twenty witnesses to testify to the condition of the night. The consensus of their testimony was that there was nothing particularly unusual about the night. It was moonless but starlit and, at worst, there may have been a slight sprinkling well before 1 A.M., but not enough to wet the road. Gardner also produced witnesses from various units that marched in the general area that night and none experienced any particular problems.

The most damaging witness against Porter was Confederate Brigadier General Jubal Early, a brigade commander in Ewell's division. It was Ewell who fought Hooker at Bristoe during the day of the twenty-seventh, and it was Ewell who Pope feared would renew the fight at daylight on the twenty-eighth. It was because of Ewell that Pope sent for Porter, directing him to be at Bristoe at daylight. However, Ewell did not renew the fight. Rather, during the night of the August 27–28, he retired up the road adjacent to the railroad to Manassas. Thus, the very night that Porter testified he could not march, and on the very same road (but ten miles above), Ewell, including Early's brigade, did march. Early testified that the march posed no particular problem.

The Five Specifications

The next five charges and specifications all involved a common element of proof; that is, Porter failed to bring his corps into action on the twenty-ninth of August.

The full text of the charges and specifications is contained in chapters 5, 6, and 7. In short, they were:

(1) Porter failed to bring his corps into action in response to Pope's joint order to him and McDowell of that morning.

(2) Porter failed to attack the enemy in response to Pope's peremptory order of 4:30 P.M.

(3) Porter not only failed to attack to aid his compatriots, but shamefully retreated.

(4) Knowing that a severe action of great consequence was taking place nearby, Porter failed to attack.

(5) Believing that Pope's nearby force was being defeated, Porter did not go to their aid, but retreated.

Any defense would have to be that Porter either did bring his corps into action, or that he could not for some good reason. A defense for number 2 above could be that he received Pope's 4:30 order to attack too late in the day for him to implement it before dark. At least two of the five charges entailed the element that he knew Pope's nearby forces were heavily engaged. A defense could be that he did not know. And lastly, at least two of the five indicated that he retreated. A defense could be either that he did not retreat, or had a compelling reason for doing so.

What Was in Front of Porter at Dawkins Branch on August 29?

In the original trial, Porter did not know the magnitude of the enemy force in front of him when he came to a halt at Dawkins Branch between 11 A.M. and noon on August 29, 1862. There was some skirmishing fire, a few cannon shots, and a cloud of dust ahead indicating an enemy build-up.

The board hearing did much to clarify the matter. It was Stuart's cavalry that Porter initially encountered. Stuart's official report of the battle that was entered into evidence stated:

> Robertson's vedettes had found the enemy approaching from the direction of Bristoe Station toward Sudley. The prolongation of his line of march would have passed through my position which was a very fine one for artillery as well as observation, and struck Longstreet in the flank. I waited his approach long enough to ascertain that there was at least an army corps, at the same time keeping detachments of cavalry dragging brush down the road from the direction of Gainesville, so as to deceive the enemy—a ruse which Porter's report shows was successful—and notified the commanding general, then opposite me on the turnpike, that Longstreet's flank and rear were seriously threatened, and of the importance of the ridge I then held. Immediately upon receipt of that intelligence Jenkins, Kempers and D. R. Jones' brigades and several pieces of

artillery were ordered to me by General Longstreet, and being placed in position fronting Bristoe, awaited the enemy's advance....[3]

Stuart himself was dead, so he could not testify. However, two members of his staff, Major White and the chaplain, the Reverend Landstreet, testified before the board on October 21, 1878. They both testified that they heard Stuart give the order to drag the brush to create the dust clouds. It was thus established that the clouds of dust, which played such an important part of Porter's (and Pope's) estimate of the situation were, at least in part, a ruse.

Pope's order to Porter on the morning of August 29 to take the Gainesville road stated that Pope did not expect Longstreet's force to arrive before the next evening at the earliest. However, Porter no sooner arrived at Dawkins Branch than he was advised that one of Longstreet's five divisions had been sighted earlier that morning passing through Gainesville, less than four miles ahead. In the trial of 1862, it was never firmly established what role this division played that date, or if any of the other of the five divisions of Longstreet had also arrived.

On July 9, 1878, the man who should have known better than any other where Longstreet's troops were on the twenty-ninth, Longstreet himself, was called to testify before the board. He testified that he commanded twenty-five thousand men that day, broken down into five divisions. He said that four of the five divisions were through Thoroughfare Gap early that morning, and that the fifth division under Gen. Anderson, containing four to five thousand men, joined him that night.

He testified that the four divisions were within supporting distance of Jackson by 9 A.M. and deployed for battle by 11 A.M. His line was at an angle from Jackson's and ran toward the south (i.e., toward Porter's position). (See map 17.) There was a gap of about three or four hundred yards between Jackson's right flank and Longstreet's left. Longstreet occupied this gap with artillery. Then came in order the divisions of Hood, Kemper, and Jones. Wilcox's division was kept in reserve. It was thus Jones's division that was closest to Porter.

Lee wanted Longstreet to make an immediate attack. Longstreet requested that he first make a personal reconnaissance. Longstreet noted Porter's force and considered that an attack by him (Longstreet) would be hazardous. He, however, considered his position a good defensive one. He testified that had Porter attempted to move across his front to Groveton, he could have broken him up; had Porter attacked him any time after 12 noon, he would have "annihilated"[4] him.

Major White and Chaplain Landstreet of Stuart's staff testified that there was actually sufficient distance between Longstreet's lines and those of Porter for Porter to have marched his corps to Groveton across Longstreet's front. They testified that, once Porter crossed Dawkins Branch, he would soon come

Map 17—Early Afternoon August 29
(What Was in Front of Porter)

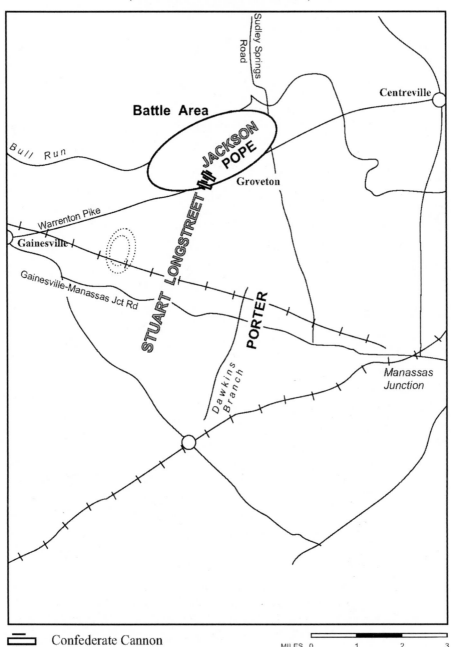

Confederate Cannon

MILES 0   1   2   3

Map 18—Deats Road

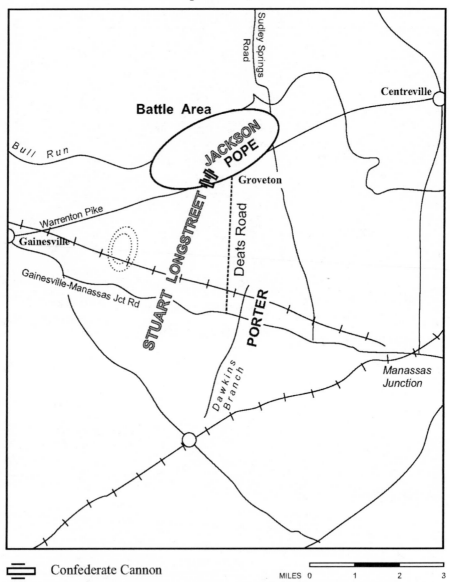

to a secondary country road, called Deats road, that ran all the way across from the Gainesville–Manassas Junction road to the Warrenton pike (see map 18). They said that this road was forward of Longstreet's lines, unguarded by the Confederates, and shielded from view from Longstreet's lines by forests.

There are a number of reasons to rebut the hypothesis that Porter could have used this road. First, Porter repeatedly tried to send scouts through the woods to his right to reach Pope at Groveton, but these were always stopped by the Confederates that infested the woods. Thus, it is evident that Confederates were on both sides of Deats road. Secondly, although parts of Deats road were shielded from the view of Longstreet's lines, others were not. And, finally, the road ultimately led past Longstreet's artillery posted between his and Jackson's line. If Porter merely wanted to join Pope, a far safer route would have been the Sudley Springs road.

Confederate Gen. Jubal Early testified before the board on October 12. In addition to his testimony, a description of the situation existing on August 29, 1862, made by him in 1874, was admitted into evidence. Early's story was as follows:

Jackson was aware of and concerned by the approach of a Union force moving up from the direction of Manassas Junction (the Porter-McDowell column). He posted Early with his own brigade, augmented by that of Hayes, just north of the Warrenton-Centreville turnpike, beyond his own far right (in the direction of Gainesville). He gave Early two missions: first, Early was to deploy two regiments as skirmishers on the far side of the turnpike in the direction of the approaching Union column and keep it under observation. Second, Early was to ensure the turnpike to Gainesville was kept open in anticipation of the arrival of Longstreet's troops.

Early in the day (time unspecified), Gen. Early's skirmishers began exchanging shots with the advancing Union column. By about 11 A.M., Early observed the head of Longstreet's column approaching on the turnpike from the direction of Gainesville. Between 11 and 12 o'clock, this force built up so rapidly between Early's position and the approaching Union column he was observing that, by noon, Early believed there were so many Confederate troops between Jackson's flank and the Union column that his mission was complete and his two brigades no longer required. Thus, without waiting for orders, he vacated his position and rejoined Jackson's main body.

One may thus conclude that it was established before the board that on August 29, at the time McDowell parted from Porter, there was a force of twenty thousand Confederates on the field, separate and distinct from those that Pope was fighting, and that these twenty thousand were deployed between Pope and Porter. For Porter to reach Jackson's flank, much less attack it, he had to either defeat this force with his force of some ten thousand, or pass directly across the front of the twenty thousand-man force—a foolhardy undertaking at best.

The now famous General Gouverneur Warren, then a colonel in command of one of Sykes's brigades, testified on July 8 that no prudent commander would have marched his troops into the woods at Porter's right, across the front of Confederates that could be seen, and risk a flank attack.

The only other way that Porter could have joined the fray at Groveton on the twenty-ninth would have been to retire back down the Gainesville–Man-assas Junction road to the Sudley Springs road and then move up the Sudley Springs road to join Pope. This is, in fact, what McDowell did on the twenty-ninth and what Porter did on the thirtieth. For Porter to have done this on the twenty-ninth would have been contrary to both the orders he received from Pope and McDowell.

What Did Porter Do at Dawkins Branch on the Twenty-ninth?

The testimony produced before the board did much to flush out Porter's activities at Dawkins Branch on the twenty-ninth, and demonstrated that he was much more active in attempting to carry out Pope's (and McDowell's) orders than appeared from the testimony at his original trial.

The testimony of Gen. Daniel Butterfield was given before the board on October 1, 1878. Butterfield said that his brigade was at the head of Porter's column when it stopped at Dawkins Branch between 11 and 12 on the morning of August 29. Porter sent for Butterfield and ordered him to take his brigade and move out across Dawkins Branch and take position near a white house that he pointed out, to cover the troops that would follow, as it was planned to make an attack. Butterfield put his brigade under the command of its senior colonel, Colonel Lansing, ordered it in motion, and then preceded it with his staff to make a personal reconnaissance.

As Butterfield and his staff approached the white house, one of his aides said, "Do you propose to tackle the enemy alone?"[5] At this, Butterfield looked back, and his brigade was nowhere in sight. Butterfield said that he retired "with great rapidity and considerable temper."[6] He found that his brigade, instead of following him, had moved off into some woods on his right. He confronted the senior officer, and demanded what he meant by retiring without his orders. He was advised that Gen. Porter himself had ordered the change, and this was a result of a meeting Porter had with McDowell.

Gen. Warren had also testified before the board on July 8, 1878, that Porter's forward movement that morning had been stopped as a result of a conference Porter had with McDowell that morning.

In Porter's original trial, two members of Porter's staff each testified that, as McDowell approached Porter that morning, they heard McDowell say, "Porter, you are too far out, this is no place to fight a battle."[7] Now, at the board hearing, the petitioner produced a third witness who overheard McDowell. Major Earle, of Gen. Morell's staff, testified on September 10 that he overheard McDowell say substantially the same words as the other two witnesses testified.

Thus, at the board hearing, the petitioner produced new evidence that it was McDowell who halted Porter's advance that morning; that Porter was preparing to seize the vital ridge ahead when stopped. Exactly what was said between Porter and McDowell at their meeting that morning at Dawkins Branch, as well as what McDowell may have sent Porter after the meeting, remained in dispute.

However, as a result of additional messages originated by Porter and submitted at the board hearing, it became increasingly clear that Porter thought that McDowell was taking his divisions to plug the gap between Pope and Porter, and that Porter was expected to connect with King's division that would appear in or beyond the woods to his right.

Three additional messages from Porter to King and McDowell were entered into evidence. The very fact that Porter was addressing messages to King and to no other division commander alone implied that Porter believed that he was to coordinate his activity with that of King. Two of Porter's messages to King stated: "I found it impossible to communicate by crossing the woods to Groveton. The enemy are in great force on this road...."[8] and "I have been wandering over the woods and failed to get a communication to you. Tell how matters go with you. The enemy is in strong force in front of me...."[9]

In any event, if McDowell and Porter were to coordinate and join, from the record it would appear that Porter was more conscientious in keeping McDowell informed of his situation than McDowell was in keeping Porter informed of his. (The full text of the dispatches from Porter to McDowell and King is contained in the Report of the Board of Army Officers in the Case of Fitz-John Porter, which appears in Appendix 9.)

On the basis of testimony presented at Porter's original trial, one might conclude that Porter was lethargic on August 29, that he never visited the skirmish line to assess with his own eyes what was in his front. Capt. Pope testified that when he delivered Gen. Pope's 4:30 order to Porter, he found Porter resting on the grass, more than a mile from the front at Bethlehem Church, while Gen. Pope's battle could be heard raging off to his right.

Testimony produced before the board rebutted this picture. Colonel Charles Johnson of the Twenty-fifth New York testified on July 10 that he saw Porter on August 29 in exposed positions near the skirmish line. Lieutenant Walter Davis, a staff officer of Martindale's brigade, testified that he met Porter near the skirmish line so many times on the twenty-ninth that he considered that Porter was fully doing his duty.

Lt. Col. Locke testified on July 17 that on August 29, Porter had been suffering from dysentery, spent much of the day in the saddle, and that by the time Capt. Pope arrived with his order, was so exhausted and unwell that it was difficult for him to rise.

Thus, the petitioner introduced evidence to indicate that, indeed, Porter was vigorous in attempting to execute his orders as he perceived them—at considerable danger and discomfort to himself.

Did Porter Know That a Battle Was Raging on the Twenty-ninth?

The final two of the five specifications entailed the element that Porter knew that Pope was involved in a battle while he failed to bring his corps into action. Consequently, the petitioner introduced evidence to indicate that he did not know.

Col. Warren of Sykes's division testified that he heard nothing but distant cannonading until the close of the day. Capt. Randol of the first artillery of Sykes's division testified likewise, as did Lieutenant Walter Davis, staff officer of Martindale's brigade. Others of Porter's corps testified that they heard nothing that indicated sustained fighting or a general battle. Longstreet testified that he knew of no infantry fighting until about 5 P.M. and that no terrible battle raged that day. Others, including Confederates, testified that they were not aware of any general engagement on the twenty-ninth.

Maj. Gardner produced a plethora of witnesses who testified to major infantry fighting and major casualties on the twenty-ninth. These included Generals Heintzelman, Hooker, Sigel, and Early, as well as numerous lesser lights. Gen. Heintzelman was able to testify from a diary that he kept up at the time. Gardner even produced witnesses as far away as the far side of Porter's skirmish line who heard the combat.

However, overwhelming as Gardner's testimony was, it was really moot, as he could demonstrate from Porter's own dispatches of the day that Porter was aware of Pope's battle. Porter's dispatches to King-McDowell stated:

> The enemy are on great force on this road, and as they appear to have driven our forces back the firing of the enemy advances and ours retired, I have decided to withdraw to Manassas....[10]

> How goes the battle? It seems to go to our rear....[11]

> The firing on my right has so far retired that, as I cannot advance and have failed to get over to you, except by the route taken by King....[12]

Thus, in the case of whether or not Porter knew of Pope's battle on the twenty-ninth, we must score one for Maj. Gardner and the government.

What Time Did Captain Pope Deliver General Pope's 4:30 Order?

The original trial posed a direct conflict of evidence on the critical point of what time Capt Douglas Pope delivered his uncle's 4:30 order. Capt. Pope and Sergeant (Private at the time) Duffee, who accompanied him, testified that they gave the order to Porter at around 5 P.M. Three members of Porter's staff testified that the time of delivery was 6:30 P.M. or later. If Capt. Pope and

Sgt. Duffee are correct, Porter had ample time to implement the order before dark and is guilty. If Porter's staffers are correct, the order was delivered too late for Porter to implement it before dark, and he is innocent. In the original trial, the court chose to believe Capt. Pope and Sgt. Duffee and found Porter guilty.

In the rehearing, new evidence was produced on each side of the issue. Capt. Pope again testified that, except for a brief pause for McDowell to read the order, they covered the distance to Porter as fast as possible and without incident, and estimated the time en route as forty-five minutes or less. In the original trial, he estimated the time as about thirty minutes. If we add the forty-five minutes to the time Pope believed he departed, and he based this on the time written on the order, the delivery time would be about 5:15 P.M. Sgt. Duffee, who accompanied Pope, again backed up Pope. However, Duffee became confused in cross examination. He had testified that they met McDowell on the road to Haymarket (presumably on the Warrenton pike), and that it was two miles from their starting point to the point where they met him. Actually, they met him on the Sudley road and it was only three fourths of a mile from the starting point. Despite Duffee's confusion and contradictions, he stuck to the main theme of his story—that the trip was at a good clip and without incident.

Two witnesses came forward, however, to directly challenge the veracity of Capt. Pope. These were Captain Edward Moale and First Lieutenant Francis Jones, both of whom testified on October 3. Moale testified that after the war, in 1867, Pope, Moale, and Francis were all serving together in the Thirty-seventh Infantry on the frontier. They lived together and frequently exchanged stories about their experiences in the war. Moale recalled Pope having described his experience in delivering his message to Porter. Although Moale could not recall Pope's exact words, he said that he was certain of the substance of Pope's story. He said that Pope said that he became lost while delivering the order, that he inquired the way of some lady who, apparently purposefully, gave him false instructions. As a result, he almost wandered into Confederate lines and spent a period hiding from the Confederates in the woods. When he finally delivered the order, two hours or so had elapsed.

When asked what his relations with Pope were, Moale said that both then and now they were on a most friendly basis; that he wanted to avoid testifying, but had been summoned by the Porter team. He further stated that he did not know how the Porter team came upon him. Lieutenant Jones testified next and backed up Moale's story in all its essentials.

Capt. Pope was recalled in rebuttal. He did not personally attack Moale or Jones. He said that he had no specific recollection of having talked to them on the subject of the delivery of the order, but he may well have. If so, they must have become confused between what he said happened and what was said about what might have happened or could have happened. In any event, he stuck to the story he had provided to the board about an uneventful delivery.

Col. Ruggles, the actual drafter of the 4:30 order, testified before the board on July 17. He said that he wrote the time of 4:30 on the order blank before Gen. John Pope began to dictate the order. He then had to write up the order, make copies, seal it up, and call and hand it to a courier. The time of departure of the courier thus must have been a significant time after 4:30.

Lieutenant Alexander D. Payne testified on September 10. He had been a member of Gen. J.E.B. Stuart's staff at the time of the battle. He was a local resident of the area and knew all the roads intimately. When Porter's trial was published (and it was open to the public) and Payne learned of Capt. Pope's testimony, he carefully rode the exact route Pope said he followed, and carefully clocked the time. He testified that it required ninety-six minutes.

The petitioner produced yet another witness who said he was present when Capt. Pope delivered his order to Porter. This was Capt. Randol of the first artillery of Sykes's division. Randol testified on July 10. He said that he was present when Capt. Pope arrived and he saw Pope give the order to Porter between 6:30 and 7 P.M. He further said that he was positive of the fact.

Another witness with new testimony on the matter was William Dyer, an orderly on Gen. Pope's staff, who testified on August 29. Dyer testified that, in addition to Duffee, Col. Ruggles ordered six orderlies to accompany Capt. Pope and then to remain with Gen. Porter to serve as messengers. Dyer was one of the six and estimated that their time en route did not exceed forty-five minutes. Dyer, however, was destroyed on cross examination. He was asked to describe houses that he passed en route to Porter's headquarters. He described one that was not built until 1863, the year after his ride. Furthermore, neither Capt. Pope nor Sgt. Duffee had any recollection of Dyer having accompanied them.

Thus, the testimony before the board ended, as it had before the court, with apparently irreconcilable differences. One possible synthesis would be as follows:

(1) Capt. Pope and Sgt. Duffee actually departed at 5 P.M. rather than 4:30 P.M. as they had surmised.
(2) The time en route was actually ninety-six minutes as reported by Lieutenant Payne.
(3) The group arrived and delivered their message to Porter after 6:30 P.M. as observed by the three Porter staffers.
(4) Capt. Moale and First Lt. Jones incorrectly remembered Capt. Pope's description of the event.

Another possible synthesis is that Moale and Lieutenant Jones were correct in their remembrances and that, in consequence, Capt. Pope arrived after 6:30 P.M. as observed by the Porter staffers.

In either event, it seems that whatever the truth, it tilts in Porter's favor.

Did Porter Retreat Before the Enemy on August 29?

An element of specifications 3, 4, and 5 was that Porter not only failed to bring his corps into action on the twenty-ninth, but retreated before the enemy. The main evidence of a retreat was, of course, Porter's dispatch to King and McDowell indicating that he intended to withdraw to Manassas. But did he actually withdraw, or did he change his mind?

The petitioner produced a near clincher case that he did not retreat. Col. Warren testified on July 8 that there was no retreat on the twenty-ninth, no falling back, nor change of position, except local. Col. Charles Johnson of the Twenty-fifth New York of Morell's division testified on July 10 that Porter's corps did not retreat on the twenty-ninth. Lt. Weld of Porter's staff testified on July 16 that he saw nothing that indicated a retreat by the corps. Gen. Morell testified on July 11 that there was nothing in the nature of a retreat on the twenty-ninth, and Gen. Sykes testified the same day that he received no order to retreat on the twenty-ninth, nor did he hear of any such order being issued.

The nearest move that might be considered a retreat was conducted by Gen. Piatt's brigade. Piatt's brigade was not part of Porter's Fifth Corps, but a part of the Washington Reserve Corps that was temporarily attached to Porter. On the twenty-ninth, Porter ordered the brigade back to Manassas to take a defensive position. To have a brigade in the rear to serve as a rallying point in case the main body is forced back is a not uncommon step that a cautious and prudent commander might take.

Thus, all the commanders who would have been central figures in a retreat testified that there was no retreat.

Maj. Gardner's case that there was a retreat was anemic in the extreme. He produced witnesses such as Corporal Solomon Thomas of Morell's division, who testified on October 11. Thomas said that his division was retreating toward Manassas when an officer rode up with an order for Porter, who then directed an about face. Anyone who has participated in a large scale military operation knows that the perception of someone low on the totem pole as to what is transpiring, particularly if that one has not participated in the planning or had access to maps, is worthless. Evidence points to conceding this matter to Porter. Despite what his dispatch to King and McDowell said, he did not retreat on August 29.

What Was Porter's Attitude Toward Pope?

A number of officers close to Porter again testified that they never heard Porter say anything against Pope. Lt. Weld, Porter's aide who ate regularly with Porter, testified on July 16 that he never saw nor heard Porter display the slightest disinclination to support Pope. General Smith testified on October 16 that he saw Porter and Pope together at Centreville after the battle and that

Pope's conduct toward Porter appeared to be of the friendliest kind. Major O. D. Green testified on October 28 that he saw Pope and Porter together at Fairfax twice on August 31 and their conversation appeared friendly and amicable.

William Ormsby was a reporter of the *New York Times* at the time of Porter's court-martial and testified before the board on October 7. He said that in December 1862, during Porter's court-martial, he accompanied William Blair Lord on a visit to Porter in Porter's room during a break in the trial. At the time, Blair Lord was the official stenographer of the court, and the purpose of the visit was to get some papers that Lord needed for the record. During the conversation that ensued with Porter, Ormsby recalled Porter saying: "I warnt loyal to General Pope, I was loyal to General McClellan."[13] Ormsby could remember no other part of the conversation, but felt certain of the substance of this remark. When asked if Porter used the word "warnt" and not "wasn't," Ormsby affirmed that he did. Gen. Schofield asked Ormsby to give an idea of the tone Porter used. Was it indignant, angry, repentant, or what? Ormsby replied that it was earnest.

William Blair Lord, now the stenographer of the U.S. House of Representatives, testified on October 16. He basically corroborated Ormsby's testimony. He said that Porter made the statement almost as a soliloquy while he, Lord, was examining the papers. In Lord's recollection, Porter said: "I was not true to Pope and there is no use denying it."[14] Porter, of course, denied ever making such a statement.

Doctor Edward Paxton, a surgeon in the Fifth Corps, testified on October 14. He said that on the morning of August 28, while Porter's corps was on the road from Warrenton Junction to Bristoe in accordance with Pope's order, he overheard Porter say to one of his aides: "Tell General Morell to halt his division, I don't give a——if I don't get there on time."[15] Paxton did not know what circumstances occasioned Porter's statement.

Captain Basil P. Bowers, a captain of artillery in Milroy's brigade, testified on October 15. He said that on the day after the battle (August 31), while looking for water for his men, he wandered into the Fifth Corps' lines and was mistakenly picked up as a straggler. While being held under guard, he heard an officer, who was addressed as "General Porter," say to his aides that "General Pope will be along this way pretty soon, and I wish it to be understood that I don't want any courtesies shown to him."[16] Presently, Gen. Pope came riding along and received no salute whatsoever. General Milroy then came along, saw Bowers, and secured his release.

Porter staffers Webb, Locke, and Weld were called in rebuttal and all vehemently denied Bowers's account. Locke testified that he had never known Porter to do an ungentlemanly thing in his life.

Was one side or the other lying in this instance? Not necessarily. Commanders on business visits sometimes request that there be no honors. Pope might have requested that there be no honors for this visit.

Major General Irvin McDowell

It was widely anticipated that the appearances of Generals McDowell and Pope before the board would provide the high point of the hearings from a public interest point of view. McDowell appeared on October 10 and 11. It is true that his appearance generated more heat, passion, and theatrics than that of any other witness. Whether it provided more substance is questionable.

McDowell testified that he met Porter twice on the twenty-ninth of August and no more. Their first meeting was early that morning when Porter and his corps set out from Manassas Junction on the road to Gainesville. The second meeting took place between 11 and 12 that morning, when Porter stopped at Dawkins Branch and McDowell rode forward to confer with him.

When discussing what transpired between him and Porter at Dawkins Branch, McDowell exhibited the same faulty memory he exhibited at the court-martial in 1862–63. Despite three witnesses who testified that they overheard McDowell say, "Porter, you are too far out already, this is no place to fight a battle," or words to that effect, McDowell had no recollection of saying any such thing. He did again say that upon parting he ordered Porter to put his troops "in here," motioning to the woods at Porter's right in the direction of Groveton, while he took his own corps up the Sudley Springs road (presumably to form on Reynolds's left and Porter's right, so as to close the gap between Reynolds and Porter). McDowell contended that once they separated, Porter was confronted by no Confederate force larger than his own and there was no good reason why he did not attack.

The defense then wanted to pose a hypothetical question to McDowell. If Porter was actually confronted by an enemy force two to three times his own (as Porter thought), what then? McDowell did not want to answer. The court told him to answer. His reply was:

> If there was a force two or three times that reported by General Buford in General Porter's front, between Gainesville and Groveton, and if General Porter was advised of its existence by the capture of rebel scouts, he was excusable in not making the movement; but General Porter should either have carried out the order of General Pope as modified by him [McDowell] unless countermanded by a superior officer, or should have found out the force in front by actual test, and reported that the movement was impossible. General Porter should have made an attack of some sort; I did not tell him whether to shell, to skirmish or to attack in force; that was left to his judgment; I had confidence in Porter's energy and ability, and merely indicated to him the direction in which he was to operate, but did not prescribe how he was to operate.[17]

During the cross examination, the petitioner introduced into evidence a letter McDowell had sent to a New York paper on February 17, 1870. The letter contained an admission by McDowell that until he parted with Porter at about 12, he, as senior officer, was in charge, and blame for not attacking up to that hour rested with him. When asked why he did not attack at that time, he replied that there was then nothing to attack; the opposing lines were too far apart and hence, there was no responsibility for anyone not ordering an attack up to that time.

McDowell entered into evidence three dispatches he received from Porter on August 29 in addition to the one he entered into evidence at the original court-martial. One of the three was addressed only to Gen. McDowell and the other two were jointly addressed to Generals King and McDowell. One dispatch contained a time of origin of 6 P.M. The other two contained no times, but were obviously earlier than 6 P.M. and later than the time Porter and McDowell parted. All three dispatches had a vital bearing on the case. They confirmed that Porter was aware that a battle was going on. (The Report of the Board of Army Officers in the Case of Fitz-John Porter, which appears in Appendix 9, contains the full text of these dispatches.) The content of the 6 P.M. dispatch clearly indicated that at the time of its origin, Porter had not yet received Pope's 4:30 peremptory order to attack. At the court-martial, the prosecution had contended that Porter received Pope's order at about 5 P.M. and hence had plenty of remaining daylight in which to comply. The defense contended that it received the order after 6:30 P.M., which provided too little remaining daylight in which to comply.

Considerable time was spent on McDowell's credibility. McDowell testified that when he learned that Porter was petitioning the President for a review of his case, he advised Pope to prepare his version of the case without delay and send it to the President. This Pope did with McDowell's help. McDowell also helped distribute the paper. (An abstract of Pope's paper that appeared in the *New York Times* on October 11, 1878, is contained in Appendix 6.) The defense pointed out that the paper incorrectly quotes from Jackson's official report of the battle. Pope quoted Jackson's report as saying that he (Jackson) was so heavily pressed at 4 P.M. on August 29 that he sent to Lee for reinforcements, but Lee was then too far away to provide them. Hence, if Porter had complied with Pope's 4:30 order of the twenty-ninth and attacked Jackson, Jackson's force would have been destroyed. The petitioner correctly pointed out that Jackson's report referenced a Union attack at 4 P.M. on August 30, rather than August 29, and hence, any response or lack thereof to Pope's order of August 29 was irrelevant. McDowell readily admitted that there was such an error in Pope's report, and that he himself was responsible. He had provided Pope with the reference from Jackson's report and the error in date was his fault; however, it was an error and no more.

The cross examination of McDowell became ever more acrimonious, causing McDowell at times to rise to his feet in anger. By and large, McDowell, as in the original court-martial, was able to successfully stave off any attack by the petitioner through a combination of incisiveness, obtuseness, and loss of memory.

There was one more matter involving him that did not relate specifically to his testimony of October 10–11. In the original court-martial, there was an unreconcilable conflict of testimony between Porter's chief of staff, Lt. Col. Locke, and McDowell—and the court chose to accept McDowell's version. Locke had testified that, after McDowell and Porter had parted at noon on the twenty-ninth, Porter sent him back down the line with a message for Gen. King. Locke said that he met King in company with McDowell near Bethlehem Church; that he delivered his message, and McDowell then gave him a verbal message for Porter. The message was: "Give my regards to General Porter, and say to him that I am going to the right and will take King with me. I think he [Porter] better remain where he is; but if it is necessary for him to fall back, he can do so on my left."[18]

Locke testified that he then rushed back and gave McDowell's message to Porter. McDowell testified that he had no recollection of any such meeting with Locke and that, if he did meet with Locke, he certainly did not give him the message that Locke claimed.

The petitioner produced a man named Robert Leipold, who had been an orderly on Porter's staff in 1862. Leipold testified before the board on July 9 that on August 29, 1862, he accompanied Lt. Col. Locke on Locke's trip back to deliver Porter's message to Gen. King; that near Bethlehem Church, he saw Locke dismount, walk up to, and converse with Gen. McDowell; that he then accompanied Lt. Col. Locke when Locke rode back to Porter.

Major General John Pope

Gen. Schofield, the president of the board, and Maj. Gardner, the judge advocate-recorder, had been on a collision course almost from the beginning of the hearings. Gardner believed that witnesses should not be cross examined on testimony they gave sixteen years ago at the original court-martial. He contended that this was unfair and unprecedented; that they had been cross examined at the time, and that they should only be cross examined on the testimony they provided before the board. The petitioner's lawyers, however, persisted in attempting to cross examine witnesses on the earlier testimony. Gardner consistently objected, and Schofield consistently sided with the petitioner and overruled Gardner. The conflict came to a head in late October 1878 in the case of Gen. Pope.

Porter's lawyers wanted Pope to appear so that they could cross examine him on his earlier testimony, but refused to have him summoned as a petitioner witness. Gardner, on the other hand, said that Pope had no new evidence, and refused to have him summoned as a government witness.

Gen. Schofield intervened. He sent a telegram to Pope, then at Fort Leavenworth, Kansas, requesting him to appear as a witness. Pope replied that he wanted the same treatment as any other witness; that he would only appear if he were subpoenaed as either a petitioner witness or as a government witness (see Appendix 7 for the complete text of Pope's response). At this, Schofield directed Gardner to issue a subpoena to Pope to appear as a government witness. The secretary of war now intervened. He sent a telegram to Pope directing him to stay where he was until further instructed. Schofield now appealed to the secretary of war and to the president of the United States to compel Pope's attendance. The President decreed that it was at Pope's discretion; he could come and testify or not. Pope chose not to come and testify and there the matter lay. Pope did not testify before the board. (Appendix 8 contains a listing of witnesses at the rehearing whose testimony was considered for this chapter.)

What Did Lincoln Think of the Porter Case?

What Lincoln thought of the Porter case was really not germane to Porter's guilt or innocence. However, the board still permitted testimony on this subject, as it considered that this might be of interest to President Hayes. Two witnesses testified before the board on this subject. The first was former governor of New Jersey, William A. Newell, who testified on July 17. Newell said that he met with Lincoln in January 1863 at the White House. At the time, Newell was a congressman and said that he was an intimate of Lincoln. Newell recalled that Lincoln said he was very busy at the time of the Porter trial; that when the transcript was submitted to him for his approval, he did not have the time to examine it in detail, but had to rely on Col. Holt's summary of the case to make his decision to approve the verdict. According to Newell, Lincoln said that he had high regard for Porter, both as a gentleman and a soldier, and hoped that Porter somehow would be able to clear himself in the future.

The second witness on the subject was Lincoln's son, Robert, who testified before the board on October 14. Young Lincoln testified to a meeting he had with his father in the White House in January 1863. He was about twenty at the time, his father often confided in him, and the meeting was either shortly before or shortly after the President approved the Porter verdict. He said that his father was angered by Porter's message to McDowell stating that he (Porter) was going to retreat to Manassas, and that he considered Porter's sentence not only just but mild, and that he deserved death.

The Report

Finally the big day came when, on March 19, 1879, the board submitted its report to President Hayes. The report was lengthy and verbose. (It is in included in its entirety in Appendix 9.) There was a complete unanimity of opinion among the board members. It first reviewed the six charges and specifications of which Porter stood convicted.

The first charge and specification was the one in which Pope ordered Porter and his corps to depart Warrenton Junction at 1 A.M. on August 28 and arrive at Bristoe by daylight. Porter, in fact, did not depart until after 3 A.M., and did not arrive at Bristoe until after 10 A.M. The board produced nothing to alter these basic facts. The board did, however, point out that the order to Porter did not indicate that Porter was expected to go directly into action upon his arrival at Bristoe, nor did it indicate that there was any particular crisis to be expected at Bristoe at daylight. Rather, the order to Porter indicated that, upon arriving at Bristoe, he was expected to enter into pursuit of a departed enemy—with the possibility of later action.

The board contended that Porter was thus confronted with two choices. He could depart at 1 A.M. and have a portion of his corps arrive at Bristoe at the designated time in a fatigued and disorganized condition; or, he could effect a minor delay and have his full corps arrive somewhat later, in a rested and organized condition—capable of continuing the action visualized in the order. The board held that Porter did no more than exercise the normal degree of discretion expected of a corps commander, and, in fact, with the information available to him, his decision was the best one to meet Pope's objectives as expressed in the order.

The report next addressed the five charges and specifications that all related to Porter's failure to bring his corps into action on August 29 to aid Pope in his fight against Jackson. Here, the board unearthed new and compelling information. It established beyond any reasonable doubt, and contrary to the views of Pope and the original court-martial, that: (1) Longstreet, with four of his five divisions, had arrived at the field of combat by late morning on the twenty-ninth. (2) Porter was now confronted with a separate and distinct enemy (Longstreet) from that which confronted Pope (Jackson). (3) Porter could not come to Pope's aid without engaging in a major battle with Longstreet. (4) Had he done so, he probably would have been defeated, inasmuch as Longstreet was greatly numerically superior to him. (5) Porter, by staying where he was and threatening Longstreet's flank, prevented Longstreet from joining the fight against Pope. The board thus concluded that, not only was Porter not guilty, but it was he, in fact, who saved Pope from destruction on the twenty-ninth.

The report also indicated that the board unearthed new information relating to the time Porter received Pope's peremptory 4:30 "attack order" on the twenty-ninth. In the original trial, the court was led to believe that the order was delivered to Porter between 5 and 5:30 P.M., and that Porter thus had ample time to implement it before dark. The board produced new evidence that absolutely established that Porter did not receive the order until near dark, and thus could not implement it.

The report did not address the three charges that related to Porter's march to the battlefield on the thirtieth, for which he was acquitted. The report did, however, address Porter's and his corps' activity upon arriving on the battlefield on the thirtieth, for which there were no charges. The report described the conduct of Porter and his corps as highly commendable.

The report thus exonerated Porter of all of the charges for which he was convicted. However, it went beyond this. It was effusive in its praise of Porter:

> Thus did the gallant corps nobly and amply vindicate the character of their trusted chief and demonstrate to all the world that "disobedience of orders" and "misbehavior in the presence of the enemy" are crimes which could not possibly find place in the head or heart of him who thus commanded that corps....[19]

> These charges and specifications certainly bear no discernable resemblance to the facts of the case now established....[20]

> We believe not one among all the gallant soldiers on that bloody field was less deserving of such condemnation than he....[21]

The report concluded as follows:

> Having thus given the reasons for our conclusions, we have the honor to report, in accordance with the President's order, that in our opinion justice requires at his hands such actions as may be necessary to annul and set aside the findings and sentence of the court-martial in the case of Maj. Gen. Fitz-John Porter, and to restore him to the positions of which that sentence deprived him—such restoration to take effect from the date of his dismissal from the service.

> Very respectfully, your obedient servants,

> J. M. Schofield
> Major-General U.S. Army

> Alfred H. Terry
> Brigadier-General U.S.S. Army

> Geo. W. Getty
> Brevet Major-General, U.S. Army, Colonel Third Artillery[22]

It appeared that Porter's nightmare was finally coming to an end. But was it? In response to the report, President Hayes sent the following message to Congress:

> Executive Mansion
> Washington, June 5, 1879

> To the Senate and House of Representatives:

> I transmit herewith the 'proceedings and report' of the Board of Officers, convened by Special Order, No. 78, Headquarters of the Army, Washing-

ton, April 12, 1878, in the case of Fitz-John Porter. The report of the board was made in March last, but the official record of the proceedings did not reach me until the 3rd instant.

I have given this report such examination as satisfies me that I ought to lay the proceedings and conclusions of the board before Congress.

As I am without power in the absence of legislation to act upon the recommendation of the report further than by submitting the same to Congress, the proceedings and conclusions of the board are transmitted for the information of Congress, and such actions as in your wisdom shall seem expedient and just.

R. B. Hayes[23]

In the event, nothing more came of the Board of Officers Report during the Hayes administration and Porter's case returned to dead center. What appeared to be his best chance had come to naught.

Porter was now fifty-seven years old.

11

Grant Intervenes

It is a wonder that Porter was able to sustain his morale after this gigantic setback, but continue his efforts he did. The next President was another Civil War major general. James Garfield took office in 1881—the same James Garfield who sat as a member of the court-martial that convicted Porter in 1863. Porter now had to convince Garfield that the court's verdict was unjust. This could be tantamount to convincing Garfield that James Garfield was unjust. But then, fate stepped in again. Garfield was shot by an assassin.

Garfield was shot on July 2, 1881, just months after assuming office. He lingered on until September 19, when he finally succumbed to his wound. He was succeeded by Chester A. Arthur. Arthur was indebted to ex–President Grant, who had appointed him to the lucrative position of collector of the Port of New York back in 1871. At the time Arthur took office, the Porter case was at dead center. At this point, Grant stepped in.

In the second half of the nineteenth century, the most popular man in America was not Lincoln but Ulysses Grant, hero of the Civil War and two-term President. At the end of 1881, Grant was approaching sixty, had only three and a half more years to live, and may have been coming to grips with his mortality. He now took an interest in the Porter case. Just perhaps, he felt he was responsible for an injustice. When he was President, he could have responded to Porter's entreaties, but did not. He now took an intense interest in the case. He pored over the Schofield report and its maps for days. He became firmly convinced that Porter was innocent.

On December 22, 1881, Grant sent the following letter to President Arthur:

New York, Dec. 22, 1881.
The President, Washington, D. C.:

Dear Sir,

At the request of Gen. Fitz-John Porter, I have recently reviewed his trial and the testimony furnished before the Schofield Court of Inquiry held in 1879, giving to the subject three full days of careful reading and consideration, and much thought in the intervening time. The reading of this record has thoroughly convinced me that for these nineteen years I have been doing a gallant and efficient soldier a very great injustice in thought and sometimes speech. I feel it incumbent upon me now to do whatever lies in my power to remove from him and from his family the stain upon his good name. I feel this the more incumbent upon me than I should if I had been a corps commander only, or occupying any other command in the army than the one which I did; but as general I had it, possibly, in my power to have obtained for him the hearing which he had only got at a later day, and as President I certainly had the power to have ordered that hearing. In justification for my injustice to General Porter, I can only state that shortly after the war closed his defense was brought to my attention, but I read in connection with it a sketch of the field where his offences were said to have been committed, which I now see, since perfect maps have been made by the engineers' department of the whole field, were totally incorrect as showing the position of the two armies. I have read it in connection with the statements made on the other side against General Porter, and, I am afraid, possibly with some little prejudice in the case, although General Porter was a man whom I personally knew and liked before; but I got the impression, with many others, that there was a half-hearted support of General Pope in his campaigns, and that General Porter, while possibly not more guilty than others, happened to be placed in a position where he could be made responsible for his indifference, and that the punishment was not a severe one for such an offence. I am now convinced that he rendered faithful, efficient, and intelligent service, and the fact that he was retained in command of a corps for months after his offences were said to have been committed is in his favor. What I would ask in General Porter's behalf, from you, is, if you can possibly give the time, that you give the subject the same study and thought that I have given it, and then act as your judgment shall dictate. But, feeling that you will not have the time for such an investigation (for it would take several days' time), I would ask that the whole matter be laid before the Attorney-General for his examination and opinion. Hoping that you will be able to do this much for an officer who has suffered for nineteen years a punishment that never should be inflicted upon any but the most guilty, I am, Very truly yours,

U.S. Grant[1]

Grant did not stop at this. He sent a copy of his letter to Senator John Logan, a distinguished senator, a close friend and leader of the opposition to restoring Porter's rank. Logan had been a Union major general during the war, and had acquired a wartime reputation that was only exceeded by that of Grant, Sherman, and Sheridan. If Grant could convince Logan of Porter's innocence, it would be possible to push a bill through the senate exonerating Porter and restoring his rank.

Grant also wrote a letter to another senator friend, Senator Cameron of Pennsylvania, beseeching his assistance.

New York, Feb 4, 1882
Hon. J. D. Cameron, U.S. Senate, Washington D. C.:

Dear Sir,

It has been my intention until with the last few days to visit Washington this winter to spend some time, and there to have a conversation with you and with General Logan on the subject of the Fitz-John Porter case; but having now pretty nearly decided not to go to Washington, I have determined to write, and write to you so that you might state my position to your friends, and particularly to General Logan, and if you choose, show this letter to any such people.

When I commenced the examination of the Fitz-John Porter case as it now stands, it was with the conviction that his sentence was a just one, and that his punishment had been light for so hideous an offence; but I tried to throw off all prejudice in the case, and to examine it on its merits. I came out of that examination with the firm conviction that an entirely innocent man had been most unjustly punished. I cast no censure upon the court which tried him, because the evidence which now proves his entire innocence of disobedience of orders it was impossible to have before that court.

When I completed the investigation and came to the conclusion that I did—of his innocence—my first thought was to write to General Logan, because I regard him as my friend, and I am sure I am his, and he has made, probably, the ablest speech of his life in opposition to the bill for General Porter's restoration to the army. I thought, therefore, it was due to him that I should inform him of the conclusion that I had come to after the investigation. But as the President was just about visiting this city when my letter to him was written, and it was desired to present it to him here, I requested, in lieu of a letter to General Logan, to have a copy of my letter to the President sent to him. This was done.

You are aware that when General Logan made his speech against General Porter, it was in opposition to a bill pending in Congress. He like myself, was thoroughly convinced of the guilt of General Porter, and was therefore opposed to the bill. His investigations therefore were necessarily to find arguments to sustain his side of a pending question. I of course had no knowledge of the papers he would refer to, or would examine, to find such arguments; but I knew that he could have the testimony which was taken before the court-martial which convicted; probably also the arguments of the officer who acted as prosecutor when the case was before the Schofield court, and arguments that have been made by lawyers, J. D. Cox and others possibly, all of which were in opposition to General Porter as much as that of paid attorneys in cases before the civil courts.

But my investigation of all the facts that I could bring before me of the occurrence from the 27th of August, 1862, and from some little time prior, to the 1st of September, the same year, show conclusively that the court and some of the witnesses entirely misapprehended the position of the enemy on that day.

General Porter was convicted of disobedience of the order of General Pope's, dated at 4.30 P.M. on the 29th of August, to attack the enemy on his right flank, and in his rear, if possible. Dispatches of General Pope of that day show that he knew General Lee was coming to the support of Jackson, whom he thought commanded the only force in his front at that time; but that he could not arrive until the evening of the following day, or the morning of the day after. It was sworn to before the court that this order of 4.30 P.M. reached General Porter at about five or half-past five in the afternoon, but it must be recollected that this testimony was given from memory, and unquestionably without any idea at the time of the occurrence that they were ever to be called upon to give any testimony in the case.

Investigation shows a dispatch from General Porter, dated six o'clock of that afternoon, which makes no mention of having received the order to attack, and it is such a dispatch as could not be written without mentioning the receipt of that order, if it had been received. There is other testimony that makes it entirely satisfactory to my mind that the order was not received until about sun-down, or between sundown and dark. It was given, as stated before, to attack the enemy's right, and, if possible, to get into his rear. This was on the supposition that Jackson was there alone, as General Pope had stated he would be until the evening of the next day, or the morning of the day following. I believe that the court was convinced that on the evening of the 29th of August[,] Jackson, with his force, was there alone; but now it is proved by testimony better than sworn evidence of any persons on the Union side that by 11 o'clock A.M., of the 29th, Longstreet was up and to the right of Jackson with a force much greater than General Porter's entire force. The attack upon Jackson's right and rear was, therefore, impossible, without first wiping out the force of Longstreet. The order did not contemplate, either, a night attack, and, to have obeyed it, even if Longstreet had not been there, General Porter would have been obliged to make a night attack. But, even as it was, I find that General Porter, notwithstanding the late hour, did all he could to obey that order. He had previously given a command to General Morell, who commanded the most advanced division, or one most fronting the enemy, to throw out a skirmish line to engage the enemy, or to keep him occupied, and on the receipt of this order, although at this late hour, he immediately sent orders to General Morell to increase it from a skirmish line to a large force, and that he would be with him as soon as he could get there.

He did actually go to the front, although it was dark, to superintend this movement, and as far as possible to prevent the enemy detaching anything from his front, thus showing a desire to obey the order strictly and to the best of his ability. I find the Schofield board acquit him entirely, but throw some censure upon him for having expressed a lack of confidence in his commanding officer. Such conduct might be censured, although if every man in the army had been punished who had expressed lack of confidence in his superior officer many of our best soldiers would have been punished. But, in fact, if this was not stated in the summing up of the case by the board, I should not have found that he had expressed any such lack of confidence. On the contrary, to my mind now, he was zealous in giving a support to General Pope, and more so, possibly, for the reason that he knew among his former army associates there was a good deal of apprehension, to say the least, of his fitness for his new place. It must be recollected that General Pope was selected from a Western army and brought East to command an army where there were a great many generals who had had the experience in a previous war, and who had, like himself, a military education, and there may (improperly) have been a feeling that it was reflection upon them to go out of their own command to find a suitable commander; and it is also very probable that expression was freely given to that feeling. But it would be well to reflect what would have been the sentiment in the West if an officer from the Eastern army had been sent out to supersede all of them and to command them, and whether or not there might have not been some harsh criticisms, even by men who proved to be among our most gallant and devoted commanders. Then, too, in re-examining the case, my attention was called again to General Pope's early order in taking command of the Army of Virginia. I send you a copy of this order. You will see that it was calculated to make the army to whom it was addressed feel that it was a reflection upon their former services and former commanders, from that of a company to the commander of the whole, and that even as amiable people as General Logan and myself are would have been very apt to have made some very uncomplimentary remarks if they had been addressed by an Eastern officer sent west to command over us in our field of duty. I commenced reading up this case with the conviction that General Porter had been guilty, as found by the court, but came out of the investigation with a thorough conviction that I, and the public generally, had done him a fearful injustice, and entirely satisfied that any intelligent man, or lawyer, who will throw aside prejudice and examine the case as I have done, will come to the same conclusion.

As stated in my letter to the President, I feel it incumbent upon me, in view of the positions that I have held heretofore, and my failure then to do what I now wish I had done, to do all in my power to place General Porter right before the public and in future history, and to repair my own unintentional injustice.

I address this letter to you, knowing that you will have a desire to do just what your judgment dictates as being right in the matter, and that you will state to whomsoever it may seem to you proper and necessary my present convictions upon this case.

Very truly yours, U.S. Grant.[2]

By 1882, support for the exoneration was also welling up in the house. Strangely enough, one of the leaders in this effort was ex–Confederate Lieutenant General Joseph Wheeler, the famous cavalry leader, who was now a representative from Alabama. Wheeler had been a cadet at West Point from 1855 to 1859, and his cavalry tactics instructor had been none other than Fitz-John Porter.

President Arthur responded promptly and favorably to Grant's letter, as might be expected. On May 4, 1882, Arthur remitted that part of Porter's sentence that was ongoing. That is, he remitted the prohibition of Porter occupying any federal office of trust or gain from that day forward. Arthur thought he had the legal authority to do this much without the consent of Congress. This was a partial victory for Porter, but only partial. Porter still stood convicted and he still did not have his rank back. However, bills were now welling up through both houses of Congress, and it appeared to be only a matter of time, and short time at that, before Porter's victory was complete.

Then, when the nightmare finally seemed to be coming to an end, fate again took a strange turn. The bill exonerating Porter and restoring his rank was laid before Arthur for his signature—and he vetoed it. Arthur's veto was not related to the merits of the Porter case. Rather, it was on constitutional grounds and was on the recommendation of his attorney general. The bill created a vacancy specifically for Porter, with the understanding that Arthur appoint Porter to the vacancy. It was the president's prerogative to appoint individuals to federal positions with the advice and consent of the Senate. The attorney general believed that the bill violated these constitutional prerogatives. The Senate overrode Arthur's veto; the House could not. Porter, now approaching sixty, lost again.

Grover Cleveland won the presidency in 1884. He was the first Democrat to be elected since the Civil War, and now Porter, for the first time, was petitioning a member of his own party. In 1886, both houses of Congress again passed a bill exonerating Porter and restoring him to the ranks he had in the regular army the date he was cashiered, that is, to colonel from May 1, 1862, and to brevet brigadier general. President Cleveland signed the bill on August 5, 1886. Porter's victory was now complete, but with one small exception—the bill did not provide him with back pay.

On August 5, 1886, Porter found himself the senior colonel in the regular army on active duty and, because of his brevet, again entitled to be addressed as "general." However, he was now sixty-four years old, past the normal age of retirement, and retired two days later.

12

Porter After the Verdict

When Porter learned of Lincoln's decision on January 21, 1863, he was already forty years old. He was now excluded from the only profession he had ever known. He had entered West Point twenty-two years earlier, and had known nothing but the military since. He had risen to the rank of major general, a rank near the very top. Although there were other major generals, only two men in the history of his country had achieved higher rank. These were George Washington and Winfield Scott. Now Porter was nothing. In fact, he was less than nothing. If he were to enlist in the army as a private, he could not rise to the rank of corporal as others could. This would be a position of trust, and he was forever barred from a position of trust with the federal government. He had been a key player in his nation's greatest trial. Now he could play no role at all. He must watch from the sidelines. The shame of it all would have been enough to break most men. Porter, however, was a fighter. He resolved to right what he considered a wrong, whatever the time and effort.

Porter was not an independently wealthy man. He lived and supported his family on his general's salary. As of January 21, 1863, he had a young wife and three children under the age of six years. They resided at 66 Union Place in a fashionable area of New York City, in a lovely, large old house with a large flower garden and fountain. As of this day, his income stopped and his immediate task was to secure the means to support them. This was an era when there was no unemployment insurance and no food stamps. It was expected that in such circumstances one would be helped by one's own; that is, one's relatives. And so, Porter was helped. Initially, the help came from an aunt of his wife. Porter understood, however, that this must be short lived. He must quickly find employment that would give him a regular source of income.

Although Porter did not have money, he did have assets that could aid him in securing money. First and foremost was his prominence and his name recognition. He lived at a time when the most famous individuals were neither athletes nor entertainers. They were generals, both North and South. The front pages of the newspapers carried little other than war news. They trumpeted the successes and failures of the generals. Generals' names became household words. Among the most popular of these was none other than Fitz-John

Porter. He was the very model of a modern major general—handsome, martial, daring, and, right up to his conviction, seemingly supremely competent.

Generals had become so popular during the Civil War that four of the five presidents elected after Lincoln were Civil War generals. Despite Porter's conviction, many, if not most, considered him innocent. He was widely perceived as a victim rather than a villain. Porter, as a general, had of course demonstrated that he could handle large numbers of men and large enterprises.

Another great asset of Porter's was the fact that he had friends in high places who could unlock doors for him that remained locked to the common man. Porter, unlike say, Pope and McDowell, was a likeable man. A word often used to describe his mannerisms was "gentlemanly." His subordinate senior officers, almost to a man, remained intensely loyal to him, and many were to return to important positions after the war. Porter's friends in high places were not restricted to Americans. During the Civil War era, it was customary for European powers to place officers on the staffs of the commanding generals of warring foreign powers as observers. These officers were often of the nobility. For example, the Prince de Joinville, the Compte de Paris, and the Duc de Chartres served on the staff of McClellan. All became fast friends of Porter, and we shall meet them again later.

Two of Porter's friends played key roles in his future. George B. McClellan had been Porter's superior, mentor, hero, and a friend in the army. McClellan was relieved from command of the Army of the Potomac in November 1862 and ordered to his home in New Jersey to await further orders. Such orders never came. In July 1864, McClellan received the nomination of the Democratic Party to run against President Lincoln in the election of November 1864. McClellan thus became the titular head of the Democratic Party until the next presidential election. McClellan lost the election and took his wife on an extended trip of Europe, during which his son, George B. McClellan, Jr., was born.

McClellan and family returned from Europe in 1868, and in 1870 McClellan accepted the position of chief engineer of the Department of Docks in New York City. In 1872, he became president of the Atlantic and Great Western Railroad, and in 1878 was elected governor of New Jersey. McClellan's son, George B. McClellan, Jr., continued on as a power in New York City politics. Between 1889 and 1892 he was treasurer of the New York and Brooklyn Bridge; in 1892 was elected to the board of aldermen, and became its president in 1893. In 1894 he was elected congressman from New York City and in 1903 was elected the mayor of New York City.

Another close friend of Porter's was Theodore Randolph. Randolph was a resident of New Jersey and a very wealthy man with interests in mining and the transportation of ores. He was also president of the Morris and Essex Railroad. Randolph, like McClellan, was a Democrat and was elected to the New

Jersey General Assembly in 1859, to the New Jersey Senate in 1862, and as governor of New Jersey in 1869. After serving as governor, he represented New
Jersey in the United States Senate until his death in 1883.

In the 1860s, as today, the politics of New Jersey and New York City were
closely intertwined. In Porter's day, this was a stronghold of Democrat political power. The Port of New York, which was the largest source of revenue for
both states in the 1860s, overlaps both states. On the west side of the Hudson
River, the port is New Jersey. On the east side of the river, it is New York.
Then, as now, the port had to be jointly managed by the two states, which ultimately resulted in the present arrangement of the New York–New Jersey Port
Authority.

Thus, two of Porter's closest friends were political powerhouses in the
New Jersey–New York City area. Both were Democrats and both resided in New
Jersey. Porter was a Democrat and variously resided in New York City and
New Jersey. In New Jersey, he was Randolph's next door neighbor.

In the 1860s and 1870s, there was no civil service—federal, state, or local—
in New York. To the victors belonged the spoils, and it was the norm for powerful politicians to put their friends and supporters in lucrative positions. Two
of Porter's closest friends were in a position to do just that for him. For much
of the remainder of Porter's life, he occupied high level political patronage
positions in the area.

Porter had another large asset. He was a college graduate in an era when
only a tiny percent attended college. At the time, West Point, although a military academy, was primarily an engineering college, and Porter graduated near
the top of his class. The 1860s was a time of nation building, and Porter was
educated in a most marketable and in-demand discipline.

Porter's first gainful employment after his conviction was not a political
plum. It began in 1864, the year after his conviction. Porter was hired by a
group of New York City investors to assess the investment prospects for gold
mining in the Gregory Gulch area of Colorado. This was indeed the wild west
at the time. It took Porter fifteen days to reach the area via train, stage coach,
and horse. Porter returned with a glowing account of the prospects, and as a
result, the investors formed a corporation called the Gunnell Gold Mining
Company. Porter was appointed the company's general manager and returned
to Colorado. He now had a salary that exceeded his salary as major general.

While in Colorado, he bought mining property in his own name with
money he borrowed from his friend Theodore Randolph. The value of Porter's
property skyrocketed and Porter soon estimated its value at $80,000—a princely
sum in those days. Porter sold a portion of his holding at a large profit. It now
seemed that his days of financial distress were behind him. Porter, however,
pined for his wife and children, and in August 1865, resigned and returned to
New York. Upon his return, he purchased a twenty acre plot in New Jersey,
next to the home of his friend Theodore Randolph, built a palatial home, and

moved his family from New York. The family now employed two maids and two gardeners.

Shortly after Porter's return, he set out on a business trip to Europe to attempt to sell stock. Here, he renewed acquaintance with his royal friends from McClellan's staff, who wined and dined him lavishly. Although the trip may not have been considered a great success as a business venture, it was a huge social success and a welcome and much deserved vacation. Porter's return to New York on March 23, 1866, on the steamship *Australasian* was duly noted in the *New York Times*, along with the arrival of other notables.

Porter's next major job, or, more correctly, position, was a political plum. The State of New Jersey had budgeted more than $3,000,000 for the construction of a giant new hospital for the insane. This was to be the largest state construction project to date, and Porter was put in charge of the construction. Again, his performance proved more than satisfactory.

In 1869, Porter received a most interesting offer. It was from the Khedive (ruler) of Egypt, who offered him command of the Egyptian Army. The proffered salary was most attractive. For Porter to accept, he would have to leave the country and give up his effort for exoneration. He declined.

It is interesting to speculate what might have been had Porter accepted the Khedive's offer. As it turned out, the Khedive was soon to be in need of a good general. An individual turned up in the Egyptian Sudan in the 1870s, proclaimed himself the Mahdi (the Mohammeden anointed one), and began gathering followers. He soon was in control of most of the Sudan. The Khedive sent the Egyptian Army, under command of General William Hicks (a British general who occupied the position Porter could have had) to bring the Mahdi to heel. Hicks's army met that of the Mahdi at a place called El Obeid in November 1883. The Mahdi destroyed the Egyptian Army and killed Hicks. Would this have been the fate of Porter? We will never know.

Porter was appointed commissioner of public works for the City of New York in 1875 to fill out the final year of the term of another appointee. Porter performed in a highly creditable manner and was strongly endorsed by the business leaders of the city for a new, full four year appointment. However, this he did not receive.

Porter was soon again under financial pressure because of the legal expenses attendant to his campaign for exoneration. His friend Randolph again came to the rescue, making Porter manager of his mining interests.

In 1878, Porter received another New Jersey political plum. The Central Railroad of New Jersey was in bankruptcy and Porter was appointed receiver. This provided him a good salary for three years. In 1884 Porter was appointed police commissioner for the City of New York for a full four year term. The salary was $5,000 per year. This was at a time when a day laborer in New York earned $1.50 per day for an annual wage of less than $500.

Porter was exonerated and restored to the rank of colonel on August 5,

1886. Although he received no back pay, he was now entitled to the salary of a full colonel, and when he retired two days later, to a substantial pension for the rest of his life, the Porters were again in financial clover.

When Porter completed his term as police commissioner in 1888, he was appointed fire commissioner. He thus remained on the New York City payroll—and incidentally, near the top of that. After serving a year as fire commissioner, Porter resigned. He now took his last non-political job. It was as head of a New York City based slag, paving, and roofing company.

On August 7, 1893, Porter, now seventy-one years old, received his final political plum. He was appointed cashier of the Post Office of New York City, with an annual salary of $2,600 per year. This provided a good sinecure for the Porters in their old age. This salary, along with Porter's colonel's pension, allowed the couple, whose children were now grown and independent, to live most comfortably. Porter finally retired from all active employment in 1897 at the age of seventy-five.

By almost any standards, Porter would have been considered a success in his post-conviction life—even had he never been exonerated. He occupied positions just below the level of mayor of the biggest city in the country, and these successfully. Throughout his career, he associated on equal terms with powerful politicians and the kingpins of industry.

By all appearances, Porter's marriage was a happy one. The Porters added one more child after Porter's return from Europe, thus completing the family at two boys and two girls. All four were provided with the finest educations available. The Porters shielded their children from their problem. They never discussed Porter's conviction or campaign for exoneration in front of them until their maturity.

When Porter was finally exonerated and restored to rank in 1886, there was much jubilation in the Porter household. They received heaps of congratulatory letters and mounds of flowers. Much of it was from now old veterans of the Army of the Potomac, from privates to generals. Porter's old Fifth Corps was particularly well-represented. The Porters were even received at a reception at the White House.

Porter lived a stressful life. He had been subjected to a shame that not many men could endure. After all, how many men in U.S. history have been judicially barred from ever occupying a position of trust with the government? Porter, however, managed to maintain his equipoise until the age of seventy, when he finally suffered a nervous breakdown. However, he recovered even from this, and was to return to his old self for a period until his death.

Porter's case had a slight political tinge from the beginning and was to become more politicized as time went by. He lived in an era when a man's political party affiliation was more important to him than it is today. At the time of his trial (and forever after) Porter was a Democrat. He was also the favorite of the leading Democrat of the time, George B. McClellan. Within one and a half years of Porter's conviction, McClellan was to receive the Democratic party's nomination to run against Lincoln in the election of 1864. Many were to believe that Republican appointed Stanton rigged the court against Porter, and that Republican appointed Col. Holt tilted his summation of the case for Lincoln against Porter. Lastly, of course, Republican President Lincoln approved the sentence.

If the Republicans could demonstrate that Porter was guilty of a heinous crime, was fairly tried, justly convicted, and received a fair and even lenient sentence, it would be a plus for the Republican party. If the Democrats could demonstrate that Porter was an innocent man, railroaded by corrupt Republicans, it would be a plus for the Democrats. When Porter's relief measures periodically arose in Congress, they normally received a near party line vote; the Democrats for, the Republicans against.

By the mid 1870s, the Senate was well populated with ex–Civil War generals. Republican Senators and ex–Generals Logan and Burnside voted against Porter; the six or so ex–Confederate generals, all Democrats, voted for Porter. As a matter of fact, some of the Confederates became his most vociferous and effective supporters.

Thus as time went by, some of Porter's old friends, such as Burnside, became his opponents, and his old enemies, the Confederates, his supporters. Politics does indeed make strange bedfellows.

Porter's final vindication and restoration to rank came about in the Cleveland administration—the first administration of the Democrats in the twenty-three years since Porter was convicted.

13

What Happened to Them

In relating the final fate of each of the key players in this drama, let us start with the three witnesses whose testimony was most damaging to Porter. These were Maj. Gen. Pope, Brig. Gen. Roberts, and Maj. Gen. McDowell.

Maj. Gen. John Pope left Washington in 1863 for his new assignment as commanding general of the Department of the Northwest with his headquarters in Minnesota. Pope was out of the Civil War, discredited, widely viewed as the cause of the loss of the second battle of Manassas, and destined to spend almost the entire remainder of his career fighting Indians.

Pope was embittered. He believed until his dying day that the true cause of the loss was McClellan's foot dragging in sending him reinforcements and Porter's disobedience of his orders. Pope initially engaged in an acrimonious exchange of correspondence with General-in-Chief Henry Halleck, his hitherto patron and friend, attempting to justify his actions, blame Porter and McClellan, and resurrect his reputation. This only served to alienate Halleck.

In January 1886, Pope published a lengthy account of the second battle of Manassas in *Century* magazine. (A portion of this article is contained in Chapter 4). Even though this article was written after the contents of the Schofield report were known to Pope, the general's opinion of Porter's and McClellan's culpability remained unchanged. In the article, Pope put forward some weighty arguments to justify his position. For example, in the Schofield testimony, Longstreet contended that he could have brought overwhelming force against Porter on August 29 and, had Porter attacked, he would have destroyed him. Pope countered with the logical point that, had this been so, why did not Longstreet attack Porter?

Pope's subsequent career fighting Indians was generally considered successful and meritorious, and thus the sole blot on his long career consisted of the brief period of weeks that he commanded the Army of Virginia. Pope also achieved renown for his advocacy of fairer and more humane treatment for the Indians.

Pope retired from the army in 1888 and died at the Old Soldiers Home at Sandusky, Ohio, on September 23, 1892, at the age of seventy. Thus, although

Pope did not outlive Porter, he lived to see Porter's exoneration and restoration in rank.

Brig. Gen. Benjamin Stone Roberts, the inspector general in Pope's army, was the man who brought the charges against Porter, and was one of the principal witnesses against him. When Pope was in essence exiled to Minnesota in 1863, Roberts initially accompanied him. After fighting Indians with Pope for a year or so, Roberts was ordered back to the Civil War. He received assignments in Washington and the Gulf Coast, and ended the war in command of a cavalry division in western Tennessee. At the close of the war, Roberts received a commission as lieutenant colonel in the regular army. He served on the frontier until 1868 and was then assigned to Yale University as professor of military science. Roberts retired in 1870 and devoted his full time to manufacturing and marketing the "Roberts Repeating Rifle," which he had invented. Roberts died in Washington, D.C., on January 29, 1875, at the age of sixty-four.

By the time of the Porter trial, the military reputation of Maj. Gen. McDowell was already a shambles, both in the eyes of the rank and file and the public. Even prior to the second battle of Manassas, McDowell was widely perceived, perhaps unjustly, as responsible for the fiasco of the first battle of Manassas. Now McDowell, in the eyes of many, was being associated with the disaster of the second battle of Manassas. This, of course, if true, would be quite an accomplishment—losing the same battle twice, disastrously each time, and against an inferior force.

McDowell attempted to resurrect his reputation by requesting that a military court of inquiry examine his entire performance as a general. This was done immediately after the Porter trial. McDowell's performance was found to be entirely satisfactory, except for the night of August 28–29 when, during the second battle of Manassas, he managed to get lost and was out of touch both with his own troops and with his commander, Gen. Pope.

However, even the court of inquiry failed to resurrect McDowell's reputation among the troops. This may have been in part because of McDowell's personality. He was never popular with his men or, for that matter, with his contemporary officers. McDowell did have and did retain the confidence of both Stanton and Lincoln.

McDowell had been a key player in the war in the east from its beginning through the second battle of Manassas. However, because of his reputation, possibly unjust, as a loser, it was now evident that he could play no further role in the Civil War. Probably because of Lincoln's and Stanton's support, McDowell was given the face-saving and choice assignment of commanding general of the Department of the Pacific, with headquarters in San Francisco. McDowell remained in the west through the remainder of his military career.

At the end of the war, he was given the rank of brigadier general in the regular army and ultimately rose to the rank of major general. McDowell retired from the army in 1884 and accepted the civilian position of commissioner of parks for the city of San Francisco. He died one year later in 1885 of a heart attack at the age of sixty-seven.

Let us now turn to the members of the court-martial that convicted Porter in 1863. There were nine members of the court and a judge advocate who served as the prosecutor. All ten died before Porter, and eight of the nine members of the court did not live long enough to see Porter exonerated and his rank restored.

Maj. Gen. David Hunter, president of the court, continued on in Washington after the court-martial, when he was designated president of the military commission assigned to affix the blame for the surrender of Harpers Ferry. After the completion of the Harpers Ferry assignment, in May 1864 Hunter was assigned to command the Department of West Virginia and was thus returned to the field of combat. Hunter engaged in operations against the Confederates in the Shenandoah Valley and in south West Virginia, during which he managed to solidify his reputation as the most hated Union general in the South, with the possible exceptions of Sherman and Butler. Hunter's performance as a combat commander was less than sterling, and after only three months, probably at Grant's request, he asked to be relieved of his command. Grant replaced him with the much more capable Sheridan. This, however, was not the last of David Hunter. After the assassination of Lincoln, Stanton appointed him president of the military court tasked with judging the conspirators. Among the more controversial results of the court were the conviction of Dr. Samuel Mudd and the conviction and hanging of Mary Surratt.

Hunter retired from the army in 1866 after a long and controversial career and continued on as a resident of Washington, D.C. He died twenty years later, in 1886, at the ripe old age of eighty-four. Among Hunter's non-controversial accomplishments was the fact that he was born and died in the District of Columbia, a rarity for a general indeed.

Next in seniority to Hunter was Maj. Gen. Ethan Allen Hitchcock. He was already sixty-four years old at the time of the trial, and because of his advanced age and close and cordial association with Secretary of War Stanton, was retained in Washington for administrative duties. His primary duty became commissioner for the exchange of prisoners. He was involved with prisoner matters until the end of the war and beyond until his retirement in 1867. Hitchcock performed most creditably in this capacity. Strangely, Hitchcock spent the remainder of his life residing in the South; first in Charleston, South Carolina, and then in Sparta, Georgia. In his retirement, Hitchcock returned to his first love, writing about literary subjects. He published works on Shakespeare and others. Hitchcock died in 1870 at the age of seventy-two.

The next member of the court in seniority was Brig. Gen. Rufus King. He had been minister to the Papal States up to the outbreak of the war and, while on active duty, was on leave of absence from that position. King was an epileptic in uncertain health, and probably should not have been on active duty in

1862. During most of the second battle of Manassas, he was too ill to command his division and was succeeded by his senior brigade commander, Gen. Hatch.

King left the military soon after the court-martial and returned to his position as minister. He remained in this capacity until 1868. Upon King's return to the States, he was appointed deputy collector of customs for the port of New York City. He resigned this position in 1869 for health reasons. King remained in New York City until his death in 1876 at the age of sixty-two. The commissioner of public works for the city of New York at the time of King's death was none other than Fitz-John Porter.

Next in seniority on the court was Brig. Gen. Benjamin Mayberry Prentiss. Prentiss was one of only three non–West Point generals on the court. After the conclusion of the court, Prentiss was ordered to the command of the District of Eastern Arkansas. In this capacity, he contributed to Grant's capture of Vicksburg, which was the turning point of the war. Prentiss resigned his commission and left the army in late 1863 for family reasons and returned to resume his profession of the law.

Prentiss subsequently held a variety of low level federal posts, including pension agent, land office agent, and postmaster. He died while postmaster of Bethany, Missouri, on February 8, 1901, at the age of eighty-one. Prentiss was the last of the members of the court to die, but still pre-deceased Porter.

Next came Brigadier James Brewerton Ricketts, who stayed on in Washington after the Porter court-martial for a time in administrative duties to more fully recover from wounds he received at Antietam. On April 4, 1864, Ricketts was returned to field duty when he was assigned to command the Third Division of the Sixth Corps of the Army of the Potomac. From this point onward to the end of the war, Ricketts saw almost continuous combat. He participated in all of Grant's battles, from the Wilderness to Petersburg. His division was then rushed back by sea to fend off Early's raid on Washington. At the battle of the Monocacy, his division suffered over fifty percent casualties.

Ricketts rose to major general and to command of the Sixth Corps. The corps was next transferred to Sheridan's command and participated in Sheridan's operations in the Shenandoah Valley. Here, at the battle of Cedar Creek, Ricketts was seriously wounded for the third time.

Ricketts wanted to stay on in the post-war army but, because of his condition caused by numerous wounds, was retired in 1867 with the rank of major general. Ricketts died in Washington, D.C., on September 22, 1887, at the age of seventy.

Brig. Gen. Silas Casey, like Hitchcock, was an army old-timer, having graduated from West Point way back in 1826, nineteen years before Porter. Although Casey had been very active early in the war, having participated in McClellan's Peninsula Campaign, he was to play no further combat role after the Porter court-martial. He, like Hitchcock, was retained in Washington for administrative duties. A primary duty was as chairman of a board entrusted with examining officers to ascertain their fitness for commanding black troops. Casey pursued his duties with his usual zeal.

At the termination of the war, Casey reverted to the rank of colonel in the regular army and commanded the Ninth Infantry Regiment until his retirement in 1868. Casey died in Brooklyn, New York in 1882 at the age of seventy-five.

The next court member, Brig. Gen. James A. Garfield, achieved the greatest fame and prominence of any member of the court by far. Garfield was to become the twentieth president of the United States. After the Porter trial, Garfield was ordered to report to the Army of the Tennessee, commanded by Major General William S. Rosecrans. Garfield became fast friends with Rosecrans and was appointed his chief of staff. After considerable success, the Army of Tennessee suffered a disastrous defeat in the battle of Chickamauga in September 1863 and was bottled up in Chattanooga. Garfield, who was in no sense to blame, was called back to Washington. Garfield had been a representative in Congress from Ohio before the war, and now Lincoln convinced him that he could better serve the country and administration if he resigned from the army and returned to Congress. This Garfield did, and after seventeen years in Congress, in 1880, was elected president of the United States.

Garfield had little opportunity to make his mark as President. He was shot by an assassin just three months after taking office and succumbed to his wound on September 19, 1881, at the age of fifty.

Brig. Gen. Napoleon Bonaparte Buford was the older half-brother of Brig. Gen. John Buford, who had appeared as a witness at the court-martial. The elder Buford served all his time in the western theater before the court-martial and returned to the western theater afterwards. He served as a brigade commander in the campaign against Vicksburg, and afterwards as a garrison commander, first at Cairo, Illinois, and then at Helena, Arkansas, until the end of the war.

Buford was mustered out in August 1865 at the rank of brigadier general. He had risen to the rank of major general, but this rank was never confirmed by the Senate. Buford served for a short time as commissioner of Indian Affairs and then as inspector for the Union Pacific Railroad, then under construction. He died on March 28, 1883, at the age of seventy-six.

Brig. Gen. John Potts Slough, the junior member of the court, was a lawyer-politician and one of the three members of the court who was not a West Point graduate. Slough was military governor of the district of Alexandria, Virginia, at the time of the court-martial and continued in this position until the end of the war.

At the war's end, President Johnson appointed Slough chief justice of the New Mexico Supreme Court. Before the trial, Slough had achieved fame in New Mexico by winning the battle of Glorieta Pass in 1862. Slough, who was the second youngest member of the court-martial, was the first to die. In his new capacity as chief justice, he immediately generated many political enemies, one of whom killed him in a fight. Slough died December 17, 1867, at the age of thirty-eight. New Mexico was indeed the "wild west" at this time.

Col. Joseph Holt, the judge advocate who successfully prosecuted Porter in his court-martial, was to move on to greater things. He was the government's chief prosecutor in two more of the most famous cases of the nineteenth century. In 1863, he secured the conviction of Congressman Clement Valldingham in his treason trial, and, in 1865, was the chief prosecutor in the trial of the Lincoln assassination conspirators.

When the government created the bureau of military justice in the War Department in 1864, Holt was promoted to brigadier general and appointed its first head. In 1865, Holt was given a brevet as major general in the regular army for his faithful, meritorious, and distinguished service during the war.

Holt stayed on as head of the Bureau of Military Justice until 1875, when he retired at the age of sixty-two. He lived on in Washington, D.C., until his death in 1894 at the age of eighty-seven. Holt thus lived to see Porter's complete exoneration, but pre-deceased him by seven years.

Five generals who testified at the trial had been members of Porter's Fifth Corps and subordinate to him. All five spoke highly of Porter and did what they could to defend him within the bounds of their oaths.

The first of these was Maj. Gen. George Morell, Porter's First Division commander and the senior of the five. Morell's days in the army were nearing an end. He left the army in 1864 because of ill health and spent the remainder of his life at his home in upstate New York as a semi-invalid and then an invalid. Morell died in 1883 at the age of sixty-eight.

Brig. Gen. George Sykes was Porter's Second Division commander. Sykes participated in all the subsequent battles of the Fifth Corps in the east through the battle of Gettysburg and rose to major general and command of the Fifth Corps. In the aftermath of Gettysburg, Sykes entered into an altercation with his commander, General George Gordon Meade, about an order Meade allegedly gave. This resulted in Sykes being relieved of command of his corps and being transferred to Kansas, where he spent the remainder of the war.

In the drawdown of the army at the end of the war, Sykes received a commission of lieutenant colonel in the regular army. He rose to the rank of colonel in command of the Twentieth Infantry and died at his post at Fort Brown, Texas, on February 8, 1880, at the age of fifty-eight.

Brig. Gen. John Reynolds was not actually subordinate to Porter but to McDowell at the second battle of Manassas. Reynolds, however, had been a part of Porter's Fifth Corps during the Peninsula Campaign. Reynolds rose to the rank of major general, and in June 1863, Lincoln offered him command of the Army of the Potomac. Reynolds said that he could only accept if he were guaranteed freedom of action. Lincoln could not, of course, accept this surrender of his constitutional prerogatives as commander in chief, and Reynolds did not get the command. Neither Lincoln nor Reynolds knew at the time that Reynolds was already in the last days of his life. He was killed July 1, 1863, on the first day of the battle of Gettysburg at the age of forty.

Brig. Gen. Charles Griffin, a brigade commander in Morell's division, was a notorious loud mouth who narrowly avoided a court-martial and a fate similar to Porter's for his disparaging remarks about Pope and for his failure to bring his brigade onto the battlefield on the thirtieth. However, Griffin did subsequently rise to division command and participation as such in almost all of the major battles of the Army of the Potomac.

In the final phases of the war, Griffin was promoted to major general and assumed command of the Fifth Corps. Grant, in his memoirs, specifically mentions Griffin as one of the better corps commanders. Griffin stayed on in the post war regular army as colonel of the Thirty-fifth Infantry Regiment stationed at Galveston, Texas. Here, he contracted yellow fever and died on September 15, 1867, at the age of forty-two.

Brig. Gen. Daniel Butterfield was a brigade commander in Morell's division. When Porter was relieved of command to stand trial, Butterfield was promoted to major general and to command of the Fifth Corps. He retained this position until Joseph Hooker was given command of the Army of the Potomac in January 1863. Hooker selected Butterfield as his chief of staff and the two became fast drinking friends.

When Hooker was relieved by Meade in June 1863, Meade retained Butterfield as chief of staff even though he did not like him, because it was a time of crisis. Butterfield was wounded on July 3 at the battle of Gettysburg, which gave Meade the opportunity he sought to divest himself of Butterfield. Upon Butterfield's recovery, he was assigned to the command of his old friend, Hooker, who was now corps commander in the Army of the Cumberland. Butterfield remained with Hooker until June 1864 when illness forced him to leave the field.

Butterfield remained in the army as a colonel after the end of the war and was assigned to recruiting duty in New York City, where he had lucrative business interests. Butterfield resigned in 1870 to accept the position of head of the U.S. Sub-treasury in New York and to resume his association with the American Express Corporation. Butterfield remained in New York until his death at the age of sixty-nine.

There are a number of unusual factoids associated with Butterfield. He was the only one of the Fifth Corps generals that testified at Porter's trial who was not a West Point graduate. Yet, Butterfield is buried at West Point and has the most ornate monument on the grounds. Butterfield's military accomplishments were many, including winning the Congressional Medal of Honor. Yet, today he is mostly remembered as the composer of the bugle call "Taps," which is played at every military funeral. Butterfield is the only main player in the

Porter trial to survive Porter, but he did this by only fifty-seven days. Butterfield died on July 17, 1901.

Major Generals George B. McClellan and Ambrose Burnside were the two senior generals to testify at Porter's trial. McClellan, as commanding officer of the Army of the Potomac, was Porter's commanding officer up until the date Porter reported in to Pope. Burnside, as the senior officer stationed on the lower Rappahannock, was Porter's on-the-scene superior from the time Porter debarked at Aquia until he reported to Pope. McClellan was Porter's friend and patron, Burnside his friend. Both testified at the trial as character witnesses.

McClellan was relieved as commanding general of the Army of the Potomac on November 5, 1862, the same day that Porter was relieved as commander of the Fifth Corps and ordered to stand trial. McClellan was ordered to his home in New Jersey to await further orders. Such orders never came. The next we hear of McClellan was when he was nominated by the Democratic party as their candidate in the presidential race of 1864. McClellan resigned his commission to compete for the presidency. Had the war turned in favor of the Confederates by election time, it is entirely possible that McClellan would have become the seventeenth and youngest president of the United States. However, the contrary happened. By election day November 1864, it was evident to all that the Union was winning. Lincoln won big and McClellan carried only three states.

After the election, McClellan and his wife took an extended tour of Europe, during which their son, George B. McClellan, Jr., was born. After the McClellans returned to the states, in 1870 he accepted the position of chief engineer in the newly formed New York City Department of Docks. In 1872, he became president of the Atlantic and Great Western Railroad. He then entered politics and was elected governor of New Jersey in 1878. After his term as governor, McClellan spent much of his time writing his memoirs. He died on October 29, 1885, at the age of fifty-eight.

George B. McClellan had all the qualities necessary to become one of the great men in American history. However, he also had a couple of additional qualities that prevented him from doing so. Each time he reached the door stoop of greatness, as the old saying goes, he came up "a day late and a dollar short."

The name of George B. McClellan lived on after him in the person of his namesake son, who achieved fame in his own right. The young McClellan was mayor of New York City from 1904 to 1909 and lived until November 30, 1940, during the Roosevelt administration.

Lincoln appointed Maj. Gen. Ambrose Burnside commanding general of the Army of the Potomac on November 9, 1862, over Burnside's objections. Burnside believed he was not qualified, and subsequent events tended to support his opinion. After a tenure of less than ninety days and the Union defeat at the battle of Fredericksburg and Burnside's infamous "mud march," Burnside was relieved and transferred to head the Department of Ohio. Here Burnside achieved some military successes in east Tennessee.

In the spring of 1864, Burnside, with his Ninth Corps, was ordered back east to assist Grant in his campaign against Lee. Burnside participated in all the battles from the Wilderness to the siege of Petersburg, where Grant's army became bogged down in the trench war against the Confederates.

This point is a crucial moment in Burnside's career. Among Burnside's troops was a regiment consisting mostly of Pennsylvania coal miners, headed by Colonel Henry Pleasants. Pleasants approached Burnside and said that his men could dig a tunnel under the Confederate lines, pack it with explosives, blow a gaping hole in the Confederate line, and then march on through to Richmond. Burnside thought it a splendid idea and the miners set to work. The big day came on July 30, 1864. The explosion was set off and it worked to perfection. There was a huge crater, a gaping hole in the Confederate line, and the way was open to Richmond. Burnside then marched his men into the crater—but they could not get out the other side and were slaughtered. This caused Burnside to be relieved from command, and he ultimately resigned in April 1865.

Burnside had a splendid post-war civilian career. He became a railroad president, a president of a locomotive factory, a three-time governor of Rhode Island, and a U.S. senator from Rhode Island, a position he held up to the time of his death in 1881 at the age of fifty-seven. Burnside was and is still considered one of Rhode Island's favorite sons.

Some of the lesser lights went on to other successful enterprises. Lt. Col. Thomas C. H. Smith, aide to Gen. Pope, was a damaging witness against Porter. It was he who testified as to Porter's "sneers" when Porter was referring to Pope. Smith was not a military professional with pre-war service, but a lawyer who entered wartime service only a year before the Porter trial. His military career after the Porter trial was highly successful. He was promoted to brigadier general of volunteers and subsequently commanded the Department of Wisconsin. He then served as inspector general of the Department of Missouri until the end of the war. Smith remained in the regular army after the war as paymaster. He retired in 1883 and died in 1897 at the age of seventy-eight. He thus lived to see the man whose reputation he had had so damaged fully exonerated.

Lt. Col. Frederick T. Locke, Porter's faithful chief of staff, remained on as the Fifth Corps chief of staff under subsequent commanders until near the end of the war. He participated in all of the major battles of the Army of the Potomac and was promoted to colonel. In the final phases of the war, he was cited for gallantry at the battle of Five Forks and given a brevet as brigadier general.

Capt. Drake DeKay, the Pope aide who delivered the order to Porter the night of August 27 to march to Bristoe by daylight, is remembered today by Civil War buffs as the Civil War personage with the largest signature. For this reason, DeKay's signatures trade on the Civil War relics market for a greater price than that of most generals.

Pope's long suffering chief of staff, David Ruggles, was a pre-war regular officer and a West Point graduate. Ruggles continued to serve on staff duty after he parted ways with Pope when Pope was ordered to Minnesota. He first served as assistant adjutant general of the Army of the Potomac during its Maryland Campaign, then on special duty with the War Department, and finally as adjutant general of the Army of the Potomac. Ruggles received brevets to colonel and to brigadier general for gallantry.

Ruggles stayed on in the post-war regular army, rising to the rank of brigadier general. He retired in 1879. He spent the remainder of his life as governor of the Old Soldiers Home. Ruggles died in 1904 at the age of seventy-one and is buried in Arlington National Cemetery.

14

A Conspiracy to Convict?

Ever since the Porter court-martial, voices have been heard that contend that there was a conspiracy to convict Porter; that the court was stacked with persons hostile to him; that they knew they were expected to convict him; that they did so and then received their promised rewards.

The basic case for the conspiracy theorists was as follows: The real target was McClellan. McClellan was hugely popular in the Army of the Potomac and was becoming increasingly powerful politically. In fact, he was to become the next candidate for president of the Democratic Party. McClellan had appointed friends such as Porter and Franklin to leading positions in the Army of the Potomac. Even if he were removed from command, his influence would continue. If his appointees could be discredited, McClellan would be discredited.

The conspiracy theorists put forth the following evidence: Porter was ordered to stand trial within days of McClellan's removal as commanding general of the Army of the Potomac. At least five, and perhaps six, members of the court-martial would have been ineligible to serve on a jury in almost any state because of possible prejudice or association with the matter for which Porter was being judged.

Hitchcock had been a competitor of McClellan for the position of commanding general of the Army of the Potomac. Hunter was a close friend of Pope, Porter's chief accuser. Casey had been humiliated by Porter when Porter refused to accept him as a division commander in his corps even though Casey had been nominated for the post by the War Department. King and Ricketts had both been parties to the very matters for which Porter was standing trial, and the conduct of both was under a cloud. Furthermore, they were the chief subordinates of McDowell, who was one of the prosecution's main witnesses. Garfield had been a house guest of Salmon Chase, the secretary of the treasury at the very time of his appointment to the court, and Chase was a vociferous advocate of Porter's conviction.

Furthermore, the theorists contended, the court members were subsequently rewarded for securing Porter's conviction. They point out that on the very day after Porter's conviction, the War Department forwarded promotions for Slough, Prentiss, Casey, and Buford to the Senate for confirmation, and other court members were given choice assignments.

Arguments have also been made to rebut the conspiracy theorists. First, if the objective in part was to remove McClellan's influence in the Army of the Potomac, other actions were very much inconsistent. The replacement chosen for McClellan was Ambrose Burnside, a long time McClellan friend. Next, McClellan's good friend, William Buel Franklin, not only was not court-martialed, but was actually moved up in authority in the Army of the Potomac from corps commander to "grand division" commander.

As regards the members of the court, Porter was given the opportunity to challenge each member, and he chose to challenge none. Furthermore, Porter requested that all proceedings of the court be open to the public, and this request was granted. As for the selection of the members of the court, it looks very much like the chief criterion for selection was availability. Eight of the nine selected happened to be in Washington for one reason or another at the time of their selection. None of the nine were in command of any combat troops. Hitchcock and Casey were on regular long term desk assignments in Washington. Buford was at a desk job in Washington recuperating from an illness, and Ricketts was at a desk job in Washington recuperating from a wound. Prentiss was in Washington awaiting an assignment after having been exchanged as a prisoner, and Garfield was between assignments in Washington. Slough was the military governor of Alexandria, a suburb of Washington, and Hunter, as previously pointed out, was in Washington, having been relieved of his position in the South for cause.

Regarding the supposed awards given to the court members for their conviction of Porter, it is possible that as many as four court members voted for his acquittal. Under the Articles of War, only a simple five to four majority was required for his conviction. Inasmuch as the vote was taken under sworn secrecy, the purveyors of the alleged rewards would not know who to reward and who not to reward. As regards the promotions of the four court members, all four were actually promoted before the trial. It was the Senate confirmation of the promotions that was sought after the trial. Senate confirmation, although required, was normally a routine and *pro forma* part of the promotion process.

The so-called choice assignments given to other court members were really not that choice, and nothing noticeable in the way of a reward came to court members King, Ricketts, or Garfield.

Then too, if there was a conspiracy, one might expect something in the way of a favor for the three main persons who were most influential in securing Porter's conviction, namely, Generals Pope, McDowell, and Roberts. They did not receive any rewards, and furthermore, two of the three were disgracefully banished from any future participation in the Civil War.

To accept the hypothesis of a conspiracy, one must accept that the members of the court were corrupt. Six of the nine members of the court were graduates of West Point, and five of the six had served long and honorably in the army, often at great risk to themselves. Of the three members who were not West Point graduates, one (Prentiss) was later appointed to responsible federal positions by three separate presidents; one (Slough) became chief justice of the Territory of New Mexico; and one (Garfield) became president of the United States.

At the time of the trial, all nine court members had reached the peak of what is probably the most ethical profession in the United States—that of military officer. In the profession of officer, dishonesty in the smallest degree is not tolerated. A single lie in the line of duty would be sufficient grounds for dismissal. If that were not sufficient, Article Eighty-three of the Articles of War provided that "any commissioned officer convicted before a general court-martial of conduct unbecoming an officer and gentleman shall be dismissed from the service."[1]

One might enter the profession of the law or medicine to obtain riches, but no one selects a military career to become wealthy. The commitment must be total, and it is clearly understood that this is up to and including giving one's life if called on to do so. To accept the conspiracy theory, one would have to accept that these nine men, or at least five of them, were willing to stoop to commit a crime that many professional criminals would decline to commit— that is, to find an innocent man guilty.

There is still more to rebut the conspiracy theory. The person or persons selecting the court would have to be corrupt. This boils down to Secretary of War Edwin Stanton and the general-in-chief of the army, Henry Halleck. If Halleck did not taint the court, he would at least have had to acquiesce in Stanton's actions if Stanton did so. There is absolutely nothing in the record of Henry Halleck to indicate that he was other than a patriotic, dedicated, and honest officer. Halleck retained the full confidence of Lincoln, who was an excellent judge of character.

At the time of the conviction, it was widely believed that the conviction was just and the sentence even lenient. Grant believed Porter guilty until he became acquainted with new evidence introduced before the Schofield board. Reporters covering the trial believed him guilty, presidential assistants Hayes and Nicolay believed him guilty, and last of all, Lincoln believed him guilty. Even after the Schofield board hearings, many believed Porter guilty. General, now Senator, Logan still believed him guilty. Asa Gardner, who previously believed him innocent, now believed him guilty, and when the bill that finally restored Porter's rank was passed, approximately one third of the senators and representatives voted against it.

Conspiracy? Hardly!

15

Hero or Villain?

Now that all the evidence is in, here is a final evaluation. Was Fitz-John Porter guilty, a hero, or something in between?

The undisputed facts of charge 1, specification 1 were that between 9:30 and 10 P.M. on August 27, 1862, while at Warrenton Junction, Porter received an order from Pope to be at Bristoe (ten miles away) by daylight on the twenty-eighth, and that Porter, with the head his column, arrived at Bristoe at 10:20 A.M. on the twenty-eighth.

The original court-martial found Porter guilty of the charge and specification. The Schofield board added nothing to dispute the basic facts stated above. However, it justified Porter's action on the grounds that he did nothing more than intelligently exercise the degree of discretion that would normally be expected of a corps commander, considering the knowledge that he had and the situation that confronted him.

Pope testified that the reason he wanted Porter at Bristoe at daylight was that Hooker's troops, the only Union troops there, were almost out of ammunition and he feared that the Confederates might renew the conflict at dawn. Had the order to Porter stated such, he would no doubt have exerted every effort to get there with what he could by daylight. The order to Porter, however, said no such thing. It in no way implied that Porter would immediately enter into action upon arriving at Bristoe. Rather, it indicated a pursuit and possible later engagement. Under the circumstances, the Schofield board concluded that it was wise and prudent for Porter to bring his corps to Bristoe in a rested and organized condition, so as to be able to continue the aggressive actions visualized for the day, even at the expense of arriving late. The Schofield board also emphasized the difficulties and trial confronting Porter in making a night march, the extreme darkness of the night, the blockage of the road by wagons, and the fatigue of his troops from earlier marching up to the evening of the twenty-seventh.

Having said this, Pope's order did contain the phrase "it is necessary, on all accounts, that you should be here at daylight."[1] This was an imperative. Although it may have given Porter discretion as to when he would leave, it appeared to give him none as to when to arrive.

The first thing Porter did after reading the order was to direct that the railroad trains at Warrenton Junction be moved up the track to the break at Kettle Run so that they remained protected by his troops as they advanced. This was a totally unnecessary action and deprived Porter of the use of the rail track bed for marching his troops to Bristoe. Porter could easily have ascertained that Banks's advancing troops would arrive at Warrenton Junction before the last of his troops left to assume guard of the trains.

When Porter discussed Pope's order with his generals that night, they never discussed how they might implement the order, but rather, the degree to which they could and should implement it. Porter read the order before 10 P.M. and thus had at least three hours to act before the order called for his troops to depart. He could have made a determined effort to clear the road, but did not. At the time he read the order, most of the wagons were off the road in park. He could have sent troops to ensure they did not re-enter the road before his troops passed, but did not. He could have marked out routes for his troops to reach the road from their bivouac, but did not. Sykes commanded the more rested division and was properly directed to lead the march. However, Morell's more fatigued troops were awakened first and had to await their turn to take up the march. It was plainly evident to all Porter's generals that night that moving the artillery in the dark along the crowded road would pose the greatest problem, and could block all that followed it. Yet, Porter, instead of ordering the artillery to bring up the rear, maintained the usual marching order of one brigade of infantry followed by one battery of artillery. As might be expected, the first batteries became stuck at the outset of the march and blocked all that followed.

Should Porter have been surprised when he received Pope's order that night? By no means. He should have been anticipating some such order. Since his meeting with Pope that morning, he knew that the Confederates had arrived at the railroad in force just a few miles away between Pope and his supply base at Alexandria. He knew that Pope had departed that afternoon with Heintzelman's corps to confront the Confederates. He did not know if Pope had succeeded in driving the Confederates away or, conversely, if the Confederates defeated Pope and were now advancing upon him.

Porter knew that the Confederates were not adverse to night operations. He knew that less than a week ago, Stuart had temporarily seized Catletts, just a stone's throw from his present encampment, in a night raid and nearly captured Pope and his staff. He probably also knew that just the previous night, Jackson's troops had captured Manassas Junction in a night battle. He should have been on hair trigger alert the night of the August 27–28. He should have been expecting a call to action at any time. He should have been keeping in close touch with Pope in front of him and Banks closing up behind him throughout the evening. What was Porter's initial reaction when he received Pope's order between 9:30 and 10 P.M. that evening? He announced to his generals: "Gentlemen, there is something for you to sleep upon."[2]

As it turned out, there was no real need for Porter to be at Bristoe at dawn. There was no Confederate attack, and his troops spent the day idle at Bristoe. However, suppose the Confederates had attacked at dawn as Pope said he feared. Hooker, without ammunition, would have been defeated, and the entire Army of Virginia supply train of over two thousand wagons on the road directly behind Hooker would have been subject to destruction. This would have been a Union disaster of unprecedented magnitude and Porter would have been responsible. Was Porter then blameless because the Confederates decided as they did?

Here is another consideration. Was Pope really fearful of a dawn attack on Hooker by the Confederates, or was it something he came up with later when he decided that Porter had cost him the battle of Manassas, and he wanted to pile up the maximum charges against Porter? Pope's order to Porter said nothing about a possible Confederate attack against Hooker, or of Hooker being short of ammunition. When Capt. DeKay, Pope's aide, delivered the order to Porter, he said nothing about Hooker being short of ammunition. When Porter arrived at Bristoe the morning of the twenty-eighth and met with Pope, Pope said nothing about their luckily having avoided a Confederate dawn attack.

Pope claimed that the problem was that Hooker was nearly out of ammunition. Yet, Pope knew perfectly well that there was more than enough ammunition in rail cars at Warrenton Junction just ten miles away, and that the railroad was open and useable all the way to the break at Kettle Run, just two miles from Hooker. All the ammunition that Hooker could use could easily have been shipped to him long before dawn. Yet, in Pope's order to Porter, he said nothing about giving priority to the shipping of ammunition.

Considering all factors, the Schofield board was likely correct. Porter was not guilty of disobeying Pope's order. Yet Porter's actions were hardly heroic or meritorious. They exhibited a large degree of lethargy and incompetence.

What about the contention that Porter was ill on the twenty-ninth—that he was suffering from dysentery and could barely stand up; that, under the circumstances, he did as well as any man could do; that actually he should be commended? Porter properly recognized that this was no defense. A military organization is designed to function twenty-four hours per day, seven days per week, regardless of the degree of disaster that may befall it. In a military organization, no two officers are equal. There is a hierarchy from highest in rank to lowest. If a commander cannot function, it is his duty to turn over command to the next in rank. If Porter could not function, it was his duty to turn command of his corps over to Morell.

The five specifications described in Chapter 5 all relate to the same basic fact—Porter's failure to bring his ten thousand man corps into action on August 29, even though he was within three miles of Pope's battle with Jackson and could hear the sounds of battle. One of the five specifications related to Porter's failure to enter into action even after Pope, at 4:30 P.M., peremptorily and unambiguously ordered him to do so immediately.

The basic undisputed facts of the situation were as follows: Porter was ordered by Pope to move his corps down the Gainesville–Manassas Junction road toward Gainesville until his forces merged with those of Pope, who was moving down the Warrenton pike toward Gainesville, presumably pursuing a retreating Jackson. However, Porter encountered enemy resistance at Dawkins Branch, about three miles short of Gainesville, and stopped; and Jackson stopped Pope at Groveton, about three miles short of Gainesville. Thus, both the forces of Porter and Pope were stopped, each three miles from their meeting point, and with a distance of about two to three miles between the two forces. Porter could hear the sound of Pope's battle through the woods to his right, but never brought his corps into action during the day.

The original court-martial found Porter guilty on all five counts. The Schofield board, however, was able to introduce new matter. It was able to show conclusively that, contrary to Pope's views, four of Longstreet's five Confederate divisions were already through Thoroughfare Gap and deploying for action by the time Porter arrived at Dawkins Branch and Pope attacked Jackson at Groveton. Thus, contrary to Pope's view, Porter was confronted with a separate and distinct force from Jackson's that was superior to his own, and consequently could not simply march across the two to three miles separating his force from Pope's and attack Jackson in the flank.

When Porter arrived at Dawkins Branch at 11:30 A.M. on the twenty-ninth and encountered the enemy, he immediately deployed his men for action. He directed Butterfield's brigade to advance and seize the dominating ridge that joined the Gainesville–Manassas Junction road and the Warrenton pike that was about one mile in front in the direction of Gainesville. This was the logical and correct thing to do. Had Butterfield succeeded, the scales for Pope's battle would have been vastly tilted in Pope's favor. We will never know if Butterfield could have seized the ridge. He never tried. At this point, along came McDowell, Porter's senior. According to the sworn testimony of three witnesses, McDowell said, "Porter you are too far out already, this is no place to fight a battle."[3] What did McDowell mean when he said, "You are too far out?" He meant that in his opinion, Porter was getting ahead of Pope, who was presumably advancing on the converging Warrenton pike, and Porter was already too close to Gainesville. Porter's advance was stopped, and he took a defensive position while the rebel forces ahead of him and to his right rapidly built up.

Porter could not now go ahead or to his right to help Pope against Jackson. He could, of course, have gone back to the junction of the Sudley Springs road and moved up the Sudley Springs road to join Pope (see map 17). This is what McDowell did and this, in fact, was what Pope ordered Porter to do on the following day, the thirtieth. However, to do this on the twenty-ninth would have been contrary to both the orders Porter received from Pope and those he received from McDowell. His last orders from Pope were to move down the Gainesville–Manassas Junction road until his forces merged with those of Pope. His last orders from McDowell were to "put your force in here"[4] while McDowell was presumably trying to bring his corps in to Porter's right to plug the gap between Porter and Pope. Furthermore, it is perfectly clear from Pope's actions and testimony that he wanted Porter on the Gainesville–Manassas Junction road. It was only via this road that Porter could reach Jackson's flank and rear as Pope desired. Thus, on the twenty-ninth Porter could not move forward, he could not move to his right, and his orders forbade him from moving back and up the Sudley Springs road to join Pope. Porter, by staying where he was, performed a useful function for Pope. He tied down large numbers of rebel troops that otherwise might have gone to Jackson's aid on the twenty-ninth.

The Schofield board also produced new evidence to confirm that Pope's 4:30 P.M. peremptory order to Porter to attack immediately was delivered much later than previously supposed. In fact, it was delivered too late for Porter to make the attack before darkness terminated the day's activity. Thus, as the Schofield board concluded, Porter was clearly not guilty of the five specifications.

Was Porter then a hero? Were his actions of the day meritorious? Hardly. It was imperative that Porter know where Pope's left flank was if he was ever going to join with Pope. Pope's left flank could not be seen from Porter's position before Dawkins Branch because of the woods. However, according to Col. Marshall and others, it could be seen from Porter's skirmish line, which was deployed beyond Dawkins Branch. We do not know if Porter ever came close enough to the skirmish line to see for himself. Would Jackson have done so? You bet he would!

Porter never conducted a reconnaissance in force in his front to ascertain just what he was up against. He never conducted a reconnaissance in force through the woods to his right to see if it was feasible to join with Pope by that route. He never made any determined effort to establish where the right flank of the enemy facing him was, and thus perhaps attack them in their flank.

When Capt. Pope arrived with Gen. Pope's 4:30 P.M. peremptory order for Porter to attack, he found Porter resting on the ground at Bethlehem Church more than a mile from his front at Dawkins Branch. Sykes commanded Porter's rear division and according to Sykes, Porter spent the entire day with him. If Jackson or Stuart or Sheridan were in command of a large body of troops unengaged and within sound of a major battle involving their comrades, would they have been resting on the ground far from the front? Hardly. Although Porter was innocent of the five specifications, his performance was hardly heroic or meritorious and, again, showed a large smattering of lethargy and incompetence.

The fourth and fifth specifications to charge 1 related to Porter's failure to bring Piatt's and Griffin's brigades to the battlefield on the thirtieth in response to Pope's order. As we will recall, both brigades took a wrong turn at an intersection while en route to the battlefield. Piatt thus appeared only late in the day to participate in the final phases of the battle, and Griffin did not appear at all. Porter was found innocent of both charges by the original court-martial because he had directed both brigades to appear as required.

One might say that the failure of the two brigades was just a mistake, or an accident, and thus this episode did not reflect on Porter's performance. To the contrary. It was Porter's responsibility as corps commander to see that such mistakes did not happen. No good corps commander would lose almost one third of his force by a wrong turn when within sound of the battlefield. We can only judge Porter's performance in this instance as abysmal. However, Porter's performance on the battlefield during the remainder of the thirtieth was commendable.

As for Porter's performance between the time he was charged and his trial, several elements are involved. Porter was charged and relieved from command soon after the second battle of Manassas. However, at McClellan's request, he was returned to the command of his corps to serve until the current crisis was resolved, and his trial was held in abeyance. The crisis was occasioned by the Confederate invasion of Maryland, which followed their victory at Manassas. It culminated in the climactic battle of Antietam on September 17, 1862, which ended the invasion. Soon after the battle, Porter was again relieved of his command and his trial was scheduled. Only eighteen days elapsed between the commencement of the crisis after the second battle of Manassas and its termination at the battle of Antietam. What was Porter's performance during this period?

For most of the period in question, Porter's corps was held back for the defense of Washington as McClellan moved out with the Army of the Potomac toward the encounter with Lee at Antietam. Shortly before the battle, Porter was sent to join McClellan and did join him in time to participate.

McClellan's plan at Antietam was to stretch the Confederate flanks by attacks at each end of the line and then, in the final phase of the battle, to commit his reserves against the weakened Confederate center. The time of decision came in the late afternoon after a day-long battle, during which all of the Confederate reserves had been committed and the Confederate center was dangerously weakened. McClellan still had two corps that were largely un-bloodied—Porter's Fifth Corps and Franklin's Sixth. At this point, McClellan, as was his wont, consulted with Porter. Porter advised McClellan not to commit his reserves, that if he did and lost, Washington would be endangered. McClellan would not go against Porter's advice. He did not commit his reserves and the battle ended in a draw. According to most post-war analysts, including Longstreet, who was second in command to Lee in the battle, had McClellan attacked at this point, he would have won decisively. The war might have been significantly shortened.

Porter was not guilty of the charges against him and he was done an injustice by being convicted. However, we will never know whether he gave Pope his best. If he did, his best was not very good. His performance was not brilliant and it was not heroic. His subsequent performance at Antietam was a negative.

Porter's exoneration and restoration to rank was not non-controversial. About one third of the members of each house of Congress voted against the bill. Many prominent and well informed men remained convinced that Porter's original trial was fair; that he was guilty and received a just and even lenient punishment. Maj. Asa Gardner, the recorder for the Schofield board, had originally been a Porter supporter. However, after seeing all the evidence, he became convinced that Porter was guilty. Senator Logan, a man of impeccable reputation and military qualifications and thoroughly versed in the case, remained convinced that Porter was guilty. The *New York Times* reporters who covered each day of the Schofield board hearings walked away convinced that he was guilty. Lincoln assistants John G. Nicolay and John Hay both considered him guilty. And last and most important, Lincoln considered him guilty. Strangely enough, many of the most ardent supporters of Porter's vindication in Congress were ex–Confederate generals.

Thus, although Porter was officially exonerated, his reputation remains just a little tarnished to this day.

Porter was a long time sufferer from diabetes. Beginning in his mid-seventies, he began to suffer periodic life threatening attacks. The last occurred in May 1901, when Porter was seventy-nine. On May 17, an article appeared in the *New York Times* that Porter was much improved. Then just four days later, on May 21, 1901, he died.

Porter's funeral was a grand event. The funeral services were conducted on May 24 at Trinity Church in downtown Manhattan. The service was scheduled for 12 noon, but the vast church was already filling up by 11 A.M. Porter's flag-draped casket was carried in by eight non-commissioned officers of the regular army, followed by a sergeant in full dress uniform and a bugler. This was followed by ten honorary civilian pall bearers, notables all. These included W. R. Grace, the shipping magnate and twice mayor of New York; Franklin Edson, ex-mayor of New York and Congressman; prominent attorneys Anson Maltby and John C. Bullitt, who had represented Porter at the Schofield board; and other notables of industry and Tammany Hall. The funeral was attended by Porter's widow and wife of forty-four years, both of Porter's sons and their families, and one of Porter's two daughters. Numerous senior military officers were also in attendance.

Porter was buried in Greenwood Cemetery in Brooklyn with full military honors. The bugler played "Taps," composed long ago by Porter's friend and subordinate from the Fifth Corps, Gen. Daniel Butterfield, who was to follow Porter to the grave in weeks.

Porter left a substantial estate to his wife and four offspring. His will was dated June 17, 1876. In it, he appealed to his sons to continue the effort to clear his name. He proclaimed his complete innocence. He said that he was always faithful to the trust placed in him as a soldier and an officer; that he was always true and obedient to those placed over him, and to none more so than Gen. Pope in August 1862.

Porter bequeathed his gold watch, his private papers, and the sword presented to him by the Fifth Corps to his oldest and namesake son. He bequeathed the sword presented to him by the city of Boston to his younger son, Robert E. Porter, and photographs and books to his daughters, Lucia and Eveline. Porter's widow, Harriet, lived on to 1914 and received the pension that she was entitled to as the wife of a colonel, U.S. Army, retired.

In 1904, the city of Portsmouth, New Hampshire, Porter's birthplace, erected an equestrian statue of Porter in Haven Park in his honor. In 2004, the hundredth anniversary of the statue, it was refurbished and re-dedicated with great fanfare. Porter received another posthumous honor. In October 1942, a World War II liberty ship was christened the SS *Fitz-John Porter*. It was torpedoed and sank early in its career on March 1, 1943. Thus, its career was somewhat analogous to that of its namesake—except that the SS *Fitz-John Porter* did not rise again.

The author's final verdict on Porter: Not guilty, but no hero and no military genius. He was, like so many Union generals in 1862, a semi-competent still learning his trade.

16

Who Lost the Second Battle of Manassas?

One last question: who then was responsible for the Union disaster at the second battle of Manassas? The primary function of Pope's Army of Virginia was to hold off Lee's army until the Army of Virginia and the Army of the Potomac could unite. By the morning of August 29, 1862, this was all but successfully accomplished. Massive reinforcements from the Army of the Potomac, as well as from other sources, had already accumulated at Alexandria. Alexandria was just twenty-five miles from Pope at Manassas. The road from Alexandria to Manassas was open. The railroad from Alexandria to Manassas had been put back into operation as far as Sangsters Station, just five miles from Manassas. Once the forces at Alexandria united with Pope, he would have an overwhelming numerical superiority over Lee and could hardly lose.

However, Pope had become obsessed with the idea of destroying Jackson's force before it could unite with that of Longstreet. When Pope awoke on the morning of August 29, he found that he had no forces between those of Jackson and Longstreet. Now, only time and distance stood between their uniting. Realistically, Pope's chance of destroying Jackson had gone with the wind. At this point, Pope could have taken a defensive position behind Bull Run and awaited the arrival of his reinforcements. However, instead of doing so, he persisted in his attacks against Jackson, still believing that he could destroy him before Longstreet

Major General Irvin McDowell of the United States Volunteers—was he the loser of Manassas? (Courtesy the Massachusetts Commandery Military Order of the Loyal Legion and the U.S. Army Military History Institute.)

arrived. Pope was wrong and led his army to disaster. The real culprit for the Union disaster at second Manassas was not Fitz-John Porter—it was John Pope.

Before leaving the question of responsibility for the loss of the second battle of Manassas, consider a couple of might-have-beens. When Porter arrived at Dawkins Branch on the morning of August 29, he put his men in line of battle and prepared to advance. Had he done so, he might have succeeded in capturing the vital Monroe House ridge just one mile in front. Had he done so, Pope just might have won on the twenty-ninth. McDowell, however, arrived on the scene and caused Porter to cease his advance.

Let us look at another might-have-been. Had McDowell been with his divisions of Ricketts and King on the evening of August 28, instead of being lost and out of touch, he might have delayed Longstreet's passage through Thoroughfare Gap by just four more hours. Had he done so, Longstreet would not have been on the field when Porter arrived at Dawkins Branch on the morning of the twenty-ninth, and hence Porter almost certainly would have seized the vital Monroe House ridge. Again, this having been accomplished, Pope might have won on the twenty-ninth.

In conclusion, although Pope lost the battle, he might have won it but for McDowell. Thus the two leading culprits are none other than Porter's two chief accusers, Pope and McDowell.

APPENDICES

APPENDIX 1. DATA ON THE GENERALS INVOLVED IN THE PORTER CASE

	Rank	Superior (8/29/1862)	Position	Age *	Source	Class**
CONFEDERATES						
Ewell, Richard	Major General	Jackson	Division Commander	45	West Point	40
Hill, A. P.	Major General	Jackson	Division Commander	36	West Point	47
Jackson, T. J.	Major General	Lee	Corps Commander	38	West Point	46
Lee, Robert E.	General	Davis	Commanding General, Army of Northern Virginia	55	West Point	29
Longstreet, James	Major General	Lee	Corps Commander	41	West Point	42
Stuart, J. E. B.	Major General	Lee	Cavalry Commander	29	West Point	54
Taliaferro, William	Brigadier General	Jackson	Division Commander	39	Politician	
Trimble, Isaac	Brigadier General	Ewell	Brigade Commander	60	West Point	22
UNION (Involved at Manassas)						
Banks, N. P.	Major General	Pope	Second Corps Commander	46	Politician	
Bayard, George D.	Brigadier General	McDowell	Cavalry Commander	26	West Point	56
Buford, John	Brigadier General	Banks	Cavalry Commander	36	West Point	48
Burnside, A. E.	Major General	Halleck	Ninth Corps Commander	38	West Point	47
Butterfield, Daniel	Brigadier General	Morell	Brigade Commander	32	Lawyer	
Duryea, A.	Brigadier General	Ricketts	Brigade Commander	47	Businessman	
Franklin, W. B.	Major General	McClellan / Pope	Sixth Corps Commander	39	West Point	43
Griffin, Charles	Brigadier General	Morell	Brigade Commander	36	West Point	47
Halleck, Henry W.	General-in-Chief	Lincoln		47	West Point	39
Hatch, John	Brigadier General	King	Brigade Commander	40	West Point	45
Heintzelman, S. P.	Major General	Pope	Third Corps Commander Army of the Potomac	57	West Point	26
Hooker, Joseph	Major General	Heintzelman	Division Commander	47	West Point	37
Kearny, Philip	Major General	Heintzelman	Division Commander	47	Soldier of Fortune	

	Rank	Superior (8/29/1862)	Position	Age *	Source	Class**
King, Rufus	Brigadier General	McDowell	Division Commander	48	West Point	33
McClellan, George B.	Major General	Halleck	Commanding General, Army of the Potomac	35	West Point	46
McDowell, Irvin	Major General	Pope	Third Corps Commander	44	West Point	34
Morell, G. W.	Major General	Porter	Division Commander	47	West Point	35
Parke, John L.	Brigadier General	Burnside	Chief of Staff	35	West Point	49
Piatt, A. S.	Brigadier General	Sturgis / Porter	Brigade Commander	41	Newspaper Editor	
Pope, John	Major General	Halleck	Commanding General, Army of Virginia	40	West Point	42
Porter, Fitz-John	Major General	Pope	Fifth Corps Commander	40	West Point	45
Reno, Jesse	Major General	Pope	Division / Corps Commander	39	West Point	46
Reynolds, John	Brigadier General	McDowell	Division Commander	42	West Point	37
Ricketts, James	Brigadier General	McDowell	Division Commander	45	West Point	39
Roberts, B. S.	Brigadier General	Pope	Inspector General	51	West Point	35
Sigel, Franz	Major General	Pope	First Corps Commander	37	German Community Leader	
Stevens, Isaac	Major General	Reno	Division Commander	44	West Point	39
Sturgis, S. B.	Brigadier General	Porter	Commander, Reserve Corps	40	West Point	46
Sykes, George	Brigadier General	Porter	Division Commander	40	West Point	42

UNION (Members of Porter's Court-Martial)

	Rank	Superior (8/29/1862)	Position	Age *	Source	Class**
Buford, N. B.	Brigadier General			55	West Point	31
Casey, Silas	Brigadier General			55	West Point	26
Garfield, James	Brigadier General			30	Politician	
Hitchcock, E. A.	Major General			64	West Point	17
Hunter, David	Major General		President	60	West Point	24
King, Rufus ***	Brigadier General					
Prentiss, B. M.	Brigadier General			42	Businessman	
Ricketts, James ***	Brigadier General					
Slough, John Potts	Brigadier General			33	Politician	

* Age as of 8/23/1862
** Year Graduated from West Point
*** Also involved at Manassas

APPENDIX 2

Halleck's Response to Stanton's Message of August 28, 1862

Washington, August 30, 1862
Hon. E. M. Stanton, Secretary of War:

SIR: In reply to your note of last evening I have to state:

1st. That on the 30th of July I directed General McClellan to send away his sick as quickly as possible, preparatory to his moving in some direction. Receiving no answer, the order was repeated August 2. On the 3d of August I directed him to withdraw his entire army from Harrison's landing and bring it to Aquia Creek.

2d. That the order was not obeyed with the promptness I expected and the national safety, in my opinion, required. It will be seen from my telegraphic correspondence that General McClellan protested against the movement, and that it was not actually commenced till the 14th instant. It is proper to remark that the reason given for not moving earlier was the delay in getting off the sick. As shown in my correspondence, I was most earnestly pressing him to move quickly, for the reason that I felt very anxious for the safety of Washington. From all the information I could obtain I believed that the enemy intended to crush General Pope's army and attack this city. I also believed that our only safety was to unite the two armies as rapidly as possible between the enemy and Washington. The object of pushing General Pope forward to the Rapidan was simply to gain time for General McClellan's army to get into position somewhere in rear of the Rappahannock. This I at first hoped to accomplish by landing the troops of Generals Burnside and McClellan at Aquia Creek. But the time which elapsed between the arrival of these two armies compelled me to bring most of General McClellan's forces to Alexandria, as General Pope was then falling back from the Upper Rappahannock before the main body of the enemy. When General McClellan's movement was begun it was rapidly carried out; but there was an unexpected delay in commencing it. General McClellan reports the delay was unavoidable.

3d. That on the 26th August, at 11.20, I telegraphed to Major-General Franklin, at Alexandria, to march his corps by Centreville toward Warrenton and to report to General Pope. Finding that Franklin's corps had not left, I telegraphed to General McClellan on the 27th, at 10 A.M., to have it march in the direction of Manassas as soon as possible. On the same day, at 12 P.M., I again telegraphed to General McClellan that General Porter reported a general battle imminent, and that Franklin's corps should move out by forced marches, carrying three or four days provisions; to be afterwards supplied, as far as possible, by railroad. I also gave him the positions of General Pope's troops as well as I could ascertain them, and suggested the possibility that the enemy would attempt to turn his right. At 9 P.M. General McClellan telegraphed that he should retain Cox with General Franklin till next morning, and would visit my headquarters immediately. He came to my quarters soon after midnight, and left about 2 o'clock in the morning of the 28th.

At our interview I urged on him the importance of pushing forward Franklin as early as possible. Hearing about noon that General McClellan had not reached Alexandria, I telegraphed, at 12.40 P.M. (28th), to General Franklin, if he had not acted on General McClellan's order to do so on mine, and move toward Manassas Junction. At 1 P.M. General McClellan telegraphed to me that the moment Franklin could be started with a reasonable amount of artillery he should go forward. At 2.45 he telegraphed some rumors he had heard about the enemy's movements, and expressed an opinion that the troops sent from Alexandria should be in force, and with cavalry and artillery, or we should be beaten in detail. I replied at 3.30 P.M. that not a moment must be lost in pushing as large a force as possible toward Manassas, so as to communicate with General Pope before the enemy could be re-enforced. He telegraphed back at 4.45 that Franklin's corps was not in condition to move and fight a battle. At 8.50 I telegraphed to him that there must be no further delay in moving Franklin's corps toward Manassas—that they must go to-morrow morning, ready or not ready. If we delay too long to get ready there will be no necessity of going at all, for Pope will either be defeated or victorious without our aid. If there is a want of wagons, the men must carry provisions with them till the wagons can come to their relief. At 10 he replied that he had ordered Franklin's corps to move at 6 o'clock.

On the morning of the 29th, at 10.30, he telegraphed to me that Franklin's corps had started at 6 A.M., and that he could give him but two squadrons of cavalry. At 12 P.M. he telegraphed that Franklin's corps was without proper ammunition and without transportation; and again at 1 P.M. he telegraphed that in his opinion Franklin ought not to advance beyond Annandale. At 3.10 P.M. I replied that I wanted Franklin's corps to go far enough to find out something about the enemy; that perhaps he might get such information at Annandale as to prevent his going farther; that otherwise he would push on toward Fairfax. I added that "our people must move more actively and find out where the enemy is. I am tired of guesses." Late in the afternoon I heard that Franklin's corps had halted at Annandale, and that he himself had been seen in Alexandria in the afternoon. I immediately telegraphed to General McClellan at 7.50 P.M. that his (Franklin's) being in Alexandria and his corps halting at Annandale was contrary to my orders; that his corps must push forward as I directed, protect the railroad, and open our communications with Manassas. General McClellan replied at 8 P.M., referring to his previous telegrams, and said that he had not deemed it safe for Franklin to march beyond Annandale, and that he was responsible for his being in Alexandria and his corps halting at Annandale.

Early on the morning of the 30th I made inquiries of the Quartermaster-General in regard to transportation, and telegraphed at 9.40 to General McClellan that I was by no means satisfied with General Franklin's march of yesterday (29th). Considering the circumstances of the case he was very wrong in stopping at Annandale. I referred to the fact that he could have obtained transportation if he had applied for it to the Quartermaster's Department, and added: "He knew the importance of opening communication with General Pope's army, and should have acted more promptly."

The foregoing is, I believe, a correct summary of the orders and instructions given by me in regard to the movement of General Franklin's corps, my expressions of dissatisfaction, and the reasons alleged for the delays which in the result proved as unfortunate.

4th. Copies of letters, orders etc., relative to your inquiries are sent herewith.

Very respectfully, your obedient servant

H. W. Halleck
General-in-Chief

Source: U.S. War Department, *The War of the Rebellion: A Compilation of the Official Records of the Union and Confederate Armies*, Series 1, Volume 12, Part III, 739–741.

APPENDIX 3

Organization at Manassas, August 1862, and the Positions Occupied by the Generals of This Narrative

UNION

Army McClellan, Commanding General, Army of the Potomac
Pope, Commanding General, Army of Virginia

Corps Banks, Second Corps Commander (Army of Virginia)
Franklin, Sixth Corps Commander (Army of the Potomac)
Heintzelman, Third Corps Commander (Army of the Potomac)
McDowell, Third Corps Commander (Army of Virginia)
Porter, Fifth Corps Commander (Army of the Potomac)
Reno, Temporary Corps Commander (from Ninth Corps)
Sigel, First Corps Commander (Army of Virginia)

Cavalry Bayard, Cavalry Brigade Commander
Buford, Cavalry Brigade Commander

Divisions Hooker, Division Commander
Kearny, Division Commander
King, Division Commander
Morell, Division Commander
Ricketts, Division Commander
Reynolds, Division Commander
Sykes, Division Commander
Stevens, Division Commander

Brigades Butterfield, Brigade Commander
Duryea, Brigade Commander
Hatch, Brigade Commander
Griffin, Brigade Commander
Piatt, Brigade Commander

Regiments

CONFEDERATE

Army		Lee, Commanding General, Army of Northern Virginia
	Cavalry	Stuart, Cavalry Commander
	Corps	Jackson, Corps Commander
		Longstreet, Corps Commander
	Divisions	Ewell, Division Commander
		Hill, Division Commander
		Taliaferro, Division Commander
	Brigades	Trimble, Brigade Commander
	Regiments	

In both armies, an army consisted of two or more corps, a corps of two or more divisions, and a division of two or more brigades. The main difference in organization was that, in the Confederate army, the cavalry brigades were formed into a cavalry division that was directly subordinate to the army commander. In the Union army, cavalry brigades were subordinate to the corps commanders.

Burnside commanded the Ninth Corps, which was not assigned to any army.

APPENDIX 4

Porter's Messages to Burnside

Warrenton Junction,
August 27, [1862]—4 P.M.

General Burnside, Falmouth:

I send you the last order from General Pope, which indicates the future as well as the present. Wagons are rolling along rapidly to the rear, as if a mighty power was propelling them. I see no cause for alarm, though I think this order may cause it. McDowell moves to Gainesville, where Sigel now is. The latter got to Buckland Bridge in time to put out the fire and kick the enemy, who is pursuing his route unmolested to the Shenandoah, or Loudoun county. The forces are Longstreet's, A. P. Hill's, Jackson's Whiting's, Ewell's, and Anderson's (late Huger's) divisions. Longstreet is said by a deserter to be very strong. They have much artillery and long wagon trains. The raid on the railroad was near Cedar Run, and made by a regiment of infantry, two squadrons of cavalry, and a section of artillery. The place was guarded by nearly three regiments of infantry, and some cavalry. They routed the guard, captured a train and many men, destroyed the bridge, and retired leisurely down the road toward Manassas. It can be easily repaired. No troops are coming up, except new troops, that I can hear of. Sturgis is here with two regiments. Four were cut off by the raid. The positions of the troops are given in the order. No enemy in our original front. A letter of General Lee, seized when Stuart's assistant adjutant-general was taken, directs Stuart to leave a squadron only to watch in front of Hanover Junction, &c. Everything has moved up north. I find a vast difference between the troops and ours. But I suppose they were new, as they to-day burned their clothes, &c., when there was not the least cause. I hear that they are much demoralized, and needed some good troops to give them heart, and I think, head. We are working now to get behind Bull Run, and, I presume, will be there in a few days, if strategy don't use us up. The strategy is magnificent, and tactics in the inverse proportion. I would like some of my ambulances; I would like also to be ordered to return to Fredericksburg and to push toward Hanover, or with a larger force, to strike at Orange Court-House. I wish Sumner was at Washington, and up near the Monocacy with good batteries. I do not doubt the enemy have large amounts of supplies provided for them, and I believe they have a contempt for this Army of Virginia. I wish myself away from it, with all our old Army of the Potomac, and so do our companions. I was informed to-day, by the best authority, that, in opposition to General Pope's views, this army was pushed out to save the Army of the Potomac, an army that could take the best care of itself. Pope says he long since wanted to go behind the Occoquan. I am in

237

great need of ambulances, and the officers need medicines, which, for want of transportation, were left behind. I hear many of the sick of my corps are in houses on the road, very sick. I think there is no fear of an enemy crossing the Rappahannock. The cavalry are all in the advance of the rebel army. At Kelly's and Barnett's Fords much property was left, in consequence of the wagons going down for grain, &c. If you can push up the grain to-night, please do so, direct to this place. There is no grain here to-day, or anywhere, and this army is wretchedly supplied in that line. Pope says he never could get enough.

F. J. Porter

Most of this is private. But if you can get me away, please do so. Make what use of this you choose, so it does good. Don't let the alarm here disturb you. If you had a good force you could go to Richmond. A force should at once be pushed out to Manassas to open the road. Our provisions are very short.

F. J. P.

Source: U.S. War Department, *The War of the Rebellion: A Compilation of the Official Records of the Union and Confederate Armies*, Series 1, Vol. 12, Part II, Supplement, 1063.

United States Military Telegraph
From Advance 11:45 P.M. (Received August 27, 1862)

Major General Burnside:

Have just received orders from General Pope to move Sykes to-morrow to within 2 miles of Warrenton, and to call up more to same point, leaving the fords guarded by the cavalry. He says the troops in rear should be brought up as rapidly as possible, leaving only a small rear guard at Rappahannock Station, and that he cannot see how a general engagement can be put off more than a day or two. I shall move up as ordered, but the want of grain, and the necessity of receiving a supply of subsistence, will cause some delay. Please hasten back the wagons sent down, and inform McClellan, that I may know that I am doing right. Banks is at Fayetteville; McDowell, Sigel, and Ricketts at and immediately in front of Warrenton; Reno on his right; Cox joins tomorrow, Sturgis next day, and Franklin is expected. So says General Pope.

F. J. Porter
Major General

Source: Official U.S. War Department, *The War of the Rebellion: A Compilation of the Official Records of the Union and Confederate Armies*, Series 1, Vol. 12, Part II, Supplement, 1067–68.

Falmouth, August 29, 1862—1 P.M.
(Received 1 P.M. Cypher)

Maj. Gen. H. W. Halleck
General-in-Chief, and
Maj. Gen. George B. McClellan,
Alexandria:

The following just received from Porter, 4 miles from Manassas, the 28th, 2 P.M.: All that talk of bagging Jackson etc., was bosh. That enormous gap—Manassas—was left open, and the enemy jumped through, and the story of McDowell having cut off Longstreet had no good foundation. The enemy have destroyed all our bridges, burned trains, etc., and made this army rush back to look for its line of communication, and found us bare of subsistence. We are far from Alexandria, considering the means of transportation. Your supply of 40 wagons is here, but I can't find them. There is a report that Jackson is at Centreville, which you can believe or not. The enemy destroyed an immense amount of property at Manassas—cars and supplies. I expect the next thing will be a raid on our rear by way of Warrenton by Longstreet, who was cut off.

F. J. Porter
Major-General

Source: U.S. War Department, *The War of the Rebellion: A Compilation of the Official Records of the Union and Confederate Armies*, Series 1, Vol. 12, Part II, Supplement, 1069.

Bristoe, August 28, 1862—9:30 A.M.

General Burnside
Falmouth:

My command will soon be up, and will at once go into position. Hooker drove Ewell some 3 miles, and Pope says McDowell intercepted Longstreet, so that, without a long detour, he cannot join Ewell, Jackson and A. P. Hill, who are supposed to be at Manassas. Ewell's train, he says took the road to Gainesville, where McDowell is coming from. We shall be today as follows: I am on the railroad, Heintzelman on left, then Reno, then McDowell. He hopes to get Ewell, and to push to Manassas today. I hope all goes well near Washington; I think there need be no cause of fear for us. I feel as if on my own way now, and thus far have kept my command and trains well up. More supplies than I supposed on hand have been brought, but none to spare, and we must make connection soon. I hope for the best, and my lucky star is always up about my birthday, the 31st. I hope Mac's is up also. You will hear of us soon by way of Alexandria. Ever Yours,

F. J. P.

Source: U.S. War Department, *The War of the Rebellion: A Compilation of the Official Records of the Union and Confederate Armies*, Series 1, Vol. 12, Part II, Supplement, 1061–62.

Bristoe, 29th—6 A.M.
General Burnside:

Shall be off in half an hour. The messenger who brought this says the enemy had been at Centreville, and pickets were found there last night.

Sigel had severe fight last night; took many prisoners. Banks is at Warrenton Junction; McDowell near Gainesville; Heintzelman and Reno at Centreville, where they marched yesterday. Pope went to Centreville with the last two as bodyguard, at the time not knowing where was the enemy, and where Sigel was fighting—within 8 miles of him and in sight. Comment is unnecessary. The enormous trains are still rolling on. Many arrivals (animals) not having been watched (watered) for fifty hours, I shall be out of provisions tomorrow night. Your train of 40 wagons cannot be found. I hope Mac's at work, and we will soon get ordered out of this. It would seem, from proper statement of the enemy, that he was wandering around loose, but I expect they know what they are doing which is more than anyone here or anywhere knows.

F. J. Porter

Source: U.S. War Department, *The War of the Rebellion: A Compilation of the Official Records of the Union and Confederate Armies*, Series 1, Vol. 12, Part II, Supplement, 1069.

APPENDIX 5

McDowell's Request for a Court of Inquiry

Washington, September 6, 1862

His Excellency the President:

I have been informed by a Senator that he had seen a note, in pencil, written by a colonel of cavalry mortally wounded in battle, stating, among other causes, that he was dying a victim "to McDowell's treachery," and that his last request was that this note might be shown to you.

That the colonel believed this charge, and felt his last act on earth was a great public service, there can be, I think, no question.

This solemn accusation from the grave of a gallant officer, who died for his country, is entitled to great consideration; and I feel called on to endeavor to meet it as well as so general a charge, from one now no longer able to support it, can be met.

I therefore beg you to please cause a court to be instituted for its investigation. And, in the absence of any knowledge whatever as to the particular act or acts, time or place, or general conduct the deceased may have had in view, I have to ask that the inquiry be without limitation, and be upon any points and every subject which may in [any] way be supposed to have led to this belief.

That it may be directed to my whole conduct as a general officer, either under another or whilst in a separate command, whether in matters of administration or command; to my correspondence with any of the enemy's commanders or with any one within the enemy's lines; to my conduct and the policy pursued by me toward the inhabitants of the country occupied by our troops with reference to themselves or their property; and further, to any imputations of indirect treachery or disloyalty toward the nation or any individual having like myself an important trust.

Whether I have or have not been faithful as a subordinate to those placed over me, giving them heartily and to the extent of my capacity all the support in my power.

Whether I have or have not failed, through unworthy personal motives, to go to the aid of, or send re–enforcements, to my brother commanders.

That this subject of my alleged treachery or disloyalty may be fully inquired into I beg that all officers, soldiers, or civilians who know, or who think they know, of any act of mine liable to the charge in question be allowed and invited to make it known to the court.

I also beg that the proceedings of the court may be open and free to the press from day to day.

I have the honor to be, very respectfully, your most obedient servant,

Irvin McDowell.
Major-General, Commanding Third Army Corps, Army of Virginia

Source: U.S. War Department, *The War of the Rebellion: A Compilation of the Official Records of the Union and Confederate Armies*, Series 1, Vol. 12, Part I, 39.

APPENDIX 6

Abstract of Pope's Paper to President Hayes

"In order to arrive at a clear understanding of the conduct for which Fitz-John Porter was tried, convicted, and cashiered, I shall proceed to give a brief statement of the facts.... To begin, then, on August 29, 1862, a severe battle was fought on the old field of Bull Run, known as the first day of the second battle of that name.... About two-thirds of the army under my immediate eye was drawn up in line of battle perpendicular to, and on both sides of the Warrenton turnpike, the road from Bethlehem Church to Sudley Springs intersecting our line of battle diagonally near its centre.

"At about 9 o'clock on the morning of Aug. 29 Porter, then at Manassas Junction, received an order from me to move forward to Gainesville on the direct road. In compliance with that order, he arrived at the forks of the road at Bethlehem church between 11 an 12 o'clock in the day, and moved forward on the direct road to Gainesville until the rear of his column rested near the forks of the road. His corps was the Fifth Corps of the Army, and having been reinforced by Piatt's brigade of Sturges' division, numbered quite 12,000 men, very nearly one-third of the whole force within the field of battle. It contained the entire regular Army of the United States, with the exception of the few regiments serving in the West, and was provided with eight batteries of light artillery, many of them batteries of the regular Army. It was the most efficient and best disciplined corps of the entire Army, and having gone but three or four miles that day, and very little further the previous day, was by far the freshest corps on the ground. McDowell had moved in Porter's rear from Manassas Junction with his corps, but hearing, on arriving at the forks of the road, the sounds of a severe battle being fought at Groveton, passed the rear of Porter's corps and, following the road to Sudley Springs, brought his corps in upon the left of our line and immediately pushed forward into action. This brief statement of facts, which can be verified by reference to my official reports, or to the testimony in Porter's case, is necessary to a clear understanding of the situation when Porter's crime was committed. Between 3 and 4 o'clock in the day, when the battle had been raging within his hearing not less than four hours, (his corps remaining with stacked arms where McDowell left it) he wrote the following letter to Gen. McDowell, addressed to McDowell and King, who as before stated, had some hours before, urged by the sounds of the battle moved up the Sudley Springs road to take part in the engagement:

Gens. McDowell and King:

> I found it impossible to communicate by crossing the roads to Groveton. The enemy are in strong force on this road, and as they appear to have driven our forces back, the firing of the enemy having advanced, and ours retired, I have determined to withdraw to Manassas. I have attempted to communicate with McDowell and Sigel, but my messengers have run into the enemy. They have gathered artillery and cavalry and infantry, and the advancing masses of dust show the enemy coming in force. Had you not better send your train back?
>
> —Fitz-John Porter, Major-General

"In other words, Porter writes deliberately that, believing our army on his right, and within less than four miles of him, was being defeated by the enemy and driven from the field, he intends, not to strive to preserve the army from defeat by reinforcing it, but to move off to Manassas Junction, and to abandon them to the disaster he believes them to be suffering. Meantime, hearing nothing from Porter, the sound of guns I had been anxiously listening for on the enemy's right since 12 o'clock in the day, I sent him, at 4:30 P.M., an order to attack on the right flank. The delivery of this order to Porter at 5 o'clock— at least an hour and a half before sunset, and fully two hours before the battle closed for the night—was proved on his trial; but the order was in no respect obeyed, and seems to have produced no effect upon Porter, except that, instead of retreating to Manassas, according to his first intention, he only retreated part of the way—far enough to be out of sight of the enemy and out of danger. Porter did exactly what he wrote to McDowell and King he intended doing."

Extracts from reports of the operations of the rebel army on Aug. 29 follow. Gen. J.E.B. Stuart says he met the head of Longstreet's column between Haymarket and Gainesville on the morning of that day, moving down the road to take position on Jackson's right. Upon repairing to the front he connoitered, and found the Federal forces advancing in such a manner as to strike Longstreet in the flank, and reported to the Commanding General that Longstreet's flank and rear were seriously threatened; Jenkins,' Kemper's, and Jones' brigades were placed in a position to bar the advance, but the Federals withdrew toward Manassas after firing a few shots.

"It is thus seen," continues Gen. Pope, "that when Porter advanced there was really nothing in front of him except a few cavalry regiments and one battery. The advancing masses of dust, indicating that the enemy was coming in force, of which he writes in his letter, was nothing more than the dust raised by a few cavalry soldiers dragging brush up and down the Warrenton turn-pike. When Longstreet was notified, he sent three brigades, and that was all the force Porter had in his front when he retired on Manassas."

An extract from Longstreet's official report of the operations of the day confirms the danger to the flank reported by Stuart, and shows that he with-drew the three brigades upon Porter's retiring. An extract from Stonewall Jack-son's report of the operations from Aug. 15 to Sept. 5, 1862, is introduced to show that the right, centre, and left of his corps were so heavily assaulted at 4 P.M., Aug. 29, that he was forced to send to Gen. Lee for assistance, which the failure of Porter to advance enabled Longstreet to render.

"It seems, then," Gen. Pope continues, "that Jackson was so hard driven by that army which Porter considered defeated that he could not hold his ground, and sent to Gen. R. E. Lee for reinforcements. But Lee was fully 30 miles distant on the morning of that day, and it was utterly impossible for him to reinforce Jackson until a late hour of the night, long before which time the whole affair would have been ended. What saved Jackson from disastrous defeat was the very troops taken from in front of Porter when he deserted the field."

Source: "General Pope's Statement," *New York Times*, October 11, 1878.

Appendix 7

Pope's Response to Schofield

Fort Leavenworth, Oct 21, 1878

Gen. J. M. Schofield, New York

I have received your dispatch of the 17th inst., in which you state that "in view of the fact that the counsel for the petitioner have stated that they believe that justice to their client requires your presence, the board requests that you appear as a witness before them, at Governors Island next Thursday, the 24th inst." In reply I have to say that if the petitioner considers my presence as a witness necessary, he should apply to have me subpoenaed as a witness for him; only as a witness for him or for the government can I be expected with any semblance of legality, to appear as a witness in the case. To appear on a mere request of the board would be to place myself in a position not only false, but in every sense extraordinary and unknown to the practices of the civil and military tribunals of the country. While I stand ready to appear before the board in any position known to law or practice, I cannot appear as a volunteer witness in the case on mere request, and without knowledge whether I am called for by the Government or Petitioner. You state that I am requested to appear as witness because of the statement or suggestion of the petitioner. It is to be inferred that I am called as a witness for him, but this fact is not distinctly stated, nor is your telegram in the nature of a subpoena, but only a request. To a subpoena regularly issued to appear as a witness for either side, I will promptly and with pleasure respond. I am entirely willing to appear as a witness in the case, and desire simply to be placed in the same relation to the board and the parties in controversy as occupied by all the other witnesses.

John Pope
Brigadier-General, United States Army

Source: "The Fitz-John Porter Case," *New York Times*, October 25, 1878.

APPENDIX 8

List of Witnesses at the Rehearing

This list includes witnesses whose testimony is addressed in Chapter 10. Ranks are those held at the period of activity testified, and not at the date of testimony.

All dates except the final date are in 1878.

*Denotes Confederate.

JULY 8–9

Colonel G. K. Warren, Brigade Commander, Sykes's Division

JULY 9

Major General James Longstreet, Confederate Corps Commander*

JULY 10

Robert Leipold, Orderly on Porter's Staff
Colonel Charles Johnson, Twenty-fifth New York, Morell's Division
Captain Randol, First Artillery, Sykes's Division
Colonel T. Sullivan, Twenty-fourth New York, King's Division
Captain John A. Johnson, Assistant AG to General Hatch, King's Division
John B. Leachman, Guide for General Anderson*

JULY 16

Charles G. William, Aide to General D. R. Jones*
Brigadier General Cadmus Wilcox, Division Commander, Longstreet's Corps*
Lieutenant Colonel Robert Thompson, One-hundred-fifteenth Volunteers, Hooker's Division
Brigadier General John Gibbon, Brigade Commander, King's Division
Lieutenant Stephen Weld, Aide to General Porter

JULY 16–17

Colonel George D. Ruggles, Chief of Staff to General Pope

JULY 17

Ex-governor Newell of New Jersey
Lieutenant Colonel Frederick T. Locke, Chief of Staff to General Porter
Captain George Montieth, Aide to Porter

JULY 18

    Captain Judson, Assistant AG to General King

    Major Hazard Stevens, Assistant AG, First Division, Reno's Corps

    Pvt. John F. Slater, Thirtieth New York, Hatch's Brigade, King's Division

JULY 19

    Captain Horace Boughton, Thirteenth New York, Roberts's Brigade,
        Morell's Division

    Lieutenant Colonel, T.C.H. Smith, Staff of General Pope

SEPTEMBER 10

    Major Francis S. Earle, Assistant AG to General Morell

SEPTEMBER 10–11

    First Lieutenant Alexander D. Payne, General Stuart's Cavalry Division*

    First Lieutenant Walter S. Davis, Staff Officer, Martindale's Brigade

SEPTEMBER 11

    Major General George Morell, Division Commander, General Porter's Corps

    Brigadier General George Sykes, Division Commander, General Porter's
        Corps

OCTOBER 1

    Brigadier General Daniel Butterfield, Brigade Commander, Morell's Division

    Lieutenant Colonel Edward D. Fowler, Fourteenth U.S., Sykes's Division

OCTOBER 2–3

    Captain Douglas Pope, General Pope's Staff

OCTOBER 3

    First Lieutenant Francis D. Jones, Thirty-seventh Infantry

    Captain Moale, Thirty-seventh Infantry

    Colonel Orlando M. Poe, Brigade Commander, Kearny's Division

    Captain William M. Mason, Nineteenth Indiana, King's Division

OCTOBER 3–4

    Private Charles Duffee, Orderly to General Pope

OCTOBER 4

    William E. Murray, Nineteenth Indiana, King's Division

    Captain W. A. Campbell, Nineteenth Indiana, King's Division

    Major General S. P. Heintzelman, Third Corps Commander

    First Lieutenant Samuel Benjamin, Second U.S. Artillery

OCTOBER 7

    W. L. Ormsby, *New York Times* Correspondent

    Colonel Thomas F. McCoy, One-hundred-seventh Pennsylvania, Ricketts's
        Division

    Captain Charles Potter, Third Brigade, Reynolds's Division

    Captain Frederick Geck, Thirteenth New York, Morell's Division

    Captain Joseph E. Terry, Thirteenth New York, Morell's Division

    Captain Ferdinand Mehle, Thirteenth New York, Morell's Division

    Captain Mark J. Bunnell, Thirteenth New York, Morell's Division

OCTOBER 8

Major William Birney, Fifty-seventh Pennsylvania, Kearny's Division
Brigadier General Abner Doubleday, Brigade Commander, King's Division
George Shockley, Fifty-first Pennsylvania, Reno's Division
Captain William W. Blackford, Staff of General Stuart*
Colonel Henry K. Douglas, Staff of General Jackson*
Major Bushrod W. Frobell, Artillery Battery, Hood's Division*
Brigadier General S. D. Sturgis, Commander, Reserve Corps with Piatt

OCTOBER 9

Captain E. D. Roak, Seventh Pennsylvania, Ricketts's Division
Lieutenant Colonel Edwin R. Byles, Ninety-ninth Pennsylvania
Captain Charles Dwight, Second Massachusetts Volunteers, Hooker's
    Division
George A. Randall, Twenty-fourth New York, King's Division
William Bullard, Fifth Excelsior New York, Sykes's Division

OCTOBER 10–11

Major General Irwin McDowell, Commander, Third Corps

OCTOBER 11

Colonel E. C. Schriver, McDowell's Chief of Staff
Brigadier General John C. Robinson, Brigade Commander, Kearny's
    Division
Major R. R. Dows, Sixth Wisconsin, King's Division
Colonel George B. Carr, Brigade Commander, Hooker's Division
Major James M. Dun, First Maryland Cavalry, Sigel's Corps
Captain Solomon Thomas, Eighteenth Massachusetts Volunteers, Morell's
    Division
Captain George W. Mendell, Assistant AG to General Kearny
First Lieutenant William Connolly, Twenty-second Infantry

OCTOBER 12

Brigadier General Jubal Early, Brigade Commander, Ewell's Division*
Colonel Gilman Marston, First Massachusetts, Grover's Brigade, Hooker's
    Division
Colonel Gershom Mott, Sixth New Jersey, Carr's Brigade, Hooker's Division
Major Tremain, Assistant AG, Third Brigade, Hooker's Division
Captain H. C. Bosdyshell, Forty-eighth Pennsylvania, Reynolds's Division
Captain John C. Brown, Kearny's Division
Captain James Hadow, Thirty-sixth Ohio
Second Lieutenant A. T. Tiffany, Thirty-sixth Ohio
Captain John P. Taylor, First Pennsylvania Cavalry, Bayard's Brigade

OCTOBER 14

Dr. Edward Paxton, Surgeon, Fifth Corps
Second Lieutenant Robert J. McNitt, First Pennsylvania Cavalry, Bayard's
    Brigade
Private William H. Ramsey, First Pennsylvania, Bayard's Brigade

John Hoffman, First Pennsylvania Cavalry, Bayard's Brigade
William Redding
Captain John S. Mosby, Staff of General Stuart*
Robert T. Lincoln, President Lincoln's Son
Sergeant Emmor B. Cope, First Pennsylvania Reserves, Reynolds's Division
Colonel Owen Jones, First Pennsylvania Cavalry, Reynolds's Division
William H. Hope, Reynolds's Division
Sergeant John S. Hollingshead, Ninth Pennsylvania Reserves, Reynolds's
   Division
Colonel LeGrand Benedict, Second New York Volunteers, Hooker's Division
Captain M. B. Lakeman, Third Maine Infantry, Kearny's Division
Colonel M. C. McLean, Second Brigade, Schenck's Division

OCTOBER 15

Major General F. Sigel, First Corps Commander
Major General J. Hooker, Division Commander, Heintzelman's Corps
Captain J. J. Cominger, Fourteenth Regulars, Sykes's Division
Captain Robert McEldowney, Twenty-seventh Virginia, Stonewall Brigade*
Captain Basil P. Bowers, Artillery, Milroy's Brigade
Captain William M. Graham, First Regular Artillery, Sykes's Division
Major General George Morell, Division Commander, Porter's Corps

OCTOBER 16

William Blair Lord, Official Stenographer, Porter Court-martial
W.L.B. Wheeler, Farmer Living Near Battlefield
Lewis B. Cowid, Farmer Living Near Battlefield
H. Monroe, Farmer Living Near Battlefield
Colonel Charles Marshall, General Lee's Staff*
Colonel Orlando Smith, Seventy-fifth Ohio, Sigel's Corps

OCTOBER 17

First Lieutenant E. P. Brooks, Acting AG, King's Division
Franklin Stringfellow, Command Cavalry Escort For General Stuart*
A S. Webb, Staff of Porter
Lieutenant Colonel F. T. Locke, General Porter's Chief of Staff
Lieutenant Stephen Weld, General Porter Aide

OCTOBER 19

Brigadier General John H. Piatt, Brigade Commander, Reserve Corps

OCTOBER 21

Brigadier General Schenck, Division Commander, Sigel's Corps
Reverend Mr. Landstreet, General Stuart's Chaplain*
Major White, Staff of General Stuart*

OCTOBER 28

Colonel George L. Andrews, Sigel's Corps
Colonel Horatio G. Sickles, Fourth Pennsylvania Reserves, Reynolds's
   Division
Major O. D. Green, Assistant AG of Sixth Corps

NOVEMBER 23

Colonel Dobson, Third Maryland Infantry, Banks's Corps
Captain John H. Piatt, Staff of General Piatt
Mr. O'Bannion, Longstreet's Corps*
Mr. Lane, Longstreet's Corps*

JANUARY 2, 1879

William Dyer, Orderly, General Pope's Headquarters

Source: *New York Times* articles, July 1878 to January 1879.

APPENDIX 9

Report of the Board of Army Officers in the Case of Fitz-John Porter

Report of the Board of Army Officers in the Case of Fitz-John Porter

New York City, March 19, 1879.

To the honorable the Secretary of War, Washington, D, C:

Sir: We, the Board of Officers appointed by order of the President to examine the evidence in the case of Fitz-John Porter, late major general of volunteers, and to report, with the reasons for our conclusions, what action (if any), in our opinion, justice requires should be taken by the President on the application for relief in that case, have the honor to make the following report. The recorder has been directed to forward to the Adjutant-General of the Army the printed record of our proceeding, including all the evidence examined and the arguments of counsel on either side.

We have made a very thorough examination of all the evidence presented and bearing in any manner upon the merits of the case. The recorder has, under instructions from the board, sought with great diligence for evidence in addition to that presented by the petitioner, especially such as might appear to have a bearing adverse to the claims urged by him.

Due care has been exercised not to inquire into the military operations of the Army of Virginia, or the conduct of officers thereof, any further than has seemed necessary to a full and fair elucidation of the subject submitted to us for investigation. On the other hand, we have not hesitated to examine fully into all the facts, accurate knowledge of which seemed to us to be necessary to the formation of a correct judgment upon the merits of the case, and to the determination of the action which justice requires should be taken by the President on the petitioner's application for relief.

We have had the benefit of the testimony of a large number of officers of the late Confederate Army, a kind of testimony which was not available at the time of General Porter's trial by court-martial. We have also availed ourselves of the testimony of many officers and soldiers of the Union forces who were present on the battle-field, and of much documentary evidence, to throw additional light upon points not made perfectly clear in the record of evidence taken before the court-martial; and we have had the use of accurate maps of the battle-field of Manassas, constructed from recent actual surveys made, under the direction of the Chief of Engineers, by a distinguished officer of that corps, who was himself a participant in that battle.

Without such a map neither the testimony upon which General Porter was convicted nor the additional testimony submitted to this board could have been correctly understood.

The evidence which we have thus been able to examine, in addition to that which was before the court-martial, has placed beyond question many important facts which were before the subjects of dispute, and in respect to some of which radically erroneous opinions were entertained by General Porter's accusers, and doubtless by the court-martial that pronounced him guilty.

The result has been, as we believe, to establish beyond reasonable doubt all the facts essential to the formation of a correct judgment upon the merits of the case of Fitz-John Porter. We are thus enabled to report, with entire unanimity, and without doubt in our own minds, with the reasons for our conclusions, what action, in our opinion, justice required should be taken by the President on the petitioner's application for relief.

The evidence presents itself under several distinct heads, viz:

First. The imperfect, and in some respects erroneous, statements of facts, due to the partial and incorrect knowledge in possession of witnesses at the time of the court-martial, and the extremely inaccurate maps and erroneous locations of troops thereon, by which erroneous statements were made to convey still more erroneous impressions.

Second. The opinions and inferences of prominent officers based upon this imperfect knowledge.

Third. The far more complete and accurate statements of facts now made by a large number of eye-witnesses from both the contending forces.

Fourth. The accurate maps of the field of operations and the exact positions of troops thereon at different periods of time, by which statements otherwise contradictory or irreconcilable are shown to be harmonious, and opposing opinions are shown to have been based upon different views of the same military situation; and,

Finally. The conflicting testimony relative to plans of operations, interpretation of orders, motives of action, and relative degrees of responsibility for unfortunate results.

A careful consideration of all the material facts now fully established, in combination with the conflicting or inconclusive testimony last above referred to, gives rise to several diverse theories respecting the whole subject with which General Porter's case is inseparably connected. These diverse views of the subject necessarily involve in a greater or less degree the acts, motives, and responsibilities of others as well as those of the petitioner. We have considered, with great care and labor, and with our best ability, each and all of these phases in which the subject can be and has been presented, and we find that all these possible views of the subject, when examined in the light of the facts which are fully established by undisputed testimony, lead inevitably to one and the same conclusion in respect to the guilt or innocence of Fitz-John Porter of the specific charges upon which he was tried and pronounced guilty by the court-martial.

Therefore, while exposing General Porter's conduct to the test of the highest degree of responsibility which recognized military principles attached to the command he held under the circumstances in which he was placed, and the orders which he had received, we are able to take that view of the whole subject which seems to involve in the least possible degree any question as to the acts, motives, or responsibility of others.

We will now proceed to give, as concisely as we are able to do, a narrative of the events which gave rise to the charges against Maj. Gen. Fitz-John Porter, omitting the

multitude of interesting but unessential details and all facts having no necessary bearing upon his case, and limiting ourselves to a plain statement of the essential facts of
the case which have been established, as we believe, by positive proof.

While the Army of the Potomac was withdrawing from its position on the James
River in August, 1862, the Army of Virginia, under Major-General Pope, was ordered
to hold the line of the Rappahannock, and to stand on the defensive until all the forces
could be united behind that river. General Pope was given to understand that, when
this concentration was effected, Major-General Halleck, the General-in-Chief, was to
take the field in command of the combined armies. On the other hand, it appears that
Major-General McClellan, then commanding the Army of the Potomac, was given to
understand that he was to direct the operations of all the forces in Virginia, as soon as
they should be united. It appears that General Pope was notified on the 25th of August
that an active campaign was soon to be commenced, without waiting for a union of all
the forces, and under some commander other than either of those before named. But
this information appears to have been of a secret character, afterward suppressed, and
not made known to General McClellan and his subordinates until five days later, when
the order appeared from the War Department, depriving McClellan of the command
of all his troops then between the Potomac and the Rappahannock, although leaving
him in nominal command of the Army of the Potomac.

Thus General Porter, who joined General Pope's army about that time, was left
under the impression, which all had previously shared, that the operations of the army
were to continue of a defensive character until all the forces should be united and proper
preparations made for the commencement of an offensive campaign under a general
designated by the President to command the combined armies. But just then the Confederate general, Jackson, with three divisions of infantry, one of cavalry, and some
artillery, commenced his movement to turn the Union right through Thoroughfare
Gap, which Gap he passed on the 26th, and that night struck the rear of the Union army
at Bristoe and Manassas Junction. The next morning, August 27, the Union army
changed front to the rear, and was ordered to move on Gainesville, Greenwich, and
Warrenton Junction.

General Porter, with his two divisions of the Fifth Corps, arrived at Warrenton
Junction on the 27th, and there reported in person to General Pope. That afternoon
Hooker's division was engaged with the enemy at Bristoe Station; McDowell and Sigel
were moving on Gainesville, and Heintzelman and Reno on Greenwich. Banks was covering the rear below Warrenton Junction and guarding the trains in their movement
toward Manassas Junction. Porter was at first ordered to move toward Greenwich upon
the arrival of Banks at Warrenton Junction but after Hooker's engagement at Bristoe
the following order was sent him, and he received it at 9.50 P.M.:

Headquarters Army of Virginia,
Bristoe Station, August 27, 1862—6.30 P.M.

Maj. Gen. F. J. Porter,
Warrenton Junction

General: The major-general commanding directs that you start at 1 o'clock to-
night and come forward with your whole corps, or such part of it as is with
you, so as to be here by daylight tomorrow morning. Hooker has had a very
severe action with the enemy, with a loss of about 300 killed and wounded.

The enemy has been driven back, but is retiring along the railroad. We must drive him from Manassas, and clear the country between that place and Gainesville, where McDowell is. If Morell has not joined you, send him word to push forward immediately; also send word to Banks to hurry forward with all speed to take your place at Warrenton Junction. It is necessary on all accounts that you should be here by daylight. I send an officer with this dispatch who will conduct you to this place. Be sure to send word to Banks, who is on the road from Fayetteville, probably in the direction of Bealeton. Say to Banks, also, that he had best run back the railroad trains to this side of Cedar Run. If he is not with you, write him to that effect.

By command of General Pope:

George D. Ruggles,
Colonel and Chief of Staff.

P. S—If Banks is not at Warrenton Junction, leave a regiment of infantry and two pieces of artillery as a guard till he comes up, with instructions to follow you immediately upon his doing so. If Banks is not at the Junction, instruct Colonel Clary to run the trains back to this side of Cedar Run, and post a regiment and a section of artillery with it.

By command of General Pope:
George D. Ruggles, Colonel and Chief of Staff

This order plainly contemplated an aggressive movement against the enemy early on the 28th, and required the presence of General Porter's corps at Bristoe Station as early as possible in the morning, to take part in the pursuit of and attack upon the enemy.

The order did not indicate any anticipation of defensive action at Bristoe, but, on the contrary, it indicated continuous, active, and aggressive operations during the entire day of the 28th, to drive the enemy from Manassas and clear the country. Hence the troops must arrive at Bristoe in condition for such service.

The evidence clearly shows that General Porter evinced an earnest desire to comply literally with the terms of the order, and that he held a consultation with his division commanders, some of his brigade commanders, and his staff officers on the subject. One of his divisions had arrived in camp late in the evening, after a long march, and was much fatigued.

If the troops marched at 1 o'clock, none of them could have much sleep before starting, and, even if they could arrive at Bristoe by or soon after daylight, they must be in poor condition for a vigorous pursuit of the enemy, who was already some distance beyond Bristoe. But this was not regarded by General Porter as sufficient reason for hesitating to make the attempt to comply literally with the order. He still urged, against the advice of his division commanders, the necessity of implicit obedience. Then further consideration of the subject disclosed the fact that the road was filled with army trains, which had been pressing in that direction all day and as late at night as they could move, until the way had become completely blocked with wagons. The trains of the army moving back from the line of the Rappahannock had been ordered to take that road to the number of "two or three thousand." In the language of one of the most intelligent witnesses, the mass of wagons blocked together at places in the road was "like a lot of ice that jams in on the shore." The night had become very dark, or, as testified by most of the witnesses, excessively dark. It would have been difficult to march troops upon a plain and unobstructed road. It was a manifest physical impossibility to march over that road that night or to remove the obstructions in the darkness of the night. When this situation was made evident, General Porter reluctantly consented to delay the movement two hours, or until 3 o'clock. At that hour the march was commenced, but it was found that no appreciable progress could be made before daylight. Nothing was gained, or could have been gained, by the attempt to move before the dawn of day. It would have been wiser to have delayed the attempt to move until 4 o'clock.

A vigorous and persistent effort to make that march, commencing at 1 o'clock, could only have resulted in greatly fatiguing the troops and throwing them into disorder, from which they could not have been extricated until long after daylight, without making any material progress, and would thus have caused the corps to arrive at Bristoe at a later hour and in a miserable condition.

Abundant experience in situations similar to that above described leaves no room for doubt what General Porter's duty was. He exercised only the very ordinary discretion of a corps commander, which it was his plain duty to exercise, in delaying the march until 3 o'clock, and in his attempt to move at that time instead of at 4 o'clock he showed only too anxious a desire to comply with the letter of his orders.

If the order had contemplated, as has been represented, an attack by the enemy at dawn of day, then it would have been General Porter's duty to start promptly, not at 1 o'clock, but at the moment he received the order, so as to have brought at least some fragments of his infantry to Bristoe in time to aid in repelling that attack. That was the most that he could have done in any event, even by starting the moment the order was received, and then his troops would have been in no condition for any aggressive movement that day.

General Porter reached Bristoe Station as soon as practicable with his corps on the morning of the 28th, and there remained, under orders from his superior commander, until the morning of the 29th, taking no part in the operations of the 28th.

In the morning of the 28th McDowell sent Ricketts' division of his corps to Thoroughfare Gap to resist the advance of re-enforcements from the main body of Lee's army then known to be marching to join Jackson. Banks was at Warrenton Junction and Porter at Bristoe. The rest of the army moved from Gainesville, Greenwich, and Bristoe on Manassas Junction to attack Jackson at that place; but that general withdrew his forces during the night of the 27th and morning of the 28th toward Sudley and Groveton. He was followed by Heintzelman and Reno, via Centreville, and McDowell and Sigel, after having marched some distance toward Manassas, were ordered to direct their march toward Centreville. In this movement toward Centreville King's division of McDowell's corps struck the right of Jackson's force late in the afternoon, just north of the Warrenton turnpike, a mile west of Groveton. A sharp contest ensued, lasting until some time after dark, when King still held his ground on the turnpike. Reynolds was then near the right of King, Sigel on his right near the stone house, Heintzelman and Reno near Centreville; Ricketts, who had been sent in the morning to Thoroughfare Gap, was disputing with Longstreet the passage of the Gap.

Thus it was still hoped to strike Jackson a decisive blow on the morning of the 29th before re-enforcements could reach him. In the meantime the Confederate general had taken up a favorable position a little to the north and west of Groveton and Sudley to await attack.

Under these conditions General Porter, who was still at Bristoe Station, received, at 6 A.M., the following order from General Pope:

Headquarters Army of Virginia,
Near Bull Run, August 29, 1862—3 A.M.

Major-General Porter:

General: McDowell has intercepted the retreat of Jackson. Sigel is immediately on the right of McDowell. Kearny and Hooker march to attack the enemy's rear at early dawn. Major-General Pope directs you to move upon Centreville at the first dawn of day with your whole command, leaving your trains to follow. It is very important that you should be here at a very early hour in the morning. A severe engagement is likely to take place, and your presence is necessary.

I am, general, very respectfully, your obedient servant,

George D. Ruggles,
Colonel and Chief of Staff.

Under this order General Porter marched promptly with his corps toward Centreville. He had passed Manassas Junction with the head of his column, when he was halted by counter–orders, issued in consequence of a grave change which had occurred in the situation since the night before.

King had withdrawn from his position near Jackson's right, on the Warrenton turnpike, and had fallen back to Manassas Junction. Ricketts had fallen back in the night from Thoroughfare Gap to Gainesville, and thence, in consequence of the movement of King, had retired to Bristoe Station.

Thus the way had been left open for the retreat of Jackson to Thoroughfare Gap or for the advance of Longstreet from that point, and ample time had elapsed for them to effect a junction, either at the Gap or near Groveton, before a force could again be interposed to prevent it. The opportunity to attack Jackson's detached force with superior numbers had passed beyond the possibility of recall.

As soon as the withdrawal of King became known to General Pope he hastily sent a verbal message to General Porter to retrace his steps and move toward Gainesville, and soon followed this message with the following order, which was received by General Porter about 9.30 A.M.:

Headquarters Army of Virginia,
Centreville, August 29, 1862.

Push forward with your corps and King's division, which you will take with you, upon Gainesville. I am following the enemy down the Warrenton turnpike. Be expeditious or we will lose much.

John Pope, Major-General, Commanding

Under these orders General Porter advanced promptly with his corps, followed by King's division, on the direct road from Manassas Junction toward Gainesville, having knowledge of the military situation as above described.

General Porter had met General McDowell near Manassas Junction, and they had conversed with each other relative to this order, placing King's division under Porter's command. McDowell claims that it was conceded that he might go forward and command the whole force under the Sixty-second Article of War, but he desired to reunite all the divisions of his corps on that part of the field where Reynolds then was. Hence he wrote to Pope on this subject, awaited his orders, and did not exercise any command over Porter's corps until after the receipt of further orders from Pope.

When, about 11.30 o'clock, the head of Porter's column arrived at Dawkins' Branch, about 3 miles from Gainesville and 9 miles from Thoroughfare Gap, he met the enemy's cavalry advance, and captured some of Longstreet's scouts. The clouds of dust in his front and to his right, and extending back toward Thoroughfare Gap, showed the enemy coming in force, and already arriving on the field in his front.

Morell's division was at once deployed; Sykes closed up in support, King's division following. A regiment was sent forward across the creek as skirmishers, and Butterfield's brigade was started across the creek to the front, and somewhat to the right, with orders to seize, in advance of the enemy, if possible, the commanding ground on the opposite ridge, about a mile distant. Morell's division, with Sykes' in support, was ready to advance at once to the support of Butterfield.

At this stage of Porter's operations, some time between 11.30 and 12 o'clock, McDowell, in person, arrived on the field and arrested the movement Porter was making, saying to him, in the hearing of several officers, "Porter, you are too far out. This is no place to fight a battle," or words to that effect.

McDowell had received a few minutes before a dispatch from Buford, informing him that seventeen regiments of infantry, a battery, and some cavalry had passed through Gainesville at 8.45 o'clock, and moved down the Centreville road toward Groveton, and hence must have been on the field in front of Sigel and Reynolds at least two hours. The dust in Porter's immediate front and extending across toward Groveton, as well as back toward Gainesville, showed that large forces of the enemy, in addition to those reported by Buford, were already on the field. The latest information from the Confederate army showed the whole force of the enemy within reach of Gainesville by noon on the 29th. McDowell's troops (Ricketts' division and some cavalry) had delayed Longstreet's advance at Thoroughfare Gap from about noon until dark on the previous day, the 28th. Hence Lee's column had had eighteen hours by the morning of the 29th to close up in mass near the Gap, and seven hours that morning in which to march 8 miles and form line on the field of battle.

Jackson, who had been supposed anxious to retreat, and for whom the way had been left open, had not retreated, but was still holding his position of the previous evening, as if confident of adequate re-enforcements. Sigel's pursuit had been checked, where it started that morning, at Groveton.

It was certain that the head of column of Lee's main army had arrived on the field in front of Groveton at least two hours in advance of the arrival of the head of column of Porter's and McDowell's corps at Dawkins' Branch, and it was so nearly certain that the main body of Lee's army was already on the field and in line of battle as to absolutely require corresponding action. This was Porter's impression at the time, and he conveyed it to McDowell by words and gesture that left no doubt in the mind of the latter that he (Porter) believed the enemy was in force in his immediate front.

In contrast to this evident preparation of the enemy for battle only Porter's 9,000 or 10,000 men were ready for action of the 35,000 men then composing the left wing of the Union army.

Banks' Corps, 10,000, was still at Bristoe without orders to move beyond that point. Ricketts' division, 8,000, was near Bristoe, under orders to move to the front, but his men were so worn-out by constant marching, night and day, that they could not possibly be got to the field even for defensive action that day. King's division, 7,000, was just in rear of Porter, but was so fatigued as to be unfit for offensive action, and hardly able to march.

Thus this long column, stretching back from Dawkins' Branch by way of Manassas Junction to and even beyond Bristoe, had struck the right wing of the Confederate army in line of battle, while a gap of nearly 2 miles remained in the Union line between Porter and Reynolds, who was on the left of Sigel, near Groveton.

The accompanying map, marked board map No. 1, illustrates the positions of the Union troops at noon of August 29, and the probable positions of the Confederate troops at the same time, as indicated by the information then in possession of the Union generals. This map is not intended to show the actual positions of the troops at that time, but to correctly interpret the information upon which the Union generals then acted.

This was the military situation on the Union left and Confederate right of the field when McDowell arrested Porter's advance, and Porter's operations under the direct orders from Pope heretofore mentioned ceased, and, under new orders just received, Porter became subordinate to McDowell.

Not only had the effort to destroy Jackson before he could be re-enforced totally failed, but the Confederate army was on the field and in line, while the Union army was not. The time to resume defensive action, awaiting the concentration of the army, had not only arrived, but had been too long postponed.

On his way to the front McDowell had received the following order from General Pope, addressed jointly to him and Porter, and Porter had received a copy of the same order a moment before McDowell's arrival:

General Orders No. 5.

Headquarters Army Virginia,
Centreville, August 29, 1862.

Generals McDowell and Porter:

You will please move forward with your joint commands toward Gainesville. I sent General Porter written orders to that effect an hour and a half ago. Heintzelman, Sigel, and Reno are moving on the Warrenton turnpike, and must now be not far from Gainesville. I desire that as soon as communication is established between this force and your own the whole command shall halt. It may be necessary to fall back behind Bull Run, at Centreville, to-night. I presume it will be so on account of our supplies. I have sent no orders of any description to Ricketts, and none to interfere in any way with the movements of McDowell's troops, except what I sent by his aide-de-camp last night, which were to hold his position on the Warrenton pike until the troops from here should fall upon the enemy's flank and rear. I do not even know Ricketts' position, as I have not been able to find out where General McDowell was until a late hour this morning.

General McDowell will take immediate steps to communicate with General Ricketts, and instruct him to rejoin the other divisions of his corps as soon as practicable. If any considerable advantages are to be gained by departing from this order it will not be strictly carried out. One thing must be had in view, that the troops must occupy a position from which they can reach Bull Run to-night or by morning. The indications are that the whole force of the enemy is moving in this direction at a pace that will bring them here by to-morrow night or next day. My own headquarters will be for the present with Heintzelman's corps or at this place.

John Pope,
Major-General, Commanding

This order and the Sixty-second Article of War made it the duty of McDowell to command the combined corps so long as they should continue to act together and General Pope should be absent from the field. In this interpretation of the law Generals McDowell and Porter agreed, and upon it they acted at the time. Upon McDowell devolved the responsibility of modifying the joint order as its terms authorized and as the military situation seemed imperatively to require.

The terms of the order contemplating that communication should be established with the troops on the other road, or, as General McDowell interpreted it, that line should be formed in connection with those troops, that the whole command should then halt, and that the troops must not go beyond a point from which they could reach Bull Run by that night or the next morning, and the military situation, as it then appeared to them, was briefly discussed by the two generals.

The situation was exceedingly critical. If the enemy should attack, as he seemed about ready to do, Porter's two divisions, about 9,000 men, were all the force then ready to stand between Lee's main army, just arrived on the field, and McDowell's long and weary column, or the left flank of Pope's army near Groveton. McDowell was "excessively anxious" to get King's division over on the left of Reynolds, who then occupied with his small division that exposed flank; and he quickly decided that "considerable advantages" were "to be gained" by departing from the terms of the joint order, so far as to make no attempt to go farther toward Gainesville, and to at once form line with the troops then engaged near Groveton; and this departure from the strict letter of the joint order was evidently required by the military situation as it then appeared and as it did actually exist.

After this brief consultation the two generals rode together through the woods to the right about three-quarters of a mile toward Groveton, and made a personal examination of the ground. As soon as this was done, McDowell decided not to take the troops through these woods, but to separate his own corps from Porter's, take King's division (Ricketts following) around the woods by the Sudley Springs road, and thus put them in beyond the woods and on the left of Reynolds. McDowell then left Porter very hurriedly, announcing his decision, as he testified, by the words, "You put your force in here, and I will take mine up the Sudley Springs road on the left of the troops engaged at that point against the enemy," or words to that effect. Even these few words, we are satisfied, Porter did not hear or did not understand, for he called, as McDowell rode away, "What shall I do?" and McDowell gave no audible answer, but only a wave of the hand. In this state of uncertainty, according to the testimony of one of General Porter's staff officers, Porter sent a message to King's division to ascertain positively if that division was ordered away by McDowell, and, if not, to give proper orders for its action with his corps, and a reply was returned by McDowell himself that he was going to the right and should take that division with him; that Porter had better stay where he was, and, if necessary to fall back, he could do so on McDowell's left.

This testimony has given rise to much controversy; but, in our opinion, the question whether that message was or was not sent is unimportant. If it was sent, it did not differ in substance from the instructions which General McDowell testifies he had previously given to General Porter, "You put your force in here," &c. Neither could be construed as directing what Porter's action should be, but only as deciding that he should continue on that line while McDowell would take his own troops to another part of the field.

There appears to have been an understanding, derived either from previous conversation or from the terms of the joint order, that when McDowell did get King's division on the other side of the woods Morell's division on the right of Porter's corps should make such connection or establish such communication with that of King as might be practicable through the woods. None of them then knew how wide was that belt of woods, nor what was its character beyond where they had reconnoitered, nor whether the ground beyond was in possession of the enemy.

When the two generals had started to take that ride to the right Morell's troops had been ordered to follow them, and Griffin's brigade had led off after its pickets had been called in. After McDowell took his departure this movement was continued for some time and until Griffin had crossed the railroad and reached a point near halfway across the belt of woods and where the forest became dense. There the movement was arrested. This movement might have meant an attempt to stretch out Morell's line through the woods so as to connect with King's on the right or a completion of the deployment for an attack upon the enemy in front. General Porter explained it as intended for an immediate attack upon the enemy if he found he could keep King in support, and that he only desisted upon being informed that King was going away. But the attack would have been a rash one under the circumstances even with King's support. Soon after this scouts were sent on through the woods to look for King, Reynolds, Sigel, or some body of Union troops in the direction where artillery firing was heard.

Presently Griffin was withdrawn to the south side of the railroad. The enemy's artillery opened on his troops during this latter movement and was replied to by one of Morell's batteries, but few shots being fired on either side. Then Morell's division was put in defensive order to hold the ground then occupied and under cover from the enemy's artillery. The scouts sent through the woods ran upon the enemy's pickets and were driven back. This effort to get scouts through the woods was repeated from time to time until late in the afternoon, but every effort failed. The scouts were all driven back or captured. As it turned out, this resulted from the fact that King's division did not get up on the right of the woods at all. That division reached a point some distance in the rear of its position in the line about 4.30 P.M., and then, after some marching and counter-marching, was sent northward to the Warrenton pike. Thus the gap in the line which McDowell's troops were to occupy remained open all the afternoon and the margin of the timber remained in possession of the enemy's pickets.

These failures to connect or to communicate directly along the front were reported by Porter to McDowell by way of the Sudley Springs road, on which McDowell had gone. The reports were made in at least four different written dispatches, which have been preserved. The hour was named in only one, apparently the latest, at 6 o'clock in the evening. Two reports—one about 4 o'clock and the other about 6.30 P.M.—were sent to General Pope direct. Both of these were received by him, but have not been preserved. About the time General McDowell arrived on the field at Porter's position, and for an hour or two thereafter, a heavy artillery combat was going on between the Union batteries near Groveton and the Confederate artillery. During this artillery combat, and until 5 o'clock P.M., there was no infantry engagement, except skirmishing and some short and sharp contests between small portions of the opposing forces, and until 6.30 P.M. no musketry was audible to any one in Porter's corps.

On the Confederate side, as it now appears, Porter's display of troops—three brigades in line—in the early part of the afternoon had given rise to the expectation of an attack on their right. This having been reported to General Longstreet, that commander sent his reserve division (Wilcox's) from his extreme left, just north of the Warrenton turnpike, to his extreme right, on the Manassas and Gainesville road. Wilcox reached this latter position about 4 o'clock P.M., and Porter having before that time withdrawn his troops under cover, some troops from the Confederate right (D. R. Jones') were pushed to the front in the woods occupied by Porter's skirmishers, apparently to reconnoiter. This movement gave rise to the impression among Porter's officer's (Morell's division) that the enemy was about to attack about 5 P.M.

General Pope having arrived some time after noon on the field in the rear of Groveton, and General McDowell's column approaching that part of the field by the Manassas and Sudley road, an attack was ordered upon the enemy's extreme left near Sudley, and a written order was sent, dated 4.30 P.M., to Porter to attack the enemy's right, and, if possible, his rear. After some time had elapsed, General Pope ordered McDowell, with King's division and other troops, to pursue up the Warrenton turnpike the enemy, who, thus to be assailed upon both flanks, would be compelled to retreat.

The attack on Jackson's left was begun by Kearny about 5 P.M.; but the order to Porter was not delivered in time. The messenger did not find General Porter until sunset. Thus at 5 o'clock, nothing having occurred to suggest to General Porter any change in the plan indicated in the joint order to retire behind Bull Run, instead of giving battle that day, the sound of artillery near Sudley, so much apparently to the rear of Groveton, suggested to Porter, who was then at Bethlehem Church, that Sigel was retiring or perhaps being driven back, and that his artillery was then in a new position near the Sudley Springs road.

If it was true that Sigel was being driven back the military situation was extremely perilous, and Porter must instantly do what he could to avert disaster. His order to Morell, which must have been issued at that instant, shows what he proposed to do. It is as follows, viz:

General Morell:

Push over to the aid of Sigel and strike in his rear. If you reach a road up which King is moving, and he has got ahead of you, let him pass; but see if you cannot give help to Sigel. If you find him retiring, move back toward Manassas, and, should necessity require it, and you do not hear from me, push to Centreville. If you find the direct road filled, take the one via Union Mills, which is to the right as you return

F. J. Porter,
Major-General.

Look to the points of the compass for Manassas.

F. J. Porter

This movement would have left Porter with Sykes alone to hold the Manassas road and cover the retreat of Ricketts' worn-out troops, who then were stretched along the road for 4 or 5 miles both toward Sudley and back toward Manassas Junction, while Morell should cover the retreat of the center of the army. But now, before Morell had time to commence this movement, came a report from him that the enemy was coming down in force to attack both his front and flank. Porter might in a few minutes have to meet the attack of 20,000 men. The purpose to cover the retreat of Sigel must needs be abandoned. Hence Porter dispatched to Morell;

General Morell:

Hold on, if you can, to your present place. What is passing?

F. J. Porter.

Again:

General Morell:

Tell me what is passing quickly. If the enemy is coming, hold to him and I will come up. Post your men to repulse him.

F. J. Porter, Major-General.

And again, in reply to advice from Morell that they had better retire, &c:

We cannot retire while McDowell holds on.

Notwithstanding contradictory testimony, we believe it was at this time that Porter ordered Piatt's brigade, of Sturgis' command, about 800 men, to move back to Manassas Junction and take up a defensive position to cover the expected retreat.

General Porter reported to General McDowell his views and intentions in the following dispatches:

Generals McDowell and King:

I found it impossible to communicate by crossing the woods to Groveton. The enemy are in great force on this road, and as they appear to have driven our forces back, the fire of the enemy having advanced and ours retired, I have determined to withdraw to Manassas. I have attempted to communicate with McDowell and Sigel, but my messengers have run into the enemy. They have gathered artillery and cavalry and infantry, and the advancing masses of dust show the enemy coming in force. I am now going to the head of the column to see what is passing and how affairs are going, and I will communicate with you. Had you not better send your train back?

F. J. Porter, Major-General.

General McDowell or King:

I have been wandering over the woods and failed to get a communication to you. Tell how matters go with you. The enemy is in strong force in front of me, and I wish to know your designs for to-night. If left to me, I shall have to retire for food and water, which I cannot get here. How goes the battle? It seems to go to our rear. The enemy are getting to our left.

F. J. Porter, Major-General Volunteers.

General McDowell:

The firing on my right has so far retired that, as I cannot advance and have failed to get over to you except by the route taken by King, I shall withdraw to Manassas. If you have anything to communicate, please do so. I have sent many messengers to you and General Sigel and get nothing.

F. J. Porter,
Major-General

An artillery duel is going on now; been skirmishing for a long time.
F. J. P.

General McDowell:

Failed in getting Morell over to you. After wandering about the woods for a time I withdrew him, and while doing so artillery opened upon us. My scouts could not get through. Each one found the enemy between us, and I believe some have been captured. Infantry are also in front. I am trying to get a battery, but have not succeeded as yet. From the masses of dust on our left and from reports of scouts think the enemy are moving largely in that way. Please communicate the way this messenger came. I have no cavalry or messengers now. Please let me know your designs, whether you retire or not I cannot get water and am out of provisions. Have lost a few men from infantry firing.

F. J. Porter,
Major-General Volunteers
August 29, 6 P.M.

But Porter soon found the sounds of artillery had deceived him. The renewal of the firing toward Groveton showed that Pope's troops were still there. Piatt's brigade was then recalled, and no further preparations for retreat were made.

Next came to Porter about 5.30 o'clock a report from the right that the enemy was in full retreat and heavy sounds of musketry soon after showed that serious work had commenced near Groveton. Porter ordered Morell to make a strong reconnaissance to learn the truth. Morell, knowing the report must be false, at least as to the enemy in his front, prepared to support this reconnaissance with his whole division. While this preparation was being made came the long-delayed order, dated 4.30 P.M., to attack the enemy in flank or rear:

Headquarters in the Field,
August 29—4.30 P.M.

Major-General Porter:

Your line of march brings you in on the enemy's right flank. I desire you to push forward into action at once on the enemy's flank, and, if possible, on his rear, keeping your right in communication with General Reynolds. The enemy is massed in the woods in front of us, but can be shelled out as soon as you engage their flank. Keep heavy reserves and use your batteries, keeping well closed to your right all the time. In case you are obliged to fall back, do so to your right and rear, so as to keep you in close communication with the right wing.

John Pope,
Major-General, Commanding

This order, though dated at 4.30 P.M., was not received by Porter, at Bethlehem Church, before 6.30 P.M.

The evidence before the court-martial tending to show that Porter received the "'4.30" order in time to execute it is found in the testimony of the officer who carried the order, and of one of the orderlies who accompanied him. Neither of these two witnesses appears to have carried a watch, and their several statements of the time when the order was delivered were based on estimates of the time occupied by them in riding from General Pope's headquarters to the place where they found General Porter. One of them at least knew from an inspection of the order that it was dated at 4.30; he, and probably both of them, therefore assumed that it was then that they started to deliver it, and adding to that hour the estimated time occupied by them, they severally fixed the hour of delivery. It is now proved by the testimony of the officer who wrote the dispatch that "4.30" was not the hour when the messenger started, but was the hour when he began to write the dispatch, and consequently that it was after that hour that the officer started to deliver it.

It is also shown that these messengers did not and could not, if other parts of their own testimony are true, have traveled over the route which they supposed they had taken. Moreover, it was proved by unquestionable testimony that since the court-martial trial one of these witnesses had made statements and admissions inconsistent with and contradictory of his former testimony, and the other witness confessed before us that recently he had deliberately made false statements in regard to the route taken while carrying the dispatch. We have therefore felt compelled to lay the testimony of these witnesses out of the case. An attempt was made to support these witnesses by the testimony of another person, who, as it was alleged, also accompanied, as an orderly, the officer charged with the dispatch, but his testimony was so completely broken down by cross-examination that we regard it as entitled to no weight whatever.

On the other hand, the testimony of General Sykes, Lieutenant-Colonel Locke, Captain Montieth, Lieutenant Ingham, and Lieutenant Weld before the court-martial that the order in question was not delivered until about sundown, either a little before or a little after that hour, has now been supported by a new and entirely independent witness, Captain Randel [Randol], and has been singularly confirmed by the production, for the first time, of the dispatch from Porter to McDowell, dated 6 P.M., the terms of which utterly forbid the supposition that at that time Porter had received the order.

The moment this order was received Porter sent his chief of staff, Colonel Locke, to General Morell, with orders to make the attack at once. He then wrote and sent a reply to Pope, and immediately rode to the front. On his arrival there Morell had about completed his preparations for the attack under the previous order to make a reconnaissance, but darkness had already come on. It was evidently impossible to accomplish any good that night, for, even if Morell might have begun the attack before dark, Sykes could not have been got into line after the order was received. The contest at Groveton had already so far spent its force as to derive no possible aid from Morell's attack. The order was based upon conditions manifestly erroneous and directed what was impossible to be done. To push Morell's division against the enemy in the dark would have been in no sense obedience to that order. Porter wisely ordered the preparations to cease, and the troops were put into position to pass the night, picketing in all directions, for Porter had but a few mounted men, and the enemy had 2,500 cavalry near his flank.

About this time, when darkness had come on, the rear of McDowell's column of weary troops was passing by the rear of Porter's column, still several miles from their destined place on the field. The Union army was not even yet ready for battle.

The accompanying maps, marked board maps, Nos. 2 and 3, exhibit substantially the military situation at the time the 4.30 P.M. order was issued, and that which was then understood by General Pope to exist, as explained to the court-martial upon the trial of General Porter. We believe this plain and simple narrative of the events of the 29th of August clearly shows the true character of General Porter's conduct during that time. We are unable to find in that conduct anything subject to criticism, much less deserving of censure or condemnation.

Porter's duty that afternoon was too plain and simple to admit of discussion. It was to hold his position and cover the deployment of McDowell's troops until the latter, or some of them, should get into line; then to connect with them as far as might be necessary and practicable, and then, in the absence of further orders, to act in concert with those troops and others to the right.

If King's division had come up on the right, as was expected, and had advanced to attack, Porter would have known it instantly, and thus could have joined in the movement.

If the main army retired, as indicated in the joint order, it was Porter's duty to retire also, after having held his ground long enough to protect its left flank and to cover the retreat of Ricketts' troops.

Porter did for a moment entertain the purpose of trying to give aid to Sigel, who was supposed to be retiring before McDowell had got King's division up to his support. That was the nearest to making a mistake that Porter came that afternoon. But it soon enough became evident that such a purpose must be abandoned; Porter had quite his full share of responsibility where he was.

The preparations made for retreat were the ordinary soldierly dispositions to enable him to do promptly what he had good reason to expect he might be required to do at any moment and must do at nightfall.

He made frequent reports to his superiors, stating what he had done and what he had been unable to do; what his situation was in respect to the enemy in his front and the strength of the enemy there; what his impressions were from the sounds of action toward his right; how he had failed thus far to get any communications from any commander in the main army, or any orders from General Pope, asking McDowell, who was nearest to him, for such information and his (McDowell's) designs for the night; sending an aide-de-camp to General Pope for orders and receiving no reply, not even information that the 4.30 order had been sent to him; and, finally, informing his superiors that if left to himself, without orders, he would have to retire at night for food and water, which he could not get where he was. These reports were sent not only frequently, but early enough to insure the receipt of orders from Pope or correct information from McDowell, if they had any to send him, before it would be time for him to withdraw.

All these dispatches were sent in the latter part of the afternoon. They all indicated a purpose to retire only after being assured that the main army was retiring, and then to cover the retreat of the army as far as possible, or to withdraw after night-fall, as the joint order had indicated, if no further orders or information of General Pope's plans could be obtained.

There is no indication in any of those dispatches, when fairly construed, nor in anything which Porter did or said, of any intention to withdraw until after dark, unless compelled to do so by the retreat of the main army; and even then he was compelled to hold on until McDowell's troops could get out of the way, and that was not until after dark, for Ricketts' division was on the road in Porter's rear all the afternoon.

It is perfectly clear that Porter had no thought whatever of retreating from the enemy, or of withdrawing because of the enemy in his front; for when the enemy was reported advancing as if to attack his orders were: "If the enemy is coming, hold to him." "Post your troops to repulse him." "We cannot retire while McDowell holds on."

It appears to have been assumed in the condemnation of General Porter's conduct that he had some order to attack or some information of aggressive plans on the part of General Pope, or some intimation, suggestion, or direction to that effect from General McDowell, or that there was such a battle going on within his hearing, or something else in the military situation that required him to attack the enemy without orders before receiving the 4.30 P.M. order at sunset. All this was the exact reverse of the truth. General Pope's last order, General McDowell's directions while he was with General Porter, the military situation as then known to both Porter and McDowell, and the movement McDowell had decided to make to get his own troops into line of battle and the state of the action on the right of the field, all combined to absolutely forbid any attack by Porter during that entire afternoon until he received Pope's order at sunset, and even that order could not possibly have been given if the situation had been correctly understood.

An attack by him would have been a violation of the spirit of his orders and a criminal blunder, leading to inevitable disaster. In short, he had no choice as a faithful soldier but to do substantially what he did do.

The range of our investigation has not enabled us to ascertain the source of the great error which was committed in the testimony before General Porter's court-martial respecting the time of arrival of the main body of Lee's army on the field of Manassas. But the information which was in possession of the Union officers at noon of the 29th of August, and afterward published in their official reports, together with the testimony before the court-martial, affords clear, explicit, and convincing proof that the main body of that army must have been there on the field at that time.

The recent testimony of Confederate officers hardly adds anything to the conclusiveness of that proof, but rather diminishes its force, by showing that one division (Anderson's) did not arrive until the next morning; while the information in their possession at that time required the Union officers to assume that that division as well as the others had arrived on the 29th. Yet General Porter's conduct was adjudged upon the assumption that not more than one division under Longstreet had arrived on the field and that Porter had no considerable force in his front.

The fact is that Longstreet, with four divisions of full 25,000 men, was there on the field before Porter arrived with his two divisions of 9,000 men; that the Confederate General-in-Chief was there in person at least two or three hours before the commander of the Army of Virginia himself arrived on the field, and that Porter with his two divisions saved the Army of Virginia that day from the disaster naturally due to the enemy's earlier preparation for battle.

If the 4.30 order had been promptly delivered a very grave responsibility would have devolved upon General Porter. The order was based upon conditions which were essentially erroneous and upon expectations which could not possibly be realized.

It required an attack upon the enemy's flank or rear, which could not be made, and that the attacking force keep closed on Reynolds, who was far to the right and beyond reach. Yet it would have been too late to correct the error and have the order modified. That order appeared to be part of a general plan. It must be executed promptly or not at all. If Porter had made not the impossible attack which was ordered, but a direct attack upon the enemy's right wing, would he have been blameless for the fruitless sacrifice of his troops? We believe not. It is a well-established military maxim that a corps commander is not justifiable in making an apparently hopeless attack in obedience to an order from a superior who is not on the spot, and who is evidently in error in respect to the essential conditions upon which the order is based. The duty of the corps commander in such a case is to make not a real attack, but a strong demonstration, so as to prevent the enemy in his front from sending re–enforcements to other parts of his line.

This is all that Porter would have been justifiable in doing even if he had received the 4.30 order at 5 o'clock; and such a demonstration, or even a real attack made after 5 o'clock by Porter alone, could have had no beneficial effect whatever upon the general result. It would not have diminished in the least the resistance offered to the attacks made at other points that afternoon. The display of troops made by Porter earlier in the afternoon had all the desired and all possible beneficial effect. It caused Longstreet's reserve division to be sent to his extreme right in front of Porter's position. There that division remained until about 6 o'clock—too late for it to take any effective part in the operations at other points of the line.

A powerful and well-sustained attack by the combined forces of Porter's corps and King's division upon the enemy's right wing, if it had been commenced early in the afternoon, might have drawn to that part of the field so large a part of Longstreet's force as to have given Pope some chance of success against Jackson; but an attack by Porter alone could have been but an ineffective blow, destructive only to the force that made it, and, followed by a counter–attack, disastrous to the Union army. Such an attack, under such circumstances, would have been not only a great blunder, but, on the part of an intelligent officer, it would have been a great crime.

What General Porter actually did do, although his situation was by no means free from embarrassment and anxiety at the time, now seems to have been only the simple, necessary action which an intelligent soldier had no choice but to take. It is not possible that any court-martial could have condemned such conduct if it had been correctly understood. On the contrary, that conduct was obedient, subordinate, faithful, and judicious. It saved the Union army from disaster on the 29th of August.

This ends the transactions upon which were based the charges of which General Porter was pronounced guilty; but some account of the part taken by him and his corps in the events of the following day, August 30, which gave rise to a charge which was withdrawn, is necessary to a full understanding of the merits of the case.

At 3 A.M. of the 30th General Porter received the following order, and in compliance with it promptly withdrew from his position in presence of the enemy and marched rapidly by the Sudley road to the center of the battle-field, where he reported to General Pope for orders:

Headquarters Army of Virginia,
In the Field, near Bull Run, August 29, 1862—8.50 P.M.

Maj. Gen. F. J. Porter:

General: Immediately upon receipt of this order, the precise hour of receiving which you will acknowledge, you will march your command to the field of battle of to-day and report to me in person for orders. You are to understand that you are expected to comply strictly with this order, and to be present on the field within three hours after its reception, or after daybreak to-morrow morning.

John Pope,
Major-General, Commanding

(Received August 30, 3.30 am)

At first sight it would appear that in this prompt and unhesitating movement under this order General Porter committed a grave fault. He was already on the field of battle, confronting the enemy in force, and holding a position of vital importance to the security of Pope's army; while the latter appeared from the order to be wholly in the dark respecting these all-important facts. It is true the order was most positive, imperative, and also distrustful in its terms. But those very terms served to show only the more forcibly that the order was based upon a total misapprehension of the essential facts, without which misapprehension it would not seem possible that such an order could have been issued. The well-established military rule is that such an order must never be obeyed until the commander who gave it has been informed of his error and given an opportunity to correct it; but, upon close examination, the opposite view of Porter's conduct under this order appears to be the just one.

Porter had repeatedly reported to McDowell the presence of the enemy in large force in his front. Presumably these reports had gone to Pope, as one of them had in fact. Porter had also sent an aide-de camp with a written message to Pope about 4 P.M., and had sent a written reply to the 4.30 P.M. order after 6.30 P.M. These last two dispatches have not been preserved by General Pope, and hence their contents are not known to us; but we are bound to presume that they reported the situation as Porter then knew it, and as he had frequently reported it to McDowell, and the last of these dispatches, in reply to the 4.30 P.M. order, was later than the latest of those in which Porter had spoken of any intention to fall back. Hence Porter had already given to his superior all the information which it was possible for him to give, and nothing remained for him but to obey the order. This movement of Porter's corps on the morning of the 30th was the beginning of the unfortunate operation of that day. This corps, which had been protecting the left flank of Pope's army, was withdrawn from its important position, leaving the left wing and flank exposed to attack by greatly superior force of the enemy, brought to the center of the field and then ordered "in pursuit of the enemy."

Special Orders No—
August 30, 1862—12 m.
Headquarters, Near Groveton

The following forces will be immediately thrown forward in pursuit of the enemy and press him vigorously during the whole day. Major-General McDowell is assigned to the command of the pursuit; Major-General Porter's corps will push forward on the Warrenton turnpike, followed by the divisions of Brigadier-Generals King and Reynolds. The division of Brigadier-General Ricketts will pursue the Hay Market road, followed by the corps of Major-General Heintzelman. The necessary cavalry will be assigned to these columns by Major-General McDowell, to whom regular and frequent reports will be made. The general headquarters will be somewhere on the Warrenton turnpike.

By command of Major-General Pope:
George D. Ruggles,
Colonel and Chief of Staff

Headquarters Third Corps, Army of Virginia,
August 30, 1862.

Major-General McDowell, being charged with the advanced forces ordered to pursue the enemy, directs me to inform you that your corps will be followed immediately by King's division, supported by Reynolds. Heintzelman, with his corps, preceded by Ricketts' division, will move on your right, on the road from Sudley Springs to Hay Market. He is instructed to throw out skirmishers to the left, which is desirable you should join with your right. General McDowell's headquarters will be at the head of Reynolds' division, on the Warrenton road. Organize a strong advance to precede your command, and push on rapidly in pursuit of the enemy until you come in contact with him. Report frequently. Bayard's brigade will be ordered to report to you; push it well to the left as you advance.

Very respectfully, your obedient servant,
Ed. Schriver
Colonel and Chief of Staff

Major-General Porter,
Commanding, &c.

These orders led to an attack upon the Confederate left wing, Jackson's command, made mainly by Butterfield's and Barnes' brigades, of Morell's division, and by Sykes' division, which is described as follows by the Confederate generals:

[Extract from General Lee's report of operations of the Army of Northern Virginia, battle of Manassas]

Headquarters Army of Northern Virginia,
March 6, 1863.

Sir: ... About 3 P.M. the enemy, having massed his troops in front of General Jackson, advanced against his position in strong force. His front line pushed forward and a fierce and bloody struggle ensued. A second and third line, of great strength, moved up to support the first, but in doing so came within easy range of a position a little in advance of Longstreet's left. He immediately ordered up two batteries, and two others being thrown forward about the same time by Col. S. D. Lee, under their well-directed and destructive fire the supporting lines were broken and fell back in confusion. Their repeated efforts to rally were unavailing, and Jackson's troops, being thus relieved from the pressure of overwhelming numbers, began to press steadily forward, driving the enemy before them. He retreated in confusion, suffering severely from our artillery, which advanced as he retired. General Longstreet, anticipating the order for a general advance, now threw his whole command against the Federal center and left....

I have the honor to be, very respectfully, your obedient servant,

R. E. Lee,
General.

[Extract from the report of General James Longstreet, October 10, 1862.]

During the day Col. S. D. Lee, with his reserve artillery placed in the position occupied the day previous by Colonel Walton, engaged the enemy in a very severe artillery combat. The result was, as the day previous, a success. At 3:30 o'clock in the afternoon I rode to the front for the purpose of completing arrangements for making a diversion in favor of a flank movement then under contemplation. Just after reaching my front line I received a message for re-enforcements for General Jackson, who was said to be severely pressed. From an eminence near by one portion of the enemy's masses attacking General Jackson were immediately within my view and in easy range of batteries in that position. It gave me an advantage that I had not expected to have, and I made haste to use it. Two batteries were ordered for the purpose, and one placed in position immediately and opened. Just as this fire began I received a message from the commanding general informing me of General Jackson's conditions and his wants. As it was evident that the attack against General Jackson could not be continued ten minutes under the fire of these batteries, I made no movement with my troops....

[Extract from the report of General Jackson of operations from August 15 to September 5, 1862.]

Headquarters Second Corps, Army of Northern Virginia,
April 27, 1863.

General: After some desultory skirmishing and heavy cannonading during the day the Federal infantry, about 4 o'clock in the evening, moved from under cover of the wood and advanced in several lines, first engaging the right, but soon extending its attack to the center and left. In a few moments our entire line was engaged in a fierce and sanguinary struggle with the enemy. As one line was repulsed another took its place and pressed forward as if determined, by force of numbers and fury of assault, to drive us from our positions. So impetuous and well sustained were these onsets as to induce me to send to the commanding general for re-enforcements; but the timely and gallant advance of General Longstreet on the right relieved my troops from the pressure of overwhelming numbers, and gave to these brave men the chances of a more equal conflict. As Longstreet pressed upon the right the Federal advance was checked, and soon a general advance of my whole line was ordered.

T. J. Jackson,
Lieutenant-General.

As Longstreet's army pressed forward to strike Pope's exposed left wing and flank, Warren, with his little brigade, sprang into the gap and breasted the storm until but a handful of his brave men were left alive. Then Sykes, with his disciplined brigades, and Reynolds, with his gallant Pennsylvania Reserves, seized the commanding ground in rear, and, like a rock, withstood the advance of the victorious enemy and saved the Union army from rout.

Thus did this gallant corps nobly and amply vindicate the character of their trusted chief, and demonstrate to all the world that "disobedience of orders" and "misbehavior in the presence of the enemy" are crimes which could not possibly find place in the head or heart of him who thus commanded that corps.

These events of the 30th of August were excluded from the evidence before the court-martial that tried General Porter; but justice requires that they should be mentioned here as having an important bearing upon the question of animus, which was so strongly dwelt upon in the review of Porter's case by the Judge-Advocate-General.

The foregoing is the simple history of the part taken by Porter and his corps in the events which gave rise to the following charges and specifications, findings and sentence, and executive action.

These charges and specifications certainly bear no discernible resemblance to the facts of the case as now established. Yet it has been our duty to carefully compare with these facts the views entertained by the court-martial, as shown in the findings and in the review of the case which was prepared for the information of the President by the Judge-Advocate-General who had conducted the prosecution, and tends to clearly perceive every error into which the court-martial was led. We trust it is not necessary for us to submit in detail the results of this comparison, and that it will be sufficient for us to point out the fundamental errors, and to say that all the essential facts in every instance stand out in clear and absolute contrast to those supposed facts upon which General Porter was adjudged guilty.

The fundamental errors upon which the conviction of General Porter depended may be summed up in few words. It was maintained, and apparently established to the satisfaction of the court-martial, that only about one-half of the Confederate Army was on the field of Manassas on the 29th of August, while General Lee, with the other half, was still beyond the Bull Run Mountains; that General Pope's army, exclusive of Porter's corps, was engaged in a severe and nearly equal contest with the enemy, and only needed the aid of a flank attack which Porter was expected to make to insure the defeat and destruction or capture of the Confederate force in their front under General Jackson; that McDowell and Porter, with their joint forces, Porter's leading, had advanced toward Gainesville until the head of their column had reached a point near the Warrenton turnpike, where they found a division of Confederate troops, "seventeen regiments," which Buford had counted as they passed through Gainesville, marching along the road across Porter's front, and going toward the field of battle at Groveton; that McDowell ordered Porter to at once attack that column thus moving to join Jackson, or the flank and rear of the line if they had formed in line, while he would take his own troops by the Sudley Springs road and throw them upon the enemy's center near Groveton; that Porter, McDowell having then separated from him, disobeyed that order to attack, allowed that division of the enemy's troops to pass him unmolested, and then fell back and retreated toward Manassas Junction; that Porter then remained in the rear all the afternoon, listening to the sounds of battle and coolly contemplating a presumed defeat of his comrades on the center and right of the field; that this division of the enemy having passed Porter's column and formed on the right of Jackson's line, near Groveton, an order was sent to Porter to attack the right flank or rear of the enemy's line, upon which his own line of march must bring him, but that he had willfully disobeyed, and made no attempt to execute that order; that in this way was lost the opportunity to destroy Jackson's detached force before the other wing of General Lee's army could join it, and that this junction having been effected during the night of the 29th, the defeat of General Pope's army on the 30th thus resulted from General Porter's neglect and disobedience.

Now, in contrast to these fundamental errors, the following all-important facts are fully established:

As Porter was advancing toward Gainesville, and while yet nearly 4 miles from that place and more than 2 miles from the nearest point of the Warrenton turnpike, he met the right wing of the Confederate army, 25,000 strong, which had arrived on the field that morning and was already in line of battle. Not being at that moment quite fully informed of the enemy's movements, and being then under orders from Pope to push rapidly toward Gainesville, Porter was pressing forward to attack the enemy in his front, when McDowell arrived on the field with later information of the enemy, and later and very different orders from Pope, assumed the command, and arrested Porter's advance. This latter information left no room for doubt that the main body of Lee's army was already on the field and far in advance of Pope's army in preparation for battle. General McDowell promptly decided not to attempt to go farther to the front, but to deploy his column so as to form line in connection with General Pope's right wing, which was then engaged with Jackson. To do this General McDowell separated his corps entirely from General Porter's, and thus relinquished the command and all right to the command of Porter's corps. McDowell did not give Porter any order to attack, nor did he give him any order whatever to govern his action after their separation.

It does not appear from the testimony that he conveyed to General Porter in any way the erroneous view of the military situation which was afterward maintained before the court-martial, nor that he suggested to General Porter any expectation that he would make an attack. On the contrary the testimony of all the witnesses as to what was actually said and done; the information which McDowell and Porter then had respecting the enemy, and the movement which McDowell decided to make, and did make, with his own troops, prove conclusively that there was left no room for doubt in Porter's mind that his duty was to stand on the defensive and hold his position until McDowell's movement could be completed. It would have indicated a great error of military judgment to have done or ordered the contrary, in the situation as then fully known to both McDowell and Porter.

General Pope appears from his orders and from his testimony to have been at that time wholly ignorant of the true situation. He had disapproved of the sending of Ricketts to Thoroughfare Gap to meet Longstreet on the 28th, believing that the main body of Lee's army could not reach the field of Manassas before the night of the 30th. Hence he sent the order to Porter dated 4.30 p. m. to attack Jackson's right flank or rear. Fortunately that order did not reach Porter until about sunset—too late for any attack to be made. Any attack which Porter could have made at any time that afternoon must necessarily have been fruitless of any good result. Porter's faithful, subordinate, and intelligent conduct that afternoon saved the Union army from the defeat which would otherwise have resulted that day from the enemy's more speedy concentration The only seriously critical period of that campaign, viz, between 11 A.M. and sunset of August 29, was thus safely passed. Porter had understood and appreciated the military situation, and, so far as he had acted upon his own judgment, his action had been wise and judicious. For the disaster of the succeeding day he was in no degree responsible. Whoever else may have been responsible, it did not flow from any action or inaction of his.

The judgment of the court-martial upon General Porter's conduct was evidently based upon greatly erroneous impressions, not only respecting what that conduct really was and the orders under which he was acting, but also respecting all the circumstances under which he acted. Especially was this true in respect to the character of the battle of the 29th of August. That battle consisted of a number of sharp and gallant combats between small portions of the opposing forces. Those combats were of short duration and were separated by long intervals of simple skirmishing and artillery duels. Until after 6 o'clock only a small part of the troops on either side were engaged at any time during the afternoon. Then, about sunset, one additional division on each side was engaged near Groveton. The musketry of that last contest and the yells of the Confederate troops about dark were distinctly heard by the officers of Porter's corps; but at no other time during all that afternoon was the volume of musketry such that it could be heard at the position of Porter's troops. No sound but that of artillery was heard by them during all those hours when Porter was understood by the court-martial to have been listening to the sounds of a furious battle raging immediately to his right. And those sounds of artillery were by no means such as to indicate a general battle.

The reports of the 29th and those of the 30th of August have somehow been strangely confounded with each other. Even the Confederate reports have, since the termination of the war, been similarly misconstrued. Those of the 30th have been misquoted as referring to the 29th, thus to prove that a furious battle was going on while Porter was comparatively inactive on the 29th. The fierce and gallant struggle of his own troops on the 30th has thus been used to sustain the original error under which he was condemned. General Porter was, in effect, condemned for not having taken any part in his own battle. Such was the error upon which General Porter was pronounced guilty of the most shameful crime known among soldiers. We believe not one among all the gallant soldiers on that bloody field was less deserving of such condemnation than he.

The evidence of bad animus in Porter's case ceases to be material in view of the evidence of his soldierly and faithful conduct. But it is our duty to say that the indiscreet and unkind terms in which General Porter expressed his distrust of the capacity of his superior commander cannot be defended. And to that indiscretion was due, in very great measure, the misinterpretation of both his motives and his conduct and his consequent condemnation.

Having thus given the reasons for our conclusions, we have the honor to report, in accordance with the President's order, that in our opinion justice requires at his hands such action as may be necessary to annul and set aside the findings and sentence of the court-martial in the case of Maj. Gen. Fitz-John Porter, and to restore him to the positions of which that sentence deprived him—such restoration to take effect from the date of his dismissal from the service.

Very respectfully, your obedient servants.

J. M. SCHOFIELD,
Major-General V S Army

ALFRED H. TERRY,
Brigadier-General U.S.S. Army

GEO. W. GETTY,
Brevet Major-General, U S Army, Colonel Third Artillery

Source: U.S. War Department, *The War of the Rebellion: A Compilation of the Official Records of the Union and Confederate Armies*, Series 1, Vol. 12, Part II, 513–535.

Chapter Notes

Abbreviations

OR—U.S. War Department, *The War of the Rebellion: A Compilation of the Official Records of the Union and Confederate Armies*. Series 1.

AW—Articles of War of April 10, 1862.

Chapter 1

1. OR, Volume 12, Part III, 706.

Chapter 3

1. AW, Article Nine.
2. AW, Article Fifty-two.
3. AW, Article Sixty-four.
4. AW, Article Sixty-nine.
5. OR, Vol. 12, Part 11, Supplement, 1041.

Chapter 4

1. OR, Volume 12, Part II, Supplement, p. 825.
2. Ibid., 840.
3. Ibid., 890.
4. Ibid., 928.
5. Ibid., 930.
6. Ibid., 934.
7. Ibid., 945.
8. Ibid.
9. Ibid., 943.
10. Ibid., 949.
11. Ibid., 960.
12. Ibid.
13. Ibid., 990.
14. Ibid.
15. Ibid., 991.
16. Ibid.
17. Ibid., 998.
18. Ibid.
19. Ibid.
20. Ibid., 998–999.
21. Ibid., 1000.
22. Ibid.
23. Ibid.
24. Ibid.
25. Ibid.
26. Ibid., 1001.
27. Ibid., 1007.
28. Ibid., 1009.
29. Ibid.
30. Ibid., 1030.
31. OR, Volume 12, Part II, Reports, 731.
32. Ibid.
33. OR, Volume 12, Part II, Supplement, 825.
34. Ibid.
35. John Pope, "The Second Battle of Bull Run," *Battles and Leaders of the Civil War*, Volume II, 449.

Chapter 5

1. OR, Vol. 12, Part II, Supplement, 825–827.
2. Ibid., 1068.
3. Ibid., 825.
4. Ibid., 852.
5. Ibid.
6. Ibid.
7. Ibid., 903.
8. Ibid., 853.
9. Ibid.
10. Ibid., 825.
11. Ibid., 809.
12. Ibid., 868.
13. OR, Vol. 12, Part II, 581.
14. Ibid.
15. Ibid., 825.
16. Ibid., 903.
17. Ibid., 904.
18. Ibid., 908.
19. Ibid., 909.
20. Ibid.
21. Ibid., 912–913.
22. Ibid., 914.
23. Ibid., 950.
24. Ibid.
25. Ibid., 952.
26. Ibid.
27. Ibid., 950.
28. Ibid., 1044.
29. Ibid., 950.
30. Ibid., 956.
31. Ibid., 955.
32. Ibid., 1041.
33. Ibid.
34. Ibid., 1035.
35. Ibid., 963.
36. Ibid.
37. Ibid., 1065.
38. Ibid., 1064.
39. Ibid., 986.

40. Ibid., 993.
41. Ibid., 994.
42. Ibid., 1012.
43. Ibid., 1021.
44. Ibid., 1023.
45. Ibid., 1061.
46. Ibid., 825.
47. Ibid., 956, 963.
48. Ibid., 904.
49. Ibid., 955.
50. Ibid., 972.
51. Ibid., 953.
52. Ibid., 984.
53. Ibid., 1068.
54. Ibid., 826.
55. Ibid., 1014.
56. AW, Article Fifty-two.

Chapter 6

1. OR, Vol. 12, Part II, Supplement, 825–827.
2. Ibid., 835.
3. Ibid., 854.
4. Ibid.
5. Ibid.
6. Ibid.
7. Ibid.
8. Ibid.
9. Ibid.
10. Ibid., 898.
11. Ibid., 970.
12. Ibid.
13. Ibid., 985.

Chapter 7

1. AW, Article Sixty-three.
2. OR, Vol. 12, Part III, 473–474.
3. OR, Vol. 12, Part II, 978.
4. Sandburg, *Abraham Lincoln: The War Years.* Vol. 1, 533.
5. Ibid., 534.
6. Ibid., 526.
7. Ibid., 535.
8. OR, Series 1, Vol. 12, Part II, Supplement, 1111.

9. Sandburg, *Abraham Lincoln: The War Years.* Vol. II, 29.
10. OR, Vol. 12, Part II, Supplement, 1063.
11. Ibid., 1067.
12. Ibid., 1069.
13. Ibid., 1062.
14. Ibid., 1069.
15. OR, Vol. 12, Part I, 39.

Chapter 8

1. OR, Vol. 12, Part II, Supplement, 872–873.
2. Ibid., 872.
3. Ibid., 841.
4. Ibid., 889–890.
5. Ibid., 999.
6. Ibid., 1008.
7. Ibid., 987.
8. Ibid., 971.
9. Ibid., 1003.
10. Ibid., 1018.

Chapter 9

1. OR, Vol. 12, Part II, Supplement, 1112–1133.
2. OR, Vol. 12, Part II, Supplement, 1134.
3. Ibid., 1051.
4. Ibid.
5. Ibid.
6. Ibid., 1052.

Chapter 10

1. OR, Vol. 12, Part II, 512–513.
2. Grant, *Personal Memoirs*, 568.
3. OR, Vol. 12, Part II, 736.
4. "The Porter Court-Martial," *New York Times*, July 10, 1878.
5. "Fitz-John Porter's Retrial," *New York Times*, October 2, 1878.

6. Ibid.
7. "The Porter Court-Martial," *New York Times*, September 11, 1878.
8. OR, Part II, 524.
9. Ibid., 525.
10. Ibid., 524.
11. Ibid.
12. Ibid.
13. "Fitz-John Porter's Delay," *New York Times*, October 8, 1878.
14. "Porter Not True to Pope," *New York Times*, October 17, 1878.
15. "Porter Deserves Death," *New York Times*, October 15, 1878.
16. "The Gen. Porter Inquiry," *New York Times*, October 16, 1878.
17. "Gen. Porter at Manassas," *New York Times*, October 11, 1878.
18. OR, Vol. 12, Part II, Supplement, 955.
19. OR, Vol. 12, Part II, 532.
20. Ibid.
21. Ibid., 534.
22. Ibid., 534–535.
23. Ibid., 535.

Chapter 11

1. Letter from Grant to Arthur, *General Grant's Unpublished Correspondence in the Case of Fitz-John Porter*, pp. 9–10. (Porter gift to the Library of Congress).
2. Letter from Grant to Cameron, Ibid., pp. 12–15.

Chapter 15

1. OR, Part II, Supplement, 825.
2. Ibid., 861.
3. Ibid., 956.
4. Ibid., 904.

Bibliography

Anders, Curt. *Injustice on Trial.* Zionsville, Ind.: Guild Press Emmis Publishing, LP, 2002.

Articles of War of 1806.

Civil War Times Illustrated Editors. *Great Battles of the Civil War.* New York: Gallery Books, 1984.

Commager, Henry Steele, ed. *Living History: The Civil War.* New York: Hess Press, 1950.

Cozzens, Peter, ed. *The New Annals of the Civil War.* Mechanicsburg, Pa.: Stackpole Books, 2004.

Davis, Major George B. *The Official Military Atlas of the Civil War.* Washington, D.C.: Government Printing Office, 1891.

Einsenschiml, Otto. *The Celebrated Case of Fitz-John Porter.* New York: Bobbs-Merrill, 1950.

"Fitz-John Porter's Delay." *The New York Times,* October 8, 1878.

"Fitz-John Porter's Retrial." *The New York Times,* October 2, 1878.

Franklin, General W. B. "The Sixth Corps at Second Bull Run." *Battles and Leaders of the Civil War.* Vol. II. New York: Thomas Yoseloff, Publisher, 1956.

"General Pope's Statement." *The New York Times,* October 11, 1878.

"General Porter at Manassas." *The New York Times,* October 11, 1878.

Grant, Ulysses S. *The Personal Memoirs of Ulysses S. Grant.* New York: Konecky and Konecky, 1886.

Heidler, David S. and Jeanne T., eds. *Encyclopedia of the American Civil War.* New York: W. W. Norton, 2000.

Henderson, Lt. Col. G.F.R. *Stonewall Jackson.* New York: Konecky and Konecky, 1977.

Irwin, Lt. Col. Richard B. "Washington Under Banks." *Battles and Leaders of the Civil War.* Vol. II. New York: Thomas Yoseloff, Publisher, 1956.

King, Capt. Charles. "In Vindication of General Rufus King." *Battles and Leaders of the Civil War.* Vol. II. New York: Thomas Yoseloff, Publisher, 1956.

Longstreet, General James. "Out March Against Pope." *Battles and Leaders of the Civil War.* Vol. II. New York: Thomas Yoseloff, Publisher, 1956.

Longstreet, James. *From Manassas to Appomattox.* Philadelphia: Da Capo Press, 1896.

McClellan, George B. "From the Peninsula to Antietam." *Battles and Leaders of the Civil War.* Vol. II. New York: Thomas Yoseloff, Publisher, 1956.

McClellan, H. B. *The Campaigns of Stuart's Cavalry.* Secaucus, N.J.: Blue and Grey Press, 1993.

Nevins, Allan. *War for the Union 1862–1863.* New York: Konecky and Konecky, 1960.

Pope, John. "The Second Battle of Bull Run." *Battles and Leaders of the Civil War.* Vol. II. New York: Thomas Yoseloff, Publisher, 1956.

"Porter Deserved Death." *The New York Times*, October 15, 1878.

"Porter Not True to Pope." *The New York Times*, October 17, 1878.

Sandburg, Carl. *Abraham Lincoln: The War Years.* Vol. I. New York: Harcourt, Brace, 1939.

Sandburg, Carl. *Abraham Lincoln: The War Years.* Vol. II. New York: Harcourt, Brace, 1939.

Taliaferro, General W. B. "Jackson's Raid Around Pope." *Battles and Leaders of the Civil War.* Vol. II. New York: Thomas Yoseloff, Publisher, 1956.

"The Fitz-John Porter Case." *The New York Times*, October 25, 1878.

"The General Porter Inquiry." *The New York Times*, October 16, 1878.

"The Porter Court-Martial." *The New York Times*, July 10, 1878.

"The Porter Court-Martial." *The New York Times*, September 11, 1878.

U.S. War Department. *The War of the Rebellion: A Compilation of the Official Records of the Union and Confederate Armies.* Series 1, Vol. 12, Part II. Harrisburg, Pa.: National Historical Society, 1971.

U.S. War Department. *The War of the Rebellion: A Compilation of the Official Records of the Union and Confederate Armies.* Series 1, Vol. 12, Part II, Supplement. Harrisburg, Pa.: National Historical Society, 1971.

U.S. War Department. *The War of the Rebellion: A Compilation of the Official Records of the Union and Confederate Armies.* Series 1, Vol. 12, Part II, Reports. Harrisburg, Pa.: National Historical Society, 1971.

U.S. War Department. *The War of the Rebellion: A Compilation of the Official Records of the Union and Confederate Armies.* Series 1, Vol. 12, Part III. Harrisburg, Pa: National Historical Society, 1971.

Index